RICHARD NIXON
AND THE RISE OF
AFFIRMATIVE ACTION

American Intellectual Culture

Series Editors: Jean Bethke Elshtain,
Ted V. McAllister, and Wilfred M. McClay

RICHARD NIXON AND THE RISE OF AFFIRMATIVE ACTION

The Pursuit of Racial Equality in an Era of Limits

Kevin L. Yuill

ROWMAN & LITTLEFIELD PUBLISHERS, INC.
Lanham • Boulder • New York • Toronto • Oxford

ROWMAN & LITTLEFIELD PUBLISHERS, INC.

Published in the United States of America
by Rowman & Littlefield Publishers, Inc.
A wholly owned subsidary of The Rowman & Littlefield Publishing Group, Inc.
4501 Forbes Boulevard, Suite 200, Lanham, Maryland 20706
www.rowmanlittlefield.com

PO Box 317
Oxford
OX2 9RU, UK

British Library Cataloguing in Publication Information Available

Library of Congress Cataloging-in-Publication Data

Yuill, Kevin L., 1962–
    Richard Nixon and the rise of affirmative action : the pursuit of racial equality in an era
of limits / Kevin L. Yuill.
        p. cm. — (American intellectual culture)
    Includes bibliographical references and index.
    ISBN-10: 0-7425-4997-6 (cloth : alk. paper)
    ISBN-10: 0-7425-4998-4 (pbk. : alk. paper)
    ISBN-13: 978-0-7425-4997-5 (cloth : alk. paper)
    ISBN-13: 978-0-7425-4998-2 (pbk. : alk. paper)
    1. Civil rights—Government policy—United States—History—20th century. 2.
Affirmative action programs—United States—History—20th century. 3. United States—
Politics and government—1969–1974. 4. Nixon, Richard M. (Richard Milhous), 1913–
I. Title. II. Series.
JC599.U5Y85 2006
331.13'3097309047—dc22   2006000044

Printed in the United States of America

⊗™ The paper used in this publication meets the minimum requirements of American
National Standard for Information Sciences—Permanence of Paper for Printed Library
Materials, ANSI/NISO Z39.48-1992.

Contents

Part 3: Affirmative Action and the New Liberalism

List of Acronyms

AFL-CIO	American Federation of Labor
ANS	Annotated News Summaries
CAP	Community Action Project
CGGC	Committee on Government Contract Compliance
CORE	Congress of Racial Equality
CR	Congressional Record
CSC	Civil Service Commission
EEO	Equal Employment Opportunity(ies)
EEOC	Equal Employment Opportunities Commission
GOP	Grand Old Party (Republican Party)
GPO	General Post Office
HEW	Health, Education, and Welfare (Department of)
HRH	Harry Robbins Haldeman
HUD	Housing and Urban Development (Department of)
LOC	Library of Congress
NAACP	National Association for the Advancement of Colored People
NPMP	Nixon Presidential Materials Project
PCGC	President's Committee on Government Contracts
PCGCC	President's Committee on Government Contract Compliance
POF	President's Own Files
PPF	President's Personal Files
PPPUS	Public Papers of the Presidents of the United States
SMOF	Staff Member and Office Files
SNCC	Student Nonviolent Coordinating Committee

USCRC   United States Civil Rights Commission
WHCCR   White House Conference on Civil Rights
WHCF   White House Central Files
WHSF   White House Special Files

Introduction:
"An Almost Hopeless Holding Action"

D AYS AFTER THE PASSAGE of the Philadelphia Plan, the first affirmative action program insisting on "goals and timetables" of minorities hired, President Richard M. Nixon pondered a news summary reporting that black leaders charged the administration with "genocide." The pessimistic summary, which stated "(i)t is hard to see how we can make much ground here," jolted the President, who had put some effort into ensuring the survival of the Philadelphia Plan. Nixon scrawled in the margin of the report: "E [Nixon's aide John Ehrlichman, who dealt with domestic issues]—I completely agree—It is an almost hopeless holding action at best. Let's limit our public action and $ - to the least we can get away with."[1]

Few at the time, or indeed since, have noted the change in direction in Nixon's policy yet, to use his own expression, this was one way that the thirty-seventh president gave history a "nudge."[2] Throughout that year—1970—Nixon began to abandon the great crusades of the 1960s aimed at destroying or radically reforming the ghettos. Always slightly cynical about the prospects of successfully integrating either housing or education, Nixon backed away from busing and placed a moratorium on federal action against discrimination in housing and neighborhoods. That Nixon effectively launched affirmative action at the same time as he decided to shut down most civil rights efforts is the central question with which research for this book began. How can we make sense of this apparently paradoxical turn of events?

While he did not develop the Philadelphia Plan, and even though he almost appeared to turn his back on it in the run up to the 1972 election, Nixon was undoubtedly the "sire of affirmative action," as Dean Kotlowski put it.[3] He defended it in Congress in 1969, developed "set asides," extended the remit of affirmative action to state and local government as well as colleges and universities, and expanded the list of beneficiaries of the policy. From 1970, his administration oversaw a massive expansion of these programs in both government and private companies. But Nixon also followed his own (and others') advice and backed away from the civil rights promises of the 1960s, creating a difficulty for historians and political scientists.

It is the inability of the existing scholarship to provide a satisfactory answer to Nixon's apparently paradoxical civil rights actions that necessitates a deeper intellectual history of the period. Recent scholarship dealing with civil rights policy during the Nixon years has emphasized important precedents for affirmative action set by civil rights activists, the Johnson administration, elements within the Democratic Party, and bureaucrats with sympathy for civil rights goals. This study, while not denying their significance, stresses instead Nixon's actions in establishing the trajectory of affirmative action. But they must be understood within the historical context of a transformation of the normative structure of American liberalism, for affirmative action rose as a response to changing circumstances. Thus, this book highlights this shifting context of American liberalism—as Sidney Milkis termed it, the "reshaping of liberalism"—in the 1970s.[4] The postwar premises of liberalism in relation to race, examined in the first section of this book, prevented serious consideration of the adoption of mandatory affirmative action policies by the federal government. By the late 1960s, pervasive questioning meant that new bases for authority—new sets of assumptions, new models of leadership—had to be found. Nixon and his policies contributed to this reshaping but the sometimes unexpected consequences of his actions—not the least of which is affirmative action—must also be understood within this broader set of circumstances.

This book is a mix of history and theory and the general approach on these pages is to make the relevant history more theoretical and relevant theory more historical. It builds upon important work by Hugh Davis Graham and John David Skrentny by examining the history of affirmative action during Nixon's tenure in light of the theories of Jürgen Habermas and John Rawls, particularly in terms of a pervasive crisis of legitimacy stalking the United States at the time. It tells the story of Nixon's actions in relation to the growth of affirmative action policy within what might be described as a comprehensive renegotiation of the terms of American liberalism.

Affirmative action is nothing if not controversial; even its definition excites controversy. The phrase has meant different things at different times since at least the Civil War. If we restrict the definition for the present to hiring, promoting, awarding contracts or admitting specific numbers (or ranges of numbers) of minorities or women for the purpose of creating equal opportunities (in the past, class rather than racial divisions were the subject of calls for affirmative action), it gets no easier.

Viewing affirmative action as essentially a continuum, a result of constantly building pressure, misses subtle but extremely important changes in the objectives underlying the policy. Its continuity lies in its existence as a policy response (or, more usually, a potential policy response) to the perception that equality of opportunity—that important aspect of Americanness pointed to by de Tocqueville—could not be guaranteed by American civil society. But affirmative action played very different roles at different times; this book emphasizes four different phases of affirmative action, each appropriate to its own historical set of circumstances.

First, in its relation to racial divisions, preferential treatment in employment began as a generally localized *demand* made by civil rights groups from the 1930s on. Second, it was a voluntaristic, hopeful, and informal policy *response* to civil rights demands (not just specific demands for quotas) formulated both by private companies and by the Kennedy/Johnson administrations. Third, the Philadelphia Plan began as an experimental, tentative, and limited regulatory policy response by Nixon to the specific problems of construction employment within cities with large black populations. Other experimental plans proposed extending purported beneficiaries to ethnic groups such as the Irish. Finally, affirmative action expanded to become the dominant policy model for civil rights, enforcing "goals and targets" of the numbers of minorities and/or women promoted, hired, awarded contracts, or admitted to higher education institutions. It became top-down, negotiated by managers and administrators in boardrooms and offices, using the increased financial muscle of the federal government to police programs.

The concern here is to discuss the forces effecting the transformation of the policy toward what it is today, though it is beyond the scope of this book to discuss in any real historical detail what has happened to affirmative action after the mid-1970s. These various phases of affirmative action—civil rights demand, voluntaristic plea, experimental policy, and dominant policy model—could not have existed outside their historical specificity. As the book shows, even the objections to affirmative action heard in the past differ from those heard today.

An important part of this book sets the scene for the rise of affirmative action by looking at changes to what has been called the New Deal order. Though the superficial aspects of the crisis becoming apparent at the end of the 1960s are often discussed—the consecutive summers of rioting in major cities, the campus and Vietnam-related disturbances, the counterculture, the assassinations of Martin Luther King, Jr., and Robert Kennedy, the tumultuous 1968 Democratic Party Convention—historians may have missed the importance of the deeper nature of the crisis that occurred in the latter half of the 1960s. The values and norms of the postwar period suddenly meant little; the political and cultural elite lost its authority and its legitimacy and genuinely struggled to regain it. Institutions, which had served as connections between the American nation and individual Americans, imploded. Affirmative action, it will be argued on these pages, began its official career as an elite response to an immediate crisis, as an effort to restore legitimacy to a specific area tainted by charges of institutional racism. In a few short years, it became the dominant response and an important counteracting tendency to aspects of the deeper crisis.

In fact, the crisis that existed in the 1960s and 1970s is perhaps best thought of as one of legitimacy. No real solid force of opposition to the status quo predominated or managed to coordinate the pervasive sense of disenchantment into a genuine alternative. However, the establishment felt its legitimacy was in question and moved to replace what it felt were bankrupt institutions with state intervention. The analysis of the crisis in this book leans upon German social theorist Jürgen Habermas's *Legitimation Crisis,* especially in explaining the relentless growth of affirmative action within, first, government agencies and, later, private companies. Habermas, writing in 1973, showed that in the act of legitimation (making oneself legitimate), the state undermined other institutions that had been administered informally in areas outside of direct state control. Thus it created a need for yet more legitimation as well as rapidly expanding the need for resources, as the vicious cycle continued. The Philadelphia Plan had the effect of undermining all employment systems that had no goals and targets for hiring and promoting minorities. Early affirmative action programs thus became part of the legitimation crisis.

However, as the later chapters show, affirmative action also provided a proximate solution for what was, in fact, an insoluble problem. In some ways, it became an institution itself, replacing the postwar goal of constant economic growth. Few have noted how the language of "goals and targets" directly replicates hitherto economic terms. In an era where constant economic growth was no longer seen as a panacea, or perhaps was no longer considered possible or even desirable, the national imperative of creating a more fair society has what has been called the cult of economic growth. Individual institutions can declare allegiance with this goal through affirmative action just as they did in the earlier postwar period with growth and national efficiency. Affirmative action is best understood in the context of an elite attempt at including those who have been excluded. It is an important part of a recasting of relationships that sets up those "down below" as helpless victims of objective circumstances and those above as "enablers" and advocate groups for the stricken underclasses.

Nixon, whose political virtues seem to be mistaken for vices as often as Kennedy's vices are mistaken for virtues, might fairly be viewed as the reluctant savior of the postwar liberal order. On his watch, affirmative action was redirected from a potentially transformative (though in comparison to some others, modest) civil rights demand to a watered-down bureaucratic program. He neutralized the civil rights challenge to postwar liberalism by reinterpreting demands for reform as lists of complaints and responding to them as such. If civil rights demands were reduced to a series of complaints, compensation rather than real reform was the correct response and the complaints of African Americans were no more valid than those of the so-called "white ethnics." Accordingly, Nixon experimented with extending affirmative action to Italian, Polish, and Irish Americans. He also took up the imaginary complaints of the so-called "Silent Majority," directly comparing what he imagined was their "plight" with that of African Americans. In doing so, Nixon helped create a new basis for the relationship between citizens and the federal government by shifting the role of the state. As Theodore Lowi observed at the time, "federal policy became a matter of indemnifying damages rather than righting wrongs."[5] Those looking for an origin of the "joys of victimhood," often connected to affirmative action, should look more closely at Nixon and his administration instead of pointing to the usual suspects.

It is worth outlining the structure and scope of the book at the start. What follows is based on empirical research, largely conducted at the Nixon archives, on the policy of affirmative action relating Nixon's actions and the growth of affirmative action to changing perceptions. It brings fresh material to light but provides a needed reinterpretation or reconsideration of a crucial yet still enigmatic period, president, and policy, challenging assumptions about what affirmative action really is, who it really serves, and why it is still fiercely contested, as well as shedding new light on Nixon's actions and motives. It is about national—not local—issues and concentrates on the intellectual frames on which policy makers hung their policy responses to various challenges and responses. It does not discuss in any real detail the race relations or the civil rights movement though they formed the essential background to the story of affirmative action. It is less about everyday politics than about the changing ideas and assumptions that drove them.

Its purpose is investigative rather than political. The point here is not to condemn nor congratulate president or policy. Though left and right are important actors in the story, viewing either Nixon or affirmative action on a left/right political spectrum obscures rather than clarifies what happened to affirmative action in the Nixon years. In the movie classic, *The Quiet Man*, a fight between Sean Thornton (John Wayne) and Red Will Danaher (Victor McLagen) ends inconclusively, with the two men sharing a drink, but the two cover a huge amount of ground before then. Many observers looking at affirmative action pay too much attention to the fight and not enough to the scenery changing dramatically behind it.

The "era of limits" in the title reflects what is perhaps the only political point made here. Limits of all varieties were discovered in the 1970s, following a trend in economic thought. Limits to economic growth, to progress, to what can be achieved, to knowledge, and to the reach of social policy, all reflect a subjective loss of faith in the ability of human beings to effect positive changes in their environment rather than objective "discoveries" in the late 1960s and 1970s. If there is a consensus between left and right to replace the consensus that (arguably) characterized the postwar period, it is that objective limits to what humanity can achieve exist. The right gives ground to ethical and environmental limits upon capitalism just as the left has given ground on how far social policy can transform American society. On affirmative action, conservatives have admitted that merit or efficiency should no longer be the sole basis of contract awards, college admissions, or hiring and promoting. Liberals have accepted that racial inequality should not be politicized; affirmative action programs, they agree, should remain in the hands of management elite and not be subject to democratic decision. Either position would have horrified their ideological predecessors in the 1960s. It is possible to call for the return of the spirit of optimism, experimentalism, and unlimited possibilities that characterized the 1960s while remaining extremely critical of decisions—whether the war on poverty or the war in Vietnam—perhaps informed by it.

Definitions

It is worth alerting the reader to the way that various issues are discussed below; some of the terms used are notoriously contentious. Definitions of affirmative action can be far-ranging—anything from advertising in minority newspapers to fixed percentages of minorities or women hired.[6] This book defines, for purposes of the discussion below, affirmative action as racial or gender preferences in employment, in assigning college places, and in the awarding of contracts. As Barbara Bergmann, a resolute defender of affirmative action, noted, the difference between "goals and timetables" and quotas is semantic.[7] Generally, "affirmative action" will refer to "hard" or "strong" affirmative action that involves quotas or preferences. These latter two terms are also used simply to avoid repetition.

"Liberalism" is also a problematic term, having become almost pejorative in recent years. Used here, it refers not to a position on the political spectrum but on the set of assumptions, operating procedures and principles by which the United States was governed in the postwar period up until at least the 1970s. Conservatism operated within the boundaries set by liberalism in almost all cases. Liberalism used in this book may refer to either the earlier postwar variety or what is sometimes termed "new liberalism" renegotiated in the late 1960s and 1970s, depending on the context.

The contentious term "consensus" will also be used here in relation to the postwar period up until the mid-1960s to indicate the broad agreement in American society on anticommunism and on a government role in maintaining the economic health of the country and other factors. Discussions of race, as Mary Dudziak and others have demonstrated, were avoided by officialdom as much as possible in this period for that very reason.[8] It is also used here in a dynamic sense. As Robert Dahl observed: "'Consensus,' then, is not at all a static and unchanging attribute of citizens. It is a variable element in a complex and more or less continuous process."[9] However, though the book points toward and shows the development of what might be seen as a new consensus, no new consensus was consolidated during the Nixon presidency—the endpoint for this book.[10]

In the postwar period, liberal assumptions were so dominant that conservative thought was associated with a psychological malady by more than one text.[11] As Lionel Trilling declared in 1950: "In the United States at this time liberalism is not only the dominant but even the sole intellectual tradition. For it is the plain fact that nowadays there are no conservative or reactionary ideas in general circulation."[12]

Institutions, in the abstract sense of the term—trade unions rather than the Teamsters, businesses rather than Ford Motor Company, clubs rather than the Kiwanis clubs, the presidency rather than Nixon, the expectation of constant economic growth rather than specific growth—are discussed not only because of the importance with which Gunnar Myrdal and others in the postwar years regarded them but also because so much of the story of the 1960s is the story of their loss of authority and legitimacy.

The "state" is also problematic in American discussions but refers here not to individual states but to the state in its most general application. In its most essential sense, the state is as Max Weber defined it: "the human community which (successfully) claims the monopoly of legitimate coercion."[13] This is, of course, different than the "elite" or the "establishment," with which the latter term is used interchangeably. It refers not to a specific set of people in the Mosca-Pareto "circulation of elites" sense, but also to those who wield power whether by office or influence, those with the highest stake in American society and thus the most to lose when the existing setup is threatened.

Organization

This book is organized in three sections. The first section adumbrates the approach to affirmative action during the years of growth liberalism. In particular, what I have called the Myrdalian paradigm dominated and was strengthened by the economic confidence of the era. Though affirmative action clearly existed as a strategy and policy option, it was rejected for a variety of reasons. The next section looks at the Nixon presidency, at the president's changing perspective on civil rights problems, at policy initiatives like the Philadelphia Plan, and less obvious contributions to affirmative action like revenue sharing. The last section shows how Nixon's political actions helped to transform the identity of some Americans, which in turn changed the meaning of affirmative action, and indicates how changing intellectual assumptions during Nixon's presidency not only opened the doors to affirmative action but created a need for it.

Much of this book is dedicated to tracing postwar liberal institutions, the crisis that beset them, and the new arrangements and institutions that replaced, augmented, or reinforced them. The first section of this book looks at the postwar period specifically in order to understand why affirmative action was neither employed nor campaigned for in any real sense. It also examines how these barriers to affirmative action fell. Chapter 1 looks at the Myrdalian paradigm, how it was formed, and why it was hostile to affirmative action. Chapter 2 examines the passivity of policy makers in response to racial issues and events. Chapter 3 looks at the effect the onset of the civil rights crisis had on the Myrdalian paradigm. Chapter 4 looks at the vacuum of authority and legitimacy facing Nixon as he took office. Chapter 5 details the conservative and business impetus behind the first affirmative action programs.

The second section shows the impact Nixon made. Chapter 6 discusses Nixon's personal inclinations, his personal and philosophical views on racial issues, and his justification of the Philadelphia Plan through his attachment to "the right to earn." Chapter 7 concentrates on the Philadelphia Plan, indicating that, though it became an important precedent, it did not work, unless its ostensible purpose to provide meaningful black employment in the ghettos is reduced to ludicrous levels. Chapter 8 details Nixon's policy contributions to reshaping affirmative action and discusses how a change emanating from the top in 1970 changed the administration's civil rights perspective, paving the way for more affirmative action.

The third section discusses the salience of a widespread reframing of ideas to the development of affirmative action. Chapter 9 explores the way affirmative action fit with theories and ideas popular during the Nixon years, showing how affirmative action, if not created in name, at least had an obvious role in the future imagined by John Rawls, Alvin Toffler, and those contributing to the 1972 publication, *Limits to Growth*. The final chapter deals with Nixon's attempts to form new constituencies—and to attract old ones—in order that counterweights to the demands of African Americans might be created. In doing so, he created the first real "victim" culture bemoaned by pundits today.

The Problem of Nixon and Affirmative Action Thus Far: Existing Historical Discussion

Though there are many, many texts dealing with the ever-fascinating character of Nixon, few deal with the history of affirmative action, perhaps because of the difficulty of linking up very different historical eras. Some that mention affirmative action in the contest of civil rights, normally with a pro-affirmative action perspective, understand the history within the present-day terms of the struggle over affirmative action. In other words, affirmative action is simply part of a constant struggle to ensure racial equality in the United States. Terry Anderson's *In Pursuit of Fairness*, perhaps the most comprehensive history of affirmative action, sees it as part of the pursuit of fairness from the very outset right up until *Gratz v. Bollinger* in 2004. In doing so, Anderson skips across the surface of a very large period of history, asking very few difficult questions about what fairness meant at different times or about the many contradictions that emerged. For instance, the section on Nixon can only call "incredible" the fact that in 1969 a majority of Republicans in Congress supported the Philadelphia Plan while the majority of Democrats voted against it. Moreover, Anderson apparently finds untroubling the fact that no affirmative action policies were implemented between the World War II and 1969—despite the excellent civil rights credentials of Harry S. Truman, John F. Kennedy, and Lyndon Johnson.[14]

Most other observers agree that something changed in the ten years after the 1964 Civil Rights Act. But no one seems quite sure of when or even *what* happened. In exploring the puzzle of Nixon's affirmative action, there is broad agreement that a set of values—existing in the 1940s, 1950s, and early 1960s but no longer in existence by the early 1970s—regarded government enforced quotas as taboo. However, rather than identifying the characteristics of this postwar period, existing histories of affirmative action tend to concentrate on when this taboo was overturned. Historians Stephan and Abigail Thernstrom, who published an influential book on race relations, see Lyndon B. Johnson's Howard University speech as the most important watershed in the development of affirmative action. In May 1965, speaking at Howard University, Johnson said he sought "not just freedom but opportunity . . . not just equality as a right and a theory but equality as a fact and as a result."[15] On that basis, they claim, "the Johnson administration began to reshape federal policy to include race conscious measures at odds with the civil rights statute so recently passed."[16] The move toward race-conscious, preferential policies was "quiet, gradual, and subtle. . . ." So subtle and quiet, in fact, that the Thernstroms fail to say who was actually making this move, identifying only as "shadowy insiders" those who successfully lobbied for affirmative action.[17]

Policy historian Hugh Davis Graham, who has produced the most authoritative account of the ascent of affirmative action, points to a "policy watershed" crossed between 1966 and 1968. Graham distinguishes a Phase I, where anti-discrimination measures were in place, and a Phase II, when enforcement and implementation problems shifted policy from equal treatment to equal results.[18] In another publication, Graham identifies three "new and institutionally distinct" streams of thought as being responsible for this shift, including the bureaucratic logic of "clientele capture," "(t)heoreticians of affirmative action," and judicial logic, following the courts' switch to demanding the "undoing of the effects of past discrimination."[19]

Unfortunately, the "theoreticians of affirmative action" that Graham claims contributed to the acceptance of affirmative action policy simply did not exist—or perhaps hid like the Thernstrom's "shadowy insiders"—before the Nixon presidency. Why anyone would need to theorize about a simple policy idea conceived and put into practice by government agencies during the New Deal and by the Freedman's Bureau at least one hundred years previously is not addressed by Graham.

In fact, very little was written about affirmative action until nearly a decade after the first policies were put in place. Not until Nathan Glazer published *Affirmative Discrimination* in 1975 (made up of articles published earlier) was there a book-length critique of affirmative action, let alone an extensive justificatory tract.[20] This calls into question Graham's formulation of affirmative action as a conscious, coherent policy. It is no doubt more accurate to say, as did Nixon speechwriter William Safire, of affirmative action: "Strange, fitting a philosophy to the set of deeds, but sometimes that is what must be done."[21]

The "clientele capture" formulation has some merit. That the clientele—the civil rights movement—became incorporated into the federal bureaucracy need not be contested.[22] What needs to be explained, however, is why, if affirmative action was the result of civil rights activists moving into the halls of government, very few calls for affirmative action programs were heard at the time of their "capture." Beside localized demands for quotas in large cities, and a brief national discussion on their possibility before the passage of the 1964 Civil Rights Act, during which civil rights leaders made clear their opposition to quotas, very little was heard about the issue at all.[23] Moreover, as will be demonstrated later, key civil rights movement figures ignored or opposed the Philadelphia Plan when it introduced an affirmative action policy in the construction industry in 1969.

In terms of understanding the previous period of history, in which affirmative action was not even considered an option, something must have existed that precluded quota-based policies. Whatever it was, it was disappearing or at least in crisis by the time affirmative action policies came to dominate the policy environment. John David Skrentny devotes an entire section of his book, *The Ironies of Affirmative Action,* to this very question.[24] Noting that, in fact, none of the civil rights groups asked for affirmative action before it was implemented, he asks why, if racial preference was in their interest, they did not demand it in 1964? His answer is simple: "Anything beyond color blindness had a strange, taboolike quality. Advocacy of racial preference was one of those 'third rails' of American politics: Touch it and you die."[25]

Skrentny's study concentrates on reconstructing the "historical and cultural context of policy elites." Three chapters address the problem of "understanding resistance to affirmative action." Skrentny shows the historical and ideological barriers to affirmative action and includes a discussion on what he calls "acceptable preference." This "color-blind" model of American society is compelling, particularly in Skrentny's explication of affirmative action and colorblindness as systems of thought that dominated different periods of history.[26] He sees affirmative action not as a specific set of policies but as a model or "policy paradigm."[27] He compares it with what he sees as the previous policy paradigm, the color-blind model. This usefully divides the piecemeal decisions from the arrival of affirmative action as a *system.* However, in order to understand why affirmative action could not be implemented before Nixon took the reins of the presidency, the "color-blind" paradigm must be investigated.

One point that has become clear (and will be discussed later) is that, before World War II, quota-based policies existed, implemented by the federal government and private companies. This move to create quotas provoked very little comment at the time. Beside this, official quotas dictated the "racial" nature of immigration to the United States after 1924. Presumably the color-blind paradigm simply did not operate before World War II. When did it operate, and why? Another possible problem with the "color-blind" model is that much of the color-blind rhetoric still holds true during the "affirmative action era." Justice Harry Blackmun, dissenting in the *Bakke* case, stated that America was going through a regrettable but necessary phase of "transitional inequality" that would end "within a decade at most."[28] Many other supporters of affirmative action today see their ultimate goal as a color-blind society but suppose that color-conscious policies are needed to achieve that goal.[29] Though there is undoubtedly much insight to be gained by arguing that a "color-blind" ethos prevented affirmative action from operating, we must look more closely at how this color-blind ethos operated.[30]

Skrentny's more recent book, *The Minority Rights Revolution,* deals with the formation of groups in the Nixon era and since. It asks some excellent questions about where the limits to consideration as a minority are. All of the minorities that became affirmative action beneficiaries did so with no campaign and little organizational pressure. Though Skrentny makes some very pertinent observations about the dynamics behind inclusion of specific groups, he is vague about the overall reasons for sponsorship by political figures. These issues will be taken up in Part 3.[31]

Thomas Sugrue has written about the history of affirmative action. He notes that, on both sides of the spectrum, the most influential arguments about affirmative action rest on two assumptions. First, affirmative action represented a radical departure from previous public policies to address racial inequality. Second, the policy of racial preferences destroyed a liberal consensus that dominated American politics since the New Deal. Both of these perspectives he calls "fundamentally ahistorical."[32]

Sugrue is half-right in his condemnation. Superficially, affirmative action can be seen as simply taking prior civil rights policies to their logical conclusion, enforcing what perhaps should have been enforced in the first place. But he misses the alteration of the context within which this old and somewhat obvious policy idea was implemented, and missed the effect it had on liberal policies. Though the form remains the same, the content has been completely altered, determining how policy makers implemented it.

Notes

1. Annotated News Summary (ANS), no date [it is likely to be, from its place in the file, early January 1970], News Summaries—January 1970, Box 31, ANS, Folder 2 of 4, Nixon Presidential Materials Staff: Presidential Materials Review Board: Review on Contested Documents [hereafter Contested Documents]: WHSF: SMOF: POF, NPMP.

2. In an interview in the 1980s with Joan Hoff, Nixon said he thought the "mark of a leader is whether he gives history a nudge." Joan Hoff, *Nixon Reconsidered* (New York: Basic Books, 1994), 6.

3. Dean Kotlowski, *Nixon's Civil Rights: Politics, Principle, and Policy* (London: Harvard University Press, 2001), 124.

4. Sidney M. Milkis, "Remaking Government Institutions in the 1970s: Participatory Democracy and the Triumph of Administrative Politics." *Journal of Policy History* 10, no. 1 (1998): 53–70.

5. Theodore Lowi, *The End of Liberalism: Ideology, Policy, and the Crisis of Public Authority* (New York: W. W. Norton & Company, Inc., 1969), 213.

6. Michael W. Combs and John Gruhl use the following definition: "By affirmative action, we refer to specific and result-oriented procedures that are utilized to insure that nonwhites and women are not disadvantaged in efforts to secure employment." Combs and Gruhl, eds., *Affirmative Action: Theory, Analysis, and Prospects* (Jefferson, NC: McFarland & Company, Inc., 1986).

7. Barbara R. Bergmann, *In Defense of Affirmative Action* (New York: Basic Books, 1996), 31.

8. See Arnold R. Hirsch, "Massive Resistance in the Urban North: Trumbull Park, Chicago, 1953–1966," *Journal of American History* 82, no. 2 (September 1995): 522–50; Thomas J. Sugrue, "Crabgrass-Roots Politics: Race, Rights and the Reaction against Liberalism in the Urban North, 1940–1964," *Journal of American History* 82, no. 2 (September 1995): 551–78; Rogers M. Smith, "Beyond Tocqueville, Myrdal, and Hartz: The Multiple Traditions in America," *American Political Science Review* 87 (1993): 549–66; Mary L. Dudziak, *Cold War Civil Rights: Race and the Image of American Democracy* (Princeton: Princeton University Press, 2000).

9. Robert A. Dahl, *Who Governs? Democracy and Power in an American City* (London: Yale University Press, 2005 [1961]), 316.

10. In fact, because the book relies on Nixon's presidential material, the real endpoint for historical discussion is in 1973. Those examining the archives will know that by 1974 Watergate so dominated discussion among Nixon's inner sanctum that little domestic policy direction is discernible.

11. See, for example, Richard Hofstadter, *The Paranoid Style in American Politics and Other Essays* (London: Jonathan Cape, 1965 [1952]), and Seymour Martin Lipset and Earl Raab, *The Politics of Unreason: Right Wing Extremism in America, 1790–1970* (London: Heineman, 1971).

12. Cited in Alan Brinkley, *Liberalism and Its Discontents* (London: Harvard University Press, 1998), 279.

13. Cited in Rodney Barker, *Legitimating Identities: The Self-Presentation of Rulers and Subjects* (Cambridge: Cambridge University Press, 2001), 2.

14. Terry H. Anderson, *In Pursuit of Fairness: A History of Affirmative Action* (New York: Oxford University Press, 2004).

15. Cited in Stephen Steinberg, *Turning Back: The Retreat from Racial Justice in American Thought and Social Policy* (Boston: Beacon Press, 1995), 110–11.

16. Stephan and Abigail Thernstrom, *America in Black and White: One Nation, Indivisible* (New York: Simon and Schuster, 1997), 172. Many others agree. See, for instance, Herman Belz, *Equality Transformed: A Quarter-Century of Affirmative Action* (London: Transaction Publishers, 1992).

17. Thernstrom, *America in Black and White*, 427–28.

18. Hugh Davis Graham, *The Civil Rights Era: Origins and Development of National Policy 1960–1972* (New York: Oxford University Press, 1990), 456.

19. Hugh Davis Graham, "Race, History, and Policy: African-Americans and Civil Rights Since 1964," in Hugh Davis Graham, ed., *Civil Rights in the United States* (University Park: The Pennsylvania State University Press, 1994), 12-39, esp. 19–20.

20. Nathan Glazer, *Affirmative Discrimination: Ethnic Inequality and Public Policy* (London: Harvard University Press, 1987). The first book-length justification for

affirmative action I have found is John Fleming, *The Lengthening Shadow of Slavery: A Historical Justification for Affirmative Action for Blacks in Higher Education* (Washington, D.C.: Howard University Press, 1976).

21. Cited in A. James Reichley, *Conservatives in an Age of Change: The Nixon and Ford Administrations* (Washington, D.C.: The Brookings Institution, 1981), 165. Graham lists John Rawls' *Theory of Justice* though it was published in 1971, *after* the Philadelphia Plan. None of the books he lists predate his "policy watershed" for civil rights. See Graham, "Race, History, and Policy," 19.

22. This point is made by Hanes Walton in his book, *When the Marching Stopped: The Politics of Civil Rights Regulatory Agencies* (New York: SUNY Press, 1988).

23. This point is discussed in chapter 3.

24. John D. Skrentny, *Ironies of Affirmative Action* (Cambridge, MA: The Belknap Press of Harvard University Press, 2002). See Part 1, "Understanding Resistance to Affirmative Action," 19–66.

25. Skrentny, *Ironies of Affirmative Action*, 3.

26. The "color-blindness" rule draws on the classic dissent of the first Justice Harlan in *Plessy v. Ferguson*, 163 US 537, 559.

27. See Skrentny, *Ironies of Affirmative Action*, 6–7.

28. Cited in Graham, *The Civil Rights Era*, 470.

29. See, for instance, Steinberg, *Turning Back*, and Bergmann, *In Defense of Affirmative Action*.

30. See Andrew Kull, *The Color-Blind Constitution* (London: Harvard University Press, 1992).

31. John D. Skrentny, *The Minority Rights Revolution* (Cambridge, MA: The Belknap Press of Harvard University Press, 2002).

32. Thomas J. Sugrue, "The Tangled Roots of Affirmative Action," *The American Behavioral Scientist* 41, no. 7 (April 1998): 886–96, esp. 888.

I

FROM MYRDAL TO THE KERNER COMMISSION: THE RISE AND FALL OF BARRIERS TO AFFIRMATIVE ACTION IN THE POSTWAR PERIOD

1

The Postwar Intellectual Milieu
and the Taboo Against Affirmative Action

ECONOMIST MILTON FRIEDMAN summed up the bemusement felt by many
Americans in the 1950s that race problems in the South still existed. It is
worth citing at length a piece written just after the 1957 events in Little Rock,
Arkansas, where he expressed faith that the market would overcome the irrational problems of race:

> No one who buys bread knows whether the wheat from which it was made was
> grown by a communist or a Republican, by a constitutionalist or a fascist, or, for
> that matter, by a Negro or a white. This illustrates how an impersonal market
> separates economic activities from political views and protects men from being
> discriminated against in their economic activities for reasons that are irrelevant
> to their productivity—whether these reasons are associated with their views or
> with their color.[1]

The hope and, for many, the expectation that American capitalism would
eventually destroy racial divisions between Americans was not limited to
those on the right; it informed most enlightened opinion on race at the time.
Few at the time thought that anything other than a Keynesian oiling of the
wheels (though Friedman disagreed that even this was necessary) or a redi-
rection of resources was needed to completely destroy racial divisions. Race
was exogenous to the market system; lingering racial antipathies were a hang-
over from slavery, a peculiar institution of the South. Should they be exposed
to the light of day, they would surely wither and die. Even those whose analysis of the rise of the National Socialist Party in Germany left little room for
racial optimism had their doubts assuaged by the unexpectedly huge growth

of the American economy after World War II. None of the problems after World War I reasserted themselves after this second war. Class divisions—upon which, many analyses at the time had it, racial divisions were based—became less and less a feature of American society. Even if doubts about man's capacity for reason and rationality haunted postwar thinkers, the problems of the haves and the have-nots could at least be put off by constantly increasing growth. It was this operational optimism above all that ensured that affirmative action—while its principles were understood—was not used in the postwar period.

Postwar Liberal Views on Race

Why examine liberal views on race? Quite simply, they—not conservative views—influenced the postwar world. As Daniel Bell observed, conservative thinkers were exiled to the margins after World War II. "Since World War Two had the characteristic of a 'just war' against fascism, rightwing ideologies and the intellectual and cultural figures associated with those causes, were inevitably discredited."[2] Though several writers have rightly questioned the view that American history is a continuity of liberal traditions, during the postwar period liberal precepts (set out by Louis Hartz in particular, but aided by Myrdal's "American Creed") undoubtedly dominated the intellectual landscape.[3] Most of these ideas expressed, as one of the defining thinkers of postwar liberalism put it, a "certain operational optimism with a certain historical and philosophical pessimism."[4]

Several characteristics of the dominant thinking on race in the postwar United States stand out as important when assessing why affirmative action was not implemented. First, the dominant perspective on race in the 1930s followed the communist line that racial divisions were a subdivision of economic or class divisions. Racial inequality was seen as an inherent tendency of capitalism, a branch of the division between worker and employer. However, as the United States entered World War II, a new liberal confidence asserted itself, defining itself not only against the communism of the Soviet Union but also against the racial ideas of the Nazis. Ultimately, a fresh perspective on race and race relations emerged, changing the ways that Americans viewed racial issues. In particular, this postwar liberal perspective viewed race thinking, a component of the way Americans understood themselves in the interwar years, as inimical to American traditions and values.

Thus, a revolution in the way race was understood occurred during and after the war. Racial divisions acceptable before the war were essentially redefined as problematic. In light of the Nazi experience, psychologists were enlisted to explain what appeared to leaders to be the bewildering motivations of men and women who became committed Nazis or Communists. The question of race became central to liberal critiques of American democracy. Polls undertaken had showed that most Americans had no idea why they were fighting the war. Democracy had to be redefined and reinvigorated. Ellen Herman observed: "Among the most glaring examples of how depraved public opinion could actually be, and therefore how much in need of expert management, was 'intergroup conflict.'"[5] Instead of a political understanding of problems of race that had been prevalent before the war—an essentially communist idea—the problem of racism was increasingly seen in psychological terms or moral terms.[6] If the problems were psychological or moral, the answers could not be found in bureaucratic measures.

More importantly, a new sensitivity on racial questions forced policy makers to reassess their former contention that issues of ethnic and racial discrimination were best avoided. As Elazar Barkan and, more recently, Mary Dudziak have shown, the realization that the United States would soon become deeply involved in world affairs convinced the elite that the treatment of blacks in the South might become a diplomatic Achilles heel.[7]

Gunnar Myrdal and the American Creed

Capturing the spirit of the new war-time racial liberalism, the Swedish sociologist Gunnar Myrdal defined America's treatment of African Americans as the primary aspect of the problem in the United States. He was called upon in 1938 by the Carnegie Corporation to conduct a comprehensive study of American race relations. Myrdal assembled all those with experience in researching Negro problems for his vast project while staying very much in control of the end product. The study gained in stature after the war began and mobilization against fascist ideology started in earnest. It was published in 1944 with some fanfare. Myrdal's *An American Dilemma* appears in the bibliographies of many works considering racial problems and race relations.[8] This massive two-volume tome remained the *modus operandi* for race relations for twenty years. It drew the nation's attention to the plight of African Americans and called on all Americans to vigorously work toward a solution to the dilemma.

Myrdal's work is remarkable not because of new formulations of the problem of race in the United States. *An American Dilemma* was only one of a number of works attacking previously accepted racial dogmas[9] but it was unique in its concentration on black Americans and in its assertion that the treatment of its most downtrodden minority represented a test for American democracy. What stands out about Myrdal's study is not only its sheer size and comprehensiveness but also its summation, or perhaps even definition, of liberal attitudes toward race during the war. Myrdal displayed an insight into the rise to world leadership of the United States at this juncture of history. In the final chapter, he warned that the Soviet Union would attract the international rising tide of colored people with egalitarian propaganda. The ability of the United States to counteract such propaganda, plus its international standing and security, depended upon how the race problem was handled.

Efforts to sum up the themes running throughout such a huge study, as contemporary reviewers complained, prove difficult because of the vast scope of the project. However, several themes emerged that would prove important for liberal thinking on race in the post-war period. Perhaps the strongest theme to emerge in *An American Dilemma* was that of what Myrdal identified as the "American Creed." This was a set of values that Myrdal saw as continuous throughout American history, stemming from the Enlightenment that militated towards racial equality, a tendency toward equality, justice, and fairness that was finally "realizing itself:" "The American Creed is a humanistic liberalism developing out of the epoch of Enlightenment when America received its national consciousness and its political structure."[10] Myrdal held firmly to his belief that all Americans, even the most bigoted Southerners, subscribed to this peculiarly American belief in the essential equality of humanity. He dedicated large tracts of *The American Dilemma* to proving the existence of the Creed in the South as well as in the urban North, buried as it might be beneath justifying myths of racial superiority and inferiority. In Myrdal's view, the Creed's powers attained a near magical healing power: "When the American Creed is once detected," he enthused, "the cacophony becomes a melody."[11]

A second theme was that the American race problem was national, rather than regional, and existed on the white side of the equation. Whereas in the 1930s the problem of black oppression was generally analysed as one of many in a constellation of problems emanating from economic inequality, Myrdal redefined it as a moral problem existing not in the structures of American society but in the hearts of whites. Such an analysis gave Myrdal (and other liberals) great hope for eradicating the problem: "The deeper reason for the technical simplicity of the value aspect of the Negro problem is this: From the point of view of the American Creed the status accorded the Negro in America represents nothing more and nothing less than a century-long lag of public morals."[12] The contradiction between the Creed and the practical treatment of Negroes, he insisted, led to whites harboring irrational fears and prejudices about blacks. From this, Myrdal implied that blacks need not organize themselves in order to eradicate the racial divisions that held them down.[13]

Postwar Institutions

A third theme was that American democratic institutions were basically sound and provided the best vehicles to move white Americans away from racial prejudice. During the 1930s these same institutions had become widely questioned and Myrdal sought to bolster them. American liberalism defined itself against the racism of Nazi Germany but, just as importantly, against the socialism of the Soviet Union, which had been using racial inequality in the United States as one of its key propagandistic points since 1928.[14] The American Creed expressed liberal optimism that equality of opportunity, the current embodiment of the American Dream, would create the best of all possible worlds. Though undoubtedly part of the problem, for Myrdal institutions remained the most hopeful solution to the prejudices within the hearts of white Americans, necessary to restrain the "un-democratic, un-American" tendencies within the masses. Democratic institutions must imbue the masses with "democratic values":

> The school, in every community, is likely to be a degree more broadminded than local opinion. So is the sermon in church. The national labor assembly is prone to decide slightly above the prejudice of the median member. . . . When the man on the street acts through his orderly collective bodies, he acts more as an American, as a Christian and as a humanitarian than if he were acting independently. . . .
> Through these huge institutional structures, a constant pressure is brought to bear on race prejudice, counteracting the natural tendency for it to spread and become more intense.[15]

Myrdal, in line with many liberals at the time, put forward the case for social science to play a greater role. He lectured social scientists within the United States under the heading of "Intellectual Defeatism." He railed against "the 'do nothing' tendency . . . in present day social science."[16] He noted that an educational offensive against racial intolerance "has never seriously been attempted in America."[17] However, he was optimistic that, if social science made a supreme effort, it would only be a matter of time before America would overcome its racial divide. He thought it possible that through enlightened intervention "institutions can be changed" and believed in "the improvability of man and society." Myrdal was careful not to insist that these changes should emerge *too* fast; instead, "*changes should, if possible, not be made by sudden upheavals but in gradual steps.*"[18]

Myrdal's optimism about the ability of American society to socially engineer change resonated within liberal circles during the war. Liberals' contribution to New Deal policy making and to war mobilization "proved their capacity for social engineering on the grandest scale. No problem was too great for them to handle."[19] Myrdal deliberately aimed his book at liberals; the dilemma was up to them to solve: "But with few exceptions, only the liberals have gone down in history as national heroes."[20] However, the social engineering Myrdal had in mind was essentially education. Myrdal told his readers that "the social engineering required should have its basis in a deliberate and well-planned campaign of popular education."[21] This emphasis on education of whites became a hallowed principle for race relations officials for twenty years.

Myrdal, it is important to note, inveighed against proportionalism, indicating that he was at least aware of the demand for it. He precluded the use of quotas as "unconstitutional" for the purpose of preserving individualism when he considered the question. "This norm (whereby blacks and whites share resources according to their proportions in the population) is in conflict with the Constitution, since it refers to the Negro *group* and does not guarantee *individuals* their right."[22] Throughout the book, the context within which Myrdal set the question suggested that employment quotas would have been regarded as unhelpful and unnecessary. If indeed a program of popular education was paramount, forcing affirmative action might have been counterproductive, especially as it might have jeopardized the larger project of completely eradicating racial divisions from American life.

Employment was far from the core of the problem according to Myrdal's "rank order of discrimination," a ranking of the social importance to both whites and blacks of various aspects of discrimination. The order, from the most difficult area to overcome racial divisions to the easiest, was (1) intermarriage and sexual intercourse, (2) personal relations—drinking, dancing, etc., (3) schools and churches, (4) political disenfranchisement, (5) courts, police, etc., and (6) land, credit, and jobs. Not only were jobs the least difficult barrier to breach but "(e)verything done to modify the caste order must diminish the *moral* conflict in the hearts of the Americans and thus decrease the defense needs, which give emotional energy to false racial beliefs."[23] Jobs were simply not, in Myrdal's view, a priority area for knocking down racial beliefs.

The Influence of Myrdal

Myrdal succeeded in setting the agenda for race relations. Soon after its publication, *An American Dilemma* became the most cited authority on race relations, buoyed in its authority by the increased interest in racial equality surrounding the forming of the United Nations and the attention to the problem by such noteworthy figures as Wendell Wilkie and Eleanor Roosevelt. David Southern notes that: "For twenty years, the Swede's authority was such that liberals simply cited him and confidently moved on."[24] Myrdal's influence among government and legal personnel, especially those involved in civil rights issues, seemed to know no bounds in the postwar period. The 1948 Truman initiative on civil rights, *To Secure These Rights*, capitalized the term "Creed" and quoted whole lines straight from Myrdal. One of the authors of the pamphlet, Robert Carr, told a House Committee that the aim of the report was to "restate the American Creed or the American Dream."[25] One of the first tasks that Harry Truman accomplished on civil rights was to banish racial classification from federal government paperwork. Chief Justice Earl Warren voiced the unanimous decision in favor of the plaintiff in the famous *Brown v. Board of Education* decision, citing Myrdal in footnote 2: "And see generally Myrdal, *An American Dilemma* (1944)."[26] Myrdal remained the basic text for civil rights professionals and other government authorities for many years. Harris Wofford, on joining the Civil Rights Commission set up by David Eisenhower in 1958, remembered that *An American Dilemma* and *To Secure These Rights*, were "our initial texts."[27]

Initially, dissenters from Myrdal's "American Creed" analysis of race relations were lumped into two camps: those influenced by Communist Party literature on race relations and those influenced by white Southerners. Apart from these marginal constituencies, Myrdal remained virtually unquestioned within the social science community. Nothing either communists or Southerners had to say made much impact against the inexorable tide of opinion in favor of his study. Southern liberals' published criticisms mildly chastised Myrdal for his insistence that the pace of change in the South should be forced but acknowledged the sometimes painful accuracy of his assessment of the racial situation in the South. The black intellectual Oliver C. Cox, in *Caste, Class and Race*, underscored Myrdal's perception that racial beliefs were the most important aspect holding back blacks: "If beliefs, per se, could subjugate a people, the beliefs which Negroes hold about whites could be as effective as those which whites hold against Negroes."[28] Accurate as Cox's criticisms might have been, his associations with the Communist Party ensured that they were marginalized. Herbert Aptheker attacked Myrdal's study vociferously for ignoring black culture, foreshadowing criticisms heard more recently, as well as for Myrdal's insistence that economic structure had little to do with black oppression. But the fact that Aptheker also toed the increasingly unpopular Communist Party line insured that his criticisms remained in obscurity until some years later.[29]

However, the focus changed. As the threat of irrational mobs receded in the nervous stability of the early postwar years, race was analyzed less as a problem of the "mob" than as a psychological problem within individuals. Though no fundamental rethink of race relations took place, few analyses of the problem of race appeared at all in the 1950s. Most social scientists rejected the concept of race entirely, preferring more general concepts such as "group hostility," "value difference," or "intergroup relations." Oscar Handlin was able to ask in the 1957 edition of his book, *Race and Nationality in American Life*, "What ever happened to race?"[30] As late as 1964, influential sociologist Talcott Parsons still attempted to provide a socio-psychological model within which to place racial problems: "Where such a large reservoir of repressed aggression exists but cannot be directly expressed, it tends to become 'free-floating' and to be susceptible of mobilization against various kinds of scapegoats outside the immediate situation of its genesis."[31]

Though the stress may have been different than Myrdal's, most of his assumptions about the fundamental nature of the problem remained unchallenged in social science literature. Abram Kardiner and Lionel Ovesy's influential 1951 work, *The Mark of Oppression*, emphasized on its final pages that "[i]t is the white man who requires the education."[32] Psychologist Gordon Allport, whose book on prejudice was regarded as one of the most authoritative during the 1950s, introduced the "contact theory," based on the military research of Samuel Stouffer and the study on housing by Mary Evan Collins and Morton Deutsch. The idea, entirely in line with Myrdal's assertion that the prejudice of white Americans constituted the largest part of the problem of black American inequality, was that increased contact between blacks and whites would decrease prejudice.[33] In any event, it is possible to understand Allport's optimism. The desegregation of the army, widely predicted to cause chaos, withstood the test of the Korean War, encouraging belief that a low profile effort to desegregate would provoke the least resistance. At most, government action to desegregate consisted of a series of court decisions eradicating the vestiges of federal complicity in segregation.

Beside the influence of the Myrdalian analysis of American race relations, two key developments made liberals who, before the war, had at least accepted racial quotas (to be discussed in the next chapter) think again. First, the expected economic slump after the war did not materialize; instead, the prosperity enjoyed during the war continued. Second, the heightening of anticommunist sentiment culminating in the Cold War created sensitivity and embarrassment about race problems and thus a reluctance to raise potentially divisive issues. The accompanying critique of "totalitarianism" also divested many liberals of their dedication to social engineering and led to a stress on freedom, especially from government interference.

Full Employment

The problem of black unemployment that later inspired the launch of affirmative action policies was subsumed at the time within the problem of unemployment in general. In early 1944, Franklin D. Roosevelt called for full employment and set a goal of sixty million jobs. His successor Harry Truman put forward a Full Employment bill in 1946; it was amended, after conservative claims that it was an attack on free enterprise, and appeared as the Employment Act of 1946. Liberals kept up the push for full employment, though. It remained a key liberal goal from the war to the late 1960s and addressed the worst liberal fears about the possibility of fascism occurring in the United States. The problems that many liberals felt led to fascistic governments in Europe—chronic unemployment, scarcity, poverty—threatened America, too, before the war. Harry Hopkins had reminded his boss in 1939: "With twelve million unemployed we are socially bankrupt and politically unstable. . . . The country cannot continue as a democracy with ten million or twelve million unemployed. It just can't be done."[34] As Alonzo Hamby, chronicler of liberalism during the Truman years, stated: "The nightmare of a totalitarian America, should progressivism fail to meet postwar necessities, existed constantly in the back of the liberal mind."[35] Full employment was also a cry heard on the left. Many Americans felt that large, monopolistic corporations had wielded excessive power over government policy, created artificial scarcity, fixed prices, and a "reserve army of labor" by maintaining more or less constant unemployment. Full employment would deprive proto-fascists of the conditions that fed frustrations and encouraged people to look for a scapegoat. James Patton, the president of the National Farmers Union, indicated the importance given to employment problems by a generation scarred by the Depression: "Nearly all our problems start with the possibility of mass unemployment; nearly all our solutions must start with full employment."[36]

Patton also expressed the growing feeling among liberals that the accumulating abundance of the late 1940s and 1950s, seen after the 1930s as little short of miraculous, would be the solution to many of the old problems. The wartime dream of sixty million jobs was achieved in 1947 and left behind in the ensuing years. Economic growth began to be seen not just in quantitative terms but as a solution to what had been seen as qualitative problems. The "dog-eat-dog" problems of the 1930s, the battles between the "haves" and the "have nots" that plagued history, all these might be overcome by distributing such a volume that exactly how it was distributed was not an urgent issue. Looked at another way, as long as everyone moved up constantly on the ladder of opportunity, people would not pay so much attention to which rung they were on. Godfrey Hodgson summed up the thinking at the time: "The abundant society could short-circuit the two quintessential questions of politics, the question of justice and the question of priority: Who gets what? What must we do first?"[37]

Few, outside of the extreme left and extreme right, resisted this principle as memories of the Depression faded. As economist John Kenneth Galbraith

noted, there was little ideological dissent from the principle of full employment: "Neither the Eisenhower Administration nor the Conservative min-
istries of Churchill, Eden, and Macmillan in Britain were less committed in
principle to full employment and economic expansion than their Democratic
or Labour opposition."[38] Until the late 1960s, few doubted that the United
States had the physical and moral resources to see off any of the problems that
had haunted previous generations.

This liberal postwar optimism about the old battles between classes influenced the way race relations were seen. First, complacency came about, given
that problems seemed to be resolving themselves without the pervasive social
engineering that Myrdal felt was necessary. Second, a consensus around the
desirability of racial reform existed between liberals and conservatives outside
the South. Liberals may have placed less faith in the "impersonal market" than
Milton Friedman but they agreed that the problem, like that of class divisions,
was chiefly one of the past. Policies based on redistribution, in such an atmosphere, might jeopardize this alliance of views.

Anti-Communism

Also ensuring antipathy toward government-regulated quotas was the shift toward anti-communism within liberal circles. First, an atmosphere of intense
competition lent the crusade for economic growth a patriotic pretence. The
fascination and even awe inspired by the industrialization of the Soviet Union
made liberals acutely aware of the importance of competing successfully in
economic terms. Daniel Bell, in *The End of Ideology* (1960), blamed liberal regard of communism for what he felt was an overemphasis on economic
growth: "And in this appeal, Russia and China have become models. The fascination these countries exert is no longer the old idea of the free society but
the new one of economic growth."[39]

The theory of "totalitarianism" associated State planning with Nazism and
communism. The wartime experience, commented Reinhold Niebuhr, "has
prompted the democratic world to view all collectivist answers to our social
problems with increased apprehension."[40] Defense of democratic society
meant that American institutions—separate from the State—had to be promoted and protected as the hallmarks of a free society. To implement
government-regulated affirmative action at this time would have been an
indictment of business, trade unions, churches, schools, the Democratic
Party, and countless other bulwarks against totalitarianism, all of whom had
launched campaigns to promote better treatment of African Americans. It
would have given the message to the outside world (and this audience, as

historian Mary Dudziak and others have shown, was a key liberal concern) that intervention into the private affairs of Americans by the State was both necessary and part of the solution to race problems. As a U.S. Information Agency (USIA) pamphlet published in the early 1950s noted, changes could not come from "fundamental changes in human attitudes by commands from a central source" or "alter psychology by fiat." The problem of racial prejudice ultimately could not be eradicated through law, for it was "essentially a question of evolving human relations."[41]

Not only would direct government intervention be ineffective in changing hearts and minds, it contradicted the message of freedom ringing out from Washington. Uniting both liberals and conservatives during the Cold War years was a distrust of solutions by government dictate. Harvard economist and "liberal leader" Alvin H. Hansen stressed the dangers of overcentralized planning. "We do not want a totalitarian state," he wrote. "We want freedom of enterprise . . . freedom for collective bargaining . . . freedom for cooperative action . . . freedom of choice of occupation."[42] However, during the hyper-Americanism of the McCarthy period, any suggestion of even the mildest socialist sympathies could be fatal. Liberals, no matter how sincere their antipathy to racial discrimination, shied away from advocating anything that might have been interpreted as such, including the "social engineering" called for by Myrdal.[43]

Finally, affirmative action had a direct connection with communism as the one force in American society that directly pushed for quotas during the postwar period was the Communist Party of the United States. At its sixth Congress in 1928, American Communists accepted a new doctrine defining Southern Negroes as an oppressed group and calling for the creation of a separate black nation, echoing Stalin's work advocating the right of self-determination for the oppressed minorities of the former Tsarist empire. It had first espoused demands for quotas in 1934, when it attempted to preempt the black nationalist "Don't Buy Where You Can't Work" boycotts by mounting an interracial picket demanding that black employees be hired without any white workers being fired.[44] After the war, the party continued this semi-successful tactic. Through its representative organizations, it sponsored black demands for African-American representation in employment within companies in black areas. In *Lucky Stores v. Progressive Citizens of America*, May 26, 1947, a case before a California county court that progressed to the California Supreme Court, a "communist-dominated branch of the NAACP" in Richmond, California, had picketed Lucky Stores because of alleged brutality to a shoplifter and insisted that the store's workforce approximated the black proportion of Lucky's customers. The communist-front organization, the Progressive Citizens Association, lost at the California Supreme Court, but a notable dissent was made by Roger Traynor. In his opinion, minorities "may seek economic equality either by demanding that hiring be done without reference to race or color or by demanding a certain amount of jobs for members of their group."[45] This is not to say that all requests for quotas of minority hiring emanated from the Communist Party. They emerged spontaneously among civil rights and nationalist groups. One of the original demands made by those boycotting the buses in Birmingham, Alabama, in 1956 was that a number of black bus drivers be hired. This demand, however, was later dropped.[46]

Conclusion

Though much of the scholarship agrees that some rubicon was crossed in the late 1960s, few sketch the intellectual terrain of the so-called "color-blind" period to indicate why affirmative action was not seriously considered as an option. As has been shown above, even though the door was left open to racial quotas, liberals simply refused to go through it.

The central tenets of Myrdal, which expressed postwar liberal attitudes about race so perfectly, remained almost unquestioned until the 1960s. First, race was seen as an excrescence on American life, chiefly emanating from the South. Existing American institutions were basically good, the structure sound. Second, the problem of race was essentially a white problem. White prejudice, rather than any flaws within the black community, was to blame for all racial problems. Blacks, as Kenneth Stampp put it in the 1950s, were simply "white men in black skins"; their culture was simply a reaction to their exclusion from the mainstream.[47] Third, race prejudice was a product of irrationality, usually at a low rather than a high level of society. Thus, race problems were best attacked by education and increased contact aimed at showing the irrationality of racism. Fourth, most Americans—even those in the South—knew that race prejudice was wrong, even if they resisted change. Affirmative action, given these terms, was simply not an appropriate measure. Rather than bringing the races together, it would have solidified the divide. It would also exacerbate prejudice amongst the lower—laboring—classes, lending a rationale to the racism that they knew was immoral and irrational.

Furthermore, after the war, many of the tensions that the elite feared between haves and have-nots were alleviated by constant economic growth. The demand for labor, many Americans then reasoned, would soon force even the most prejudiced employers to take on black Americans without forcing the issue. American capitalism, they then thought (and had some reason to think), would automatically begin the process of integrating all Americans. The next chapter indicates how the ideas discussed above influenced government policy on race relations.

Notes

1. Milton Friedman, "Capitalism and Freedom," in Felix Morley, ed., *Essays on Individualism* (Philadelphia: University of Pennsylvania Press, 1958), 166–90, esp. 180. Others making similar points include William G. Carleton, "The Second Reconstruction: An Analysis from the Deep South," *Antioch Review* XVIII (Summer 1958): 171–80, esp. 174]. See also J. Milton Yinger and George E. Simpson, "Can Segregation Survive in Industrial Society?" *Antioch Review* XVIII (Spring 1958): 10–20, esp. 16.

2. Cited in Kenan Malik, *The Meaning of Race: Race, History and Culture in Western Society* (London: MacMillan, 1996), 14.

3. Rogers Smith questions whether an equalitarian American Creed has ever really existed. See Rogers M. Smith, "Beyond Tocqueville, Myrdal, and Hartz: The Multiple Traditions in America," *The American Political Science Review* 87, no. 3. (September 1993): 549–66.

4. Arthur M. Schlesinger, Jr., *The Vital Center: The Politics of Freedom* (Boston: The Riverside Press, 1949), 256.

5. Ellen Herman, *The Romance of American Psychology: Political Culture in the Age of Experts* (London: University of California Press, 1995), 57.

6. See, for instance, T. W. Adorno et al., *The Authoritarian Personality* (New York: Harper and Brothers, 1950). Many of the most prominent authors on racial issues, such as Gordon Allport and Bruno Bettelheim, were psychologists.

7. Elazar Barkan, *The Retreat of Scientific Racism* (Cambridge: Cambridge University Press, 1992); Gary Gerstle, "The Protean Character of American Liberalism," *American Historical Review* 99, no. 4 (October 1994), 1045–74, esp. 1070; Mary L. Dudziak, *Cold War Civil Rights: Race and the Image of American Democracy* (Princeton: Princeton University Press, 2000). See also John D. Skrentny, *The Minority Rights Revolution* (Cambridge, MA: The Belknap Press of Harvard University Press, 2002), chapter 2, "'This Is War and This Is a War Measure': Racial Equality Becomes National Security," 43–66.

8. This is perhaps less true today because Myrdal is seen as "fatalistic and deterministic in championing the ameliorating power of government and laws to eliminate racial injustice." Robert F. Burk, *The Eisenhower Administration and Civil Rights* (Knoxville: University of Tennessee Press, 1984). See also Stanford Lyman, "Race Relations as Social Progress," in *Race in America*, ed. Herbert Hill and James E. Jones, Jr. (Madison: University of Wisconsin Press, 1993), 78–99.

9. See, for instance, Gunnar Dahlberg, *Race, Reason and Rubbish: An Examination of the Biological Credentials of the Nazi Creed* (London: Allen and Unwin, 1942) and Ruth Benedict, *Race and Racism* (London: Routledge, 1942). For an excellent discussion of the shift in thinking regarding race among anthropologists, psychologists, and sociologists occurring just before and during World War II, see Barkan, *The Retreat of Scientific Racism*.

10. Gunnar Myrdal, *An American Dilemma: The Negro Problem and American Democracy* (New York: Harper & Brothers Publishers, 1944), 8.

11. Myrdal, *An American Dilemma*, 3.

12. Myrdal, *An American Dilemma*, 24.

13. He entitles one section "A White Man's Problem" and states that: "It is thus the white majority group that naturally determines the Negro's 'place.'... The Negro's entire life and, consequently, also his opinions on the Negro problem, are, in the main, to be considered as secondary reactions to more primary pressures from the side of the dominant white majority." Myrdal, *An American Dilemma*, xlvii.

14. See Harvey Klehr, *The Heyday of American Communism: The Depression Decade* (New York: Basic Books, 1984).

15. Myrdal, *An American Dilemma*, 80.

16. Cited in David W. Southern, *Gunnar Myrdal and Black–White Relations: The Use and Abuse of An American Dilemma, 1944–1969* (London: Louisiana University Press, 1987), 58.

17. Cited in Southern, *Gunnar Myrdal and Black–White Relations*, 59.

18. Myrdal, *An American Dilemma*, 518. Emphasis in original.

19. Gerstle, "The Protean Character of American Liberalism," 1070.

20. Myrdal, *An American Dilemma*, 7.

21. Myrdal, *An American Dilemma*, 383.

22. Myrdal, *An American Dilemma*, 336. Emphasis in original.

23. Myrdal, *An American Dilemma*, 60, 110. Emphasis added.

24. The next sentence reads: "If historians need to understand the rudiments of Keynsian ecomomics to teach effectively the recent past, then they surely need to know something of Myrdal, the Keynes of American race relations." Southern, *Gunnar Myrdal and Black–White Relations*, xvi.

25. Leon Friedman, ed. *The Civil Rights Reader: Basic Documents of the Civil Rights Movement* (New York: Walker and Company, 1967), 67.

26. Cited in Southern, *Gunnar Myrdal and Black–White Relations*, 123, 127. David Levering Lewis, while agreeing on the impact of Myrdal's work, maintains that it was influential only for a decade. Lewis, "Origins and Causes of the Civil Rights Movement," in Charles Eagles, *The Civil Rights Movement in America* (London: University Press of Mississippi, 1975), 74–92.

27. Harris Wofford, *Of Kennedys and Kings: Making Sense of the Sixties* (New York: Farrar, Strauss, Giroux, 1980), 465.

28. Oliver C. Cox, *Caste, Class and Race: A Study in Social Dynamics* (New York: Doubleday, 1948), 531. Cox devoted an entire section of his book to attacking Myrdal in what was clearly the most effective contemporary critique; see 509–38.

29. Most modern-day Myrdal critics often decline to cite Aptheker's 1946 book, *The Negro People in America: A Critique of Gunnar Myrdal's An American Dilemma* (New York: Kraus Reprint, 1977). They cite instead black novelist Ralph Ellison, who voiced these same criticisms at the time in an essay which remained unpublished for some years, a fact that only underlines the omniscience of the Myrdalian model at the time of publication. Ellison, echoing Aptheker's primary point, asked, "[C]an a people ... live and develop over three hundred years simply by *reacting*?" Ralph Ellison, *Shadow and Act* (New York: Signet Books, 1966), 360.

30. Oscar Handlin, *Race and Nationality in American Life* (Boston: Little, Brown and Company, 1957 [1948]), chapter 8, "Whatever Happened to Race?" 188–207. See also Southern, *Gunnar Myrdal and Black–White Relations*, 218.

31. Talcott Parsons, "Certain Primary Sources and Patterns of Aggression in the Social Structure of the Western World," *Essays in Sociological Theory* (New York: Free Press, 1964), 308–9. Thomas F. Gossett, *Race: The History of an Idea in America* (New York: Harper and Brothers, 1964) is also useful in fleshing out this point.

32. Cited in Herman, *The Romance of American Psychology*, 190.

33. "Contacts that bring knowledge and acquaintance are likely to engender sounder beliefs about minority groups [therefore]. . . . Prejudice . . . may be reduced by equal status contact between majority and minority in the pursuit of common goals." Gordon W. Allport, *The Nature Of Prejudice* (Reading, MA: Addison-Wesley, 1954), 17.

34. Cited in Godfrey Hodgson, *In Our Time: America From World War II to Nixon* (London: MacMillan, 1977), 49.

35. Alonzo Hamby, *Beyond the New Deal: Harry S. Truman and American Liberalism* (London: Columbia University Press, 1973), 5.

36. Hamby, *Beyond the New Deal*, 9.

37. Hodgson, *In Our Time*, 51.

38. John Kenneth Galbraith, *The Affluent Society* (London: Penguin Books, 1962), 160.

39. Daniel Bell, *The End of Ideology* (Glencoe, IL: The Free Press, 1960), 373.

40. Cited in Alan Brinkley, *Liberalism and Its Discontents* (London: Harvard University Press, 1998), 86.

41. Mary L. Dudziak, *Cold War Civil Rights: Race and the Image of American Democracy* (Princeton: Princeton University Press, 2000), 51.

42. Cited in Hamby, *Beyond the New Deal*, 11.

43. As a useful background to the changes in liberalism after the war, see chapter 5, "The Two World Wars and American Liberalism," of Brinkley, *Liberalism and Its Discontents*, (79–110). See also Gareth Davies, *From Equal Opportunity to Entitlement: the Transformation and Decline of Great Society liberalism* (Lawrence: University Press of Kansas, 1996).

44. Klehr, *The Heyday of American Communism*, 341.

45. Paul D. Moreno, *From Direct Action to Affirmative Action: Fair Employment Law and Policy in America 1933–1972* (London: Louisiana State University Press, 1997), 93. Chapter 4, pp. 84–107, discusses *Hughes*. See pages 90–97 for a general discussion of the case.

46. William H. Chafe, *The Unfinished Journey: America since World War II* (New York: Oxford University Press, 1986), 163.

47. Kenneth Stampp, *The Peculiar Institution* (London: Eyre and Spottiswoode, 1964 [1956]), 8.

2

Letting Sleeping Dogs Lie: Policy Making and Affirmative Action Before Nixon

THE STANCE OF THE U.S. GOVERNMENT toward racial issues in the 1940s and 1950s broadly reflected liberal perspectives outlined in the last chapter. Faith in the ability of the market to at least postpone—if not slowly alleviate—race problems framed policy makers' response. The issue must be approached delicately, they reasoned, to prevent dangerous reactions from threatening the quiet steps being made toward racial equality. Calling attention to racial issues except for statements of intent at the highest level to assuage international critics was seen as destructive criticism at a time of great rivalry with the Soviet Union. Moreover, a hearts and minds problem required moral leadership rather than mechanical solutions. In this climate, affirmative action, though a known and available policy option throughout the period, was resisted.

When the civil rights movement began its activist approach to asserting their rights, the response of many articulate observers was a mixture of cautious approval and worry about what forces may have been unleashed. Within the civil rights question was an undoubted tension between national purpose and local structures and institutions. But, when the civil rights movement first arrived on the scene, very few were shaken from their belief in the Myrdalian precepts or from a belief that American society would eventually become racially integrated. After the Soviets launched the *Sputnik* probe, however, these precepts were not so much abandoned as practically applied with a new energy and vigor.

It was not that nobody had imagined such a policy as affirmative action. A curious aspect of the scholarship on the history of affirmative action is that it, with a few honorable exceptions, generally ignores or is unaware of all mention of affirmative action before John F. Kennedy's Executive Order 10925 of 1961. Usually, this is cited as the first mention of the phrase "affirmative action" in the context of black civil rights, emerging only after the civil rights movement had begun a concerted campaign for such rights. Nicholas Lemann, for instance, published a piece in the *New York Times Magazine* identifying Hobart Taylor, Jr., the young black lawyer in charge of drafting the executive order banning discriminatory hiring by federal contractors. Taylor told an interviewer at the Lyndon B. Johnson Library: "I put the word *affirmative* in there at that time. I was searching for something that would give a sense of positiveness to performance under that executive order, and I was torn between the words *positive action* and the words *affirmative action*. . . . And I took *affirmative action* because it was alliterative."[1] But the phrase had already been in use for nearly a century. It had been connected to civil rights since World War II. Had Taylor read the reports published by his predecessors in the Truman Contract Compliance Committee, he might have saved himself some time.

In the more distant past, the phrase routinely referred to positive action (in today's parlance, a "pro-active" response to a particular problem) from at least the middle of the nineteenth century. The earliest example of the phrase, which was perhaps valued by writers, as it was with Taylor, for its alliterative qualities, has been found by this author in *The Nation* in 1866.[2] Originally referring to assent on the part of a legislative body, it began to be associated with Progressive movement demands for government regulation.[3] It was used to call for government action to ensure equality of opportunity in the face of the perceived shortcomings of the capitalist market. During the first half of the twentieth century, this redress dealt with equal opportunity for economic classes rather than racial groups. In 1914, reformer William F. Willoughby, in an address to the American Association for Labor Legislation, called for "equalizing of opportunities" through a "fuller recognition of the province of the modern state." He reminded his audience that "real individualism can only be secured through the state recognizing that *affirmative action* on its part is necessary if this end is to be maintained.[4]

The phrase made a significant legislative appearance in the 1935 Wagner Act, again in relation to the rights of labor. There, it asked that managers take "affirmative action" to re-employ union members laid off because they joined a union.[5] Later, the phrase was used to delineate the new postwar conception of human rights. Reflecting the liberal attachment to the New Deal and the rejection of discredited laissez-faire capitalism, one United Nations (UN) report stated: "The list of fundamental freedoms thus includes not only the traditional rights of man against interference from the state, but the newer rights arising from the changed conditions of economic life and the necessity of affirmative action on the part of the state to enable the individual to be free in a highly industrialized and interdependent economic society." Later, the report elaborated: "It is, however, feasible to distinguish between the older body of political rights, directed against the interference of the state with the liberty of the individual, and the newer body of economic and social rights which call for affirmative action on the part of the state."[6]

The term first became associated with civil rights sometime in the 1940s. A Fair Employment Practices Committee (FEPC) ordered employers to cease and desist their discriminatory practices and "take the following affirmative action": (1) hire the black women and men who had filed complaints; (2) educate white workers about FEPC regulations; (3) devise and announce publicly a nondiscrimination employment and promotion policy; and (4) submit monthly reports to the FEPC.[7]

After the war, for reasons discussed in the last chapter, the emphasis on government regulations diminished as bureaucratic means of lessening race discrimination fell out of favor. The wartime espousal of augmentations of the market, associated as it was at the time with depression and war, gave way to a concerted defense of market principles in opposition to communism. However, five years after the demise of the federal FEPC in 1946, President Truman issued a further executive order to ensure that federal contractors followed policies of nondiscrimination. Truman signed Executive Order 10,308 on December 3, 1951, which provided that all government contracts and subcontracts have nondiscrimination clauses. The order also set up the President's Committee on Government Contract Compliance to ensure compliance with the order. Staffed by members of the business community, labor representatives, social workers, and federal employees, it had no powers of enforcement, however, and had to convince contracting agencies to weed out discriminating contractors. As such, its impact was negligible. On January 16, 1953, it published an obscure final report for what was apparently a very limited audience.[8] However, it called for "affirmative action" against racial discrimination in the report. After seeing encouraging signs of active nondiscrimination in the Office of Education against recalcitrant states, the Committee recommended, in an unpublished version of its report, "The Bureau of Employment Security take more affirmative action in a program to aid employers, Federal-State Employment Services, and other agencies in the maximum placement of minority group workers."[9] The published version of the report contained a use of the phrase with similar persuasive implications: "Nevertheless, the Office of Education should take more affirmative action to persuade states to conform to the enunciated policy of the Federal Government."[10] The phrase was familiar enough outside of bureaucratic agencies to occur in magazine articles in the late 1940s and 1950s.[11]

Nor was the imposition of quotas by the federal government unprecedented, as historian Paul Moreno has shown. A quota program operated within the Public Works Administration (PWA). Secretary of Labor Harold Ickes issued an order prohibiting discrimination based on race or religion in all PWA projects on September 1, 1933. In 1934, Isador Lubin of the Bureau of Labor Statistics disclosed a confidential plan by which the Labor Department would negotiate for projects that would use 50 percent Negro labor. Clark Foreman, also of the Bureau of Labor, suggested basing the proportion of Negroes in each job category upon the occupational census of 1930. The PWA put Foreman's plan into effect. No quotas were ever devised for other racial or religious groups. Ickes sent a message to the National Association for the Advancement of Colored People's (NAACP) 1935 annual conference explaining the program. The contract for the first federal housing project, in Atlanta, specified that 12 percent of the skilled labor payroll must go to Negro employees.[12] Moreno saw this action partly as a response to the Davis-Bacon Act of 1931 which required paying "prevailing wage rates," thus reducing migrant nonunion (often black) employment. In other words, these quotas may have been meant to prevent too much cheap black labor. If this is true, the NAACP raised no objections to the PWA quotas. In general, there was little objection in principle to the PWA experiments. They were successfully instituted in most cases, and met no legal challenge.[13]

Postwar policy makers struggled between the realization on a local level that employers would fail to act without regulatory action, and their commitment on a national level to Myrdalian precepts—something that was to last until the Nixon presidency. Affirmative action remained a tempting but, in the end, undesirable option for policy elites concerned about racial divisions during the 1950s and early 1960s.

The inherent problems of "voluntaristic" policies at a local level were already well-known even at this stage. It was extremely difficult to untangle the claims and counterclaims of individuals concerned, which had the effect—along with the lack of compulsive measures—of inaction on the part of employers. Moreover, overt discrimination was not seen as the major problem; instead, the problem, as Vice President Nixon would state in 1955, was "like an iceberg, only part of it is visible."[14] The Truman Committee report clearly struggled to create a role for itself. Suggestions included advertising specifically "among such groups as the physically-handicapped, upper-age groups, women, minority groups."[15] Mirroring the concerns that resulted in the Philadelphia Plan nearly twenty years later, labor groups were attacked for discriminatory practices: "The Committee recommends that the Federal Committee on Apprenticeship promulgate policies which will *exert maximum influence* to eliminate discrimination and restrictive practices from all apprenticeship programs."

Throughout these reports issued in the 1950s, phrases like "affirmative stand," "exert maximum effort," "a need for definite action," and "act positively and affirmatively" can only indicate a perception that discrimination must not only be attacked in a negative sense—by outlawing discrimination. Some sort of structural or institutional reform was needed.[16]

Eisenhower set up a new commission to replace the earlier one. In its publications designed to persuade employers to take the lead in tackling racism (Myrdal had, after all, stated: "Northern white workers are often said to start out with a feeling of strangeness and suspicion against Negroes. If they meet with a firm policy from the employer, they change, usually quickly."[17]), it is possible to see some of the assumptions behind today's affirmative action. In answer to the question, "How can an agency determine whether there was discrimination in a particular action?" a pamphlet, using the example of "Indians," put out in 1955 told staff to check the history of the employer. If said supervisor had previously, "on his own initiative," promoted or appointed other Indians, the complaint might be deemed unwarranted: "If no Indians had ever been appointed or promoted to a position such as that in question by that particular supervisor, further investigation would become necessary."[18]

When affirmative action machinery was finally installed in the 1970s, this process would become known as a "compliance review." The supervisor was assumed to discriminate (or at least to warrant further investigation) if he had appointed or promoted no Indians in the past. The implication for the employer was that if he appointed or promoted an unspecified quota of Indians, he would have fulfilled his obligation to equal opportunity policy. Certainly, racial quotas had not been made illegal as an employment policy of a private employer. The Superior Court of California, dealing with the aforementioned *Hughes* case, declared in 1950 that "it [the court] need not forbid the employer to adopt such a quota system of his own free will."[19]

Progress in combating racial discrimination, despite the declared good intentions of both federal and state governments at the time, was slow if not nonexistent. One trumpeted accomplishment of the Committee for Contract Compliance was that, in 1960, "a Negro electrician was hired for the first time in the District of Columbia by a contractor engaged in the construction of a Federal building."[20] This took place only after threatened litigation. However, such small gains still looked good in percentage terms; a second Negro electrician would constitute a 100 percent increase. Less cynically, many Americans hoped that cases like this would set an example, breaking down the prejudices of union members and employers and opening the door for more black workers. For African Americans living at the time, however, the lack of patience with such glacial progress exemplified by Martin Luther King, Jr.'s *Why We Can't Wait* must have been widespread.[21]

The theory of "institutional racism" that forms the basis to affirmative action policies, emphasizing the harm of unintentional racism through systematic exclusion of minorities using what appear to be nonracist patterns and practices as opposed to intentional discrimination, was at least partially understood in the 1950s. The New York Supreme Court, for example, in its summing up of *Holland v. Edwards* (1953) found against an employment agency that inquired into an applicant's change of name. To the agency's contention that the name change inquiry was not intentional discrimination, the court answered: "Discrimination in selection for employment based on considerations of race, creed, or color is quite apt to be a matter of refined and elusive subtlety. Innocent components can add up to a sinister totality."[22]

In a report by Eisenhower's President's Committee on Government Contracts, of which Vice President Richard Nixon was chairman, the observation was made that: "Overt discrimination, in the sense that an employer actually refuses to hire solely because of race, religion, color, or national origin is not as prevalent as is generally believed. To a greater degree, the indifference of employers to establishing a positive policy of nondiscrimination hinders qualified applicants and employees from being hired and promoted on the basis of equality."[23] Thus, the theory of "disparate impact," voiced by the Supreme Court in the 1971 *Griggs v. Duke Power Co.* ruling—at least the reasoning behind it that effects and not intentions were harmful—was familiar to policy makers in the 1950s.

Theoretically, based on Truman's Executive Order in 1948 declaring that contractors must include a nondiscrimination clause (Eisenhower renewed this clause upon taking office in 1953), the federal government had the power to cancel contracts and to debar contractors from further government contracts. Richard Nathan, in a report written for the Civil Rights Commission in 1969, claimed that several firms were debarred during the Eisenhower and Kennedy administrations.[24] Though Kennedy undoubtedly made specific the penalties for discrimination in his Executive Order, there is no evidence to support John D. Skrentny's contention that the first agency with "real power" was Kennedy's President's Committee on Equal Employment Opportunity (PCEEO). The PCEEO did have some powers but, again, without full backing in the White House, it dared not bare its teeth.[25] Whatever the case, the PCEEO failed to take significant action.

All the parts were in place: the analysis of the problem of institutional racism was at least vaguely understood in government circles, the necessity for some sort of proportional solution to the problem of employment discrimination had been grasped, and the mechanism for enforcing it existed, at least as a potential. Yet it was not used.

The only effort at initiating affirmative action policies was to cajole and coax businesses to implement programs. As one official in Truman's contract compliance committee observed, "(i)t is not the desire of the Committee to win compliance with a club. The processes of education and appeals to human decency and basic American principles will be the prime weapons against discrimination." To insist would have been to undermine faith in the ability of American business to accomplish the task itself, to admit that, far from being a rational force for progress, this American institution pushed the country away from its democratic goal of equal opportunity. Not only that, forcing Americans to accept quotas of minorities, it was thought, would not be successful: "It is a well known fact that the most effective means of obtaining compliance with any statute, regulation or order is by achieving acceptance on the part of the public. There is no budget large enough to force adherence to an unaccepted law, as witness prohibition."[26]

Contract compliance had to be "sold" to employers, the committee thought. Much of the efforts of the Truman Committee and its inheritor in the Eisenhower administration directed themselves towards explaining to employers that discrimination was bad business. For example, a pamphlet put out by the CGC warned prejudiced company directors that "a discriminatory attitude on the part of employers or employees may result in:

Cost to employers
Wasted skills
Destruction of competition
Cost to community
Destruction of employee incentives
Cost to nation
Lowered purchasing power"[27]

With the benefit of considerable hindsight, we might speculate that a more positive response on the part of employers could have been forthcoming had "widespread rioting" been added to the list. Nevertheless, it is interesting that most of these relate to economic goals, similar to the way diversity is sold today. The same document asked in a "question and answer" section whether racial proportionalism might be utilized. The peremptory treatment given the question by the pamphlet indicates that such issues were beyond serious consideration: "Should the interviewer making referrals try to send out a certain percentage or "balance" of Negro and white workers? Ans. No. Referrals based on qualifications for a job avoid the proportion consideration."[28]

In its voluntary guise, and only implemented in specific circumstances, affirmative action did not necessarily contradict the framework of racial liberalism whereby racial inequality was best addressed by convincing individual whites that racial discrimination was irrational or morally wrong. The affirmative action programs that the government employed were designed to be exemplary, aiming at cajoling and even threatening businessmen into hiring more African Americans and thus integrating them, from the top down. As Truman's Contract Compliance Committee emphasized by capitalizing the following sentence, "DEMOCRACY THRIVES ON VOLUNTARY ACTION BY MEN OF GOOD WILL. PREJUDICE IN EMPLOYMENT CAN BE DEFEATED MOST EASILY WHERE IT BREEDS—IN FACTORIES, UNIONS, AND COMMUNITIES."[29]

Within the reports issued by the Truman and Eisenhower committees, the importance of equal opportunities for black Americans was continuously stressed in light of America's role as world leader in the fight against communism. Certainly, there was awareness that many emerging third-world countries found America's race relations deeply unattractive. The Soviet Union made the race situation in the United States one of its most important propagandistic points throughout the early postwar period. The Truman committee reminded Americans that: "This is no longer the problem of several states. The spotlight of world leadership in the fight against tyranny and oppression reveals shortcomings which our enemies are exploiting on every continent." Throughout the report, various mentions of the world role of the United States were repeated, telling its readers that the country "must fortify the claim to this leadership by deeds among our own people."[30]

Why, given the high priority allegedly given to combating racial prejudice, did the report issued by the Truman committee in 1953 receive so little attention? Voting rights and racial segregation of schools and facilities attracted some attention nationally throughout the 1950s, especially after *Brown v. Board of Education* in 1954. The heightened awareness of the domestic "threat" of communism after Senator McCarthy made his widely-publicized charges made racial liberals wary of repeating or even being too sensitive to charges made by the Soviets. Labor issues might have been more sensitive than those of education, given the connection between many unions prominent in war industries and Moscow. But another answer is given in correspondence from Durward V. Sandifer, Acting Assistant Secretary for United Nations Affairs, to Robert Granville, chairman of the committee dated August 22, 1952. "One of the most persistent themes of the Communists is the alleged widespread racial discrimination practiced in the United States. This theme is only infrequently stated in terms of discrimination in employment practices. Much greater emphasis is placed upon more general charges of the denial of human rights." Thus, the committee and its recommendations, minimal though they were, could be safely ignored by Truman and the incoming Eisenhower, world attention being fixed on human rights and not employment issues.[31]

Affirmative Action and the Beginnings of the Civil Rights Movement

Underlining the reliance of social theory on Myrdal's insistence that racism was a "white man's problem," the fear when black civil rights campaigns began in the 1950s was of white resistance to change. The liberal line on civil rights expressed, above all else, the need to quell "totalitarian" tendencies that might, if unchecked, grow into mass movements. Black protest was beside the point at that stage. As Walter Jackson noted, "mass movements" in relation to civil rights implied to white liberals something akin to the Ku Klux Klan, a dangerous right-wing extremist sentiment that could target other groups besides blacks. The dangerous areas where prejudice "breeds," were the "factories, workplaces, and communities" where the white masses could be found.[32]

Operating on these assumptions and united by a common enemy, a loose coalition of Americans at least mildly approved of civil rights initiatives. In this period the factors that united them were more important than the disagreements between them, although, in the 1960s the disagreements rose to the surface.

The most committed to the cause of civil rights, of course, were black Americans themselves. Most black civil rights activists prioritized achievement of equality above the stability of the liberal order, though most felt at the time that their best hope of achieving their aims was through lobbying and pressuring liberal leaders in power. On a political level, black Americans tended to be within the Democratic New Deal coalition. Left-wing (but still anti-communist) liberals tended to welcome the civil rights protests in the 1950s. Southern white radical liberals such as James Anderson Dombrowski, Virginia and Clifford Durr, Anne and Carl Braden, and others had rallied to the cause of better treatment for blacks in the South as early as 1938 on the basis that continued segregation and devaluation of black Southerners held Southern development back. They maintained their commitment throughout the 1950s and 1960s. However, due to the climate created by McCarthyism in the South, the central organization of these liberals, the Southern Conference for Human Welfare and, later, the Southern Conference Education Fund, despite being roll calls of prominent black and white liberal activists, were barely able to sustain themselves and made, by their own admission, little impact on Southern white attitudes.[33]

More mainstream liberals initially welcomed black protests but expressed nervousness about possible responses by Southern whites. The *Nation* blended optimism with concern about the effect on the Democratic Party of such protests. The *New Republic* took an even-handed approach, publishing pieces such as "The NAACP's New Direction" by Paul Jacobs, which complained in 1956 of the growing militancy of the NAACP.[34] It also featured debates between

Southern "moderates" (defined as wishing to slow down but not entirely stop desegregation) such as Virginia State Senator Benjamin Muse and NAACP representatives such as Thurgood Marshall.[35]

Of course, to those in politics, there existed a political answer to the problem of inequality. The New Deal had successfully harnessed the votes of hitherto ignored urban immigrants, marshalling them into powerful forces and giving Italians, Eastern Europeans, and others real power. From this position of power, these immigrant groups secured resources, jobs, and other forms of patronage and launched themselves into the American mainstream. Not surprisingly, many Americans felt that giving blacks the vote would resolve their problems. Eisenhower's Attorney General Herbert A. Brownell recalled drafting a four-part civil rights bill: "We believed that once black citizens had the right to vote . . . they would have a 'level playing field' and the same opportunity to achieve their political goals as all other citizens."[36]

Others felt that racial equality would make democracy stronger and thus it was worth supporting. Seymour Martin Lipset expressed what was no doubt the consensus amongst the intelligentsia when he wrote: "Democracy is not only or even primarily a means through which different groups can attain their ends or seek the good society: *it is the good society itself.*"[37] However, even those more critical of American democracy looked upon the civil rights struggle primarily as a means to an end rather than the end itself. As the left-wing publication *Liberation* magazine put it in 1964, when the cracks were beginning to appear, "In our opinion, civil rights, vitally necessary though they are, are not an end in themselves, but a beginning towards the really good society in which man will be really equal—economically and socially *as well* as politically."[38]

The factor that united these disparate streams of liberalism was the continuing appearance of progress. African Americans, liberals, and many conservatives were able to group together under the banner of progress toward racial equality, whether they saw it as the end of the perfection of democracy, the creation of real democracy, or simply black equality. As long as progress toward it appeared to be forthcoming and the enemy of it could be clearly identified, a broad consensus (outside of most Southern whites) existed. Federal government action against the Southern recalcitrants seemed the best possible method of achieving this goal to nearly everyone that considered themselves liberal. Loren Miller, writing in the early 1960s, stated that the liberal outlook "contemplates the ultimate elimination of all racial distinctions in every phase of American life through an orderly, step-by-step process adjusted to resistance and aimed at overcoming such resistance."[39]

When civil rights movement activists began to take direct action, more moderate liberals became uneasy. While the commitment of the civil rights movement to achieving patriotic American values made liberals sympathetic, the social activism—despite its religious and nonviolent nature—made many mainstream liberals worry that instability caused by direct action might be more harmful to American democracy than the good of achieving racial equality faster. The liberal Texan Johnson aide Harry McPherson remembered Martin Luther King, Jr.'s bus boycott as "vaguely disturbing" because of the "Negroes' assertiveness, the use of the active voice on their own behalf."[40] However, most liberals welcomed the emergence of the question, confirming, as it did, their theories on the need to control irrational mobs, personified in Southern whites. They called not for mass support of the civil rights movement but for firm government action.

After *Brown,* Southern resistance began getting organized. While civil rights groups also began organizing, their existence inspired little comment, let alone revision of the Myrdalian model. As Jackson shows, only *The New Republic* contained any coverage of the Montgomery bus boycott, "an event that was greatly overshadowed in the national press by Massive Resistance." Throughout the 1950s race relations were considered legally and politically tricky but not yet intellectually problematic. Most mainstream liberal Americans felt they understood black anger but equally felt that protests and demonstrations hurt the cause by provoking white anger.[41]

Kennedy's Muscular Liberalism

John F. Kennedy's dictum, "a rising tide lifts all boats," indicated his strong commitment to the idea that constant economic progress was the best means of satisfying black demands. True, black demands were much louder in the 1960s than they were in previous years. The liberal response to this challenge to the existing institutions, however, was to regard it simply as a challenge and to redouble existing efforts. This was the meaning for liberals of Kennedy's election, as Harold Fleming observed in 1966: "The 'moral leadership' of the White House, absence of which had been so long and bitterly decried by civil rights spokesmen, was seen as an imminent reality."[42] Liberal ideas, it was felt by many, would soon be vindicated.

The civil rights movement showed a genius for exploiting the difference between liberal idealism and pragmatism in power. Kennedy was elected in 1960 to "do something" about America's problems and he had contrasted himself with the complacency of the Eisenhower years. Civil rights was among the problems identified by the Kennedy team where it was felt that executive action might be needed. Kennedy's Executive Order 10925, issued in 1961 and containing the term "affirmative action," created a new agency, the President's Committee on Equal Employment Opportunity, and provided for more stringent and explicit requirements on government contractors. Despite the new emphasis on enforcement, it created no new standards for proving discrimination. Without specific provable discrimination, little could be done against employers suspected of discriminating. The most visible aspect of the Order was the Plans for Progress program, designed to induce prominent government contractors to devise their own plans for increasing minority group hiring and employment mobility. The National Urban League's Whitney Young praised Plans for Progress in 1963 for its preferential hiring policies. However, the NAACP's Herbert Hill and Martin Luther King, Jr. were more critical.[43]

The issue of "racial preference" arose during Kennedy's tenure and was significant enough that the president felt he had to react to it, stating that he would not countenance "hard and fast quotas." He continued, "We are too mixed, this society of ours, to begin to divide on the basis of race and color."[44] Traditional liberalism and a majority in the civil rights movement rejected the notion of quotas because the Myrdalian analysis of the problem, particularly the optimistic view that white Americans would eventually be reformed away from their prejudices that had kept black Americans down through the centuries, remained largely intact.

Throughout the early 1960s, faced with the rising tempo of civil rights protests, some began to question whether the existing provisions, based on the fair employment approach of the Fair Employment Practices Committees (FEPCs) initiated by Roosevelt, were adequate. Minnesota Senator Hubert H. Humphrey introduced a bill on August 1, 1963, S.1937, which sought to "establish a broader and more comprehensive obligation of providing equal employment opportunities." Humphrey's bill hoped to go further than the fair employment approach of the state FEPCs.[45]

What was becoming apparent to all Americans shortly before the 1964 Civil Rights Act passed was that previous efforts had not yet been effective. The civil rights activism of the early 1960s, with its well of support and legions of volunteers, had proved both that existing civil rights efforts were deficient and that doing nothing would simply aggravate the problem. The bill ran into opposition from Southerners who pointed out that the legislation would simply nationalize postwar FEPC acts passed by twenty-five states shortly after the war. Southern racial conservatives like John Stennis were able to point out that the pressure for a federal act came from the failure of these other approaches. He asked "Why should we compound and enlarge the error by expanding such a law to all States?"[46] However, due precisely to the objections of Southern Democrats, the Act failed to go any further than the state FEPC laws, except in the sense that it prohibited discrimination on the basis of sex in addition to race, color, national origin, and religion (ironically, this inclusion came because of a failed spoiling tactic by Representative Howard Smith of Virginia).

Title VII of the Act, dealing with employment, gave courts power to insist on "affirmative action" by employers found to be engaging in illegal employment practices to ensure nondiscrimination in hiring, firing, and promotion. These requirements covered employers with one hundred or more employees a year after the law came into effect. It extended the regulations to those with twenty-five or more after July 2, 1967. In the proceedings leading up to the bill's passage, Southern Democrats objected to the potential for forcing firms to hire quotas of African Americans, which, they said, would negate union seniority rights. The leadership of the AFL-CIO denied this charge.

However, to blunt the Southern opposition, three provisos were included within the Act. Section 703(h) allowed employers to continue with a "bona fide seniority or merit system" and section 706(g), by disallowing the court from requiring hiring, reinstatement, advancement, etc. of employees for reasons "other than discrimination on account of race, color, religion, sex or national origin," implied that reasons of racial balance would not be legitimate. Section 703(j) was the most clear in its intentions, inveighing against "preferential treatment to any individual or to any group because of the race, color, religion, sex, or national origin of such individual or group on account of an imbalance which may exist with respect to the total number or percentage of persons of any race, color, religion, sex, or national origin employed."[47]

It is clear from the debate surrounding the passage of the 1964 Act that the use of quotas, while a possibility, had no sponsors among even the most liberal congressmen and women. Hubert Humphrey insisted that "nothing in it [the Act, at that stage a Bill] will give any power to the Commission or to any court to require hiring especially at the grass roots level, firing or promotion of employees to meet a racial quota, or to achieve a certain racial balance."[48] Senator Joseph Clark, one of the floor managers of the bill, assured his colleagues that "nothing in this bill will interfere with merit hiring or merit promotion."[49] Some, like Alexander Bickel, considering the "benevolent quota," admitted in 1962 that removing legal bars to segregation would be "ineffectual" and that "the State or the Federal government may have to legislate some degree of controlled segregation."[50] Mainstream liberals, at this time, did not consider the use of quotas as legitimate in any circumstance. When Franklin Delano Roosevelt, Jr., the Chairman of the Equal Employment Opportunities Commission (EEOC), also created by the Civil Rights Act of 1964, was asked in January 1966 about the possibility of quotas, he replied: "It is wrong even to talk about quota systems."[51]

The objections made by Southern Democrats—that under the provisions of the Act, no precise definition of what constituted employment discrimination existed—were brushed aside rather than tackled head on. Liberals continued to have faith in the ability of existing institutions to include African

Americans; the 1964 Act was designed more as a prod than a stick. They hoped that the mere appearance of civil rights legislation would induce employers to hire blacks and that the process would snowball until African Americans were represented at the same level in employment as they were in the American population.

The provisos demanded by Southerners and some Republicans caused little consternation amongst the liberal sponsors of the bill except in that they were barriers to its passage. The AFL-CIO never seriously worried that it might be adversely affected by the legislation and argued against the need for the provisos. The 1964 Civil Rights Act, though it raised the profile of affirmative action, did not change its definition.

One other consideration that, while not a key consideration in some liberal minds, was certainly considered by those involved in politics as a solid reason to resist quotas. Trade unions and African Americans made up two important Democratic constituencies. On most civil rights issues, the AFL-CIO and the individual unions took a liberal stand and backed the civil rights movement's demands. Enforced quotas, however, would threaten the unions' seniority systems. Southerners made this point when arguing against passage of the 1964 Civil Rights Act. Segregationist Governor George Wallace, campaigning for the presidency, was quite aware of this clash of interests, as he explained in May 1964 to a predominantly blue-collar audience in Baltimore. Federal officials, Wallace explained, would soon "tell an employer who he's got to employ. If a man's got one hundred Japanese-Lutherans working for him and there's one hundred Chinese-Baptists unemployed, he's got to let some of the Japanese-Lutherans go so he can make room for some of the Chinese-Baptists. And, of course, what does that do for your seniority rights? It destroys them!"[52] Though Wallace made little headway in 1964, the vehement denials that any quotas would result from the 1964 Civil Rights Act heard in Congress at least indicated the unease within the Democratic camp about potential clashes. The fear was, at the time, that labor would leave the camp.

Conclusion

In response to civil rights challenges in the 1950s and early 1960s, policy makers generally maintained their optimistic outlook, though they viewed the civil rights movement's campaign with increasing anxiety. The fragility of liberal confidence in the market to accomplish social goals was exposed at the end of the 1950s with the launching of *Sputnik* and the outbreak of disturbances at Little Rock. At the heart of the dilemma policy makers faced was whether American institutions would respond to the challenges they faced.

The more activist approach adopted by policy makers in the 1960s reflected a general sense of impatience with the Eisenhower years. However, this was a Keynesian oiling of the wheels, designed to spur the existing institutions to action, a reaffirmation of existing perspectives rather than its reconsideration. Though many thought that more action was needed, few doubted that the goal of a more equal, racially integrated society was achievable.

Affirmative action remained an obvious but unused option for the authorities in the postwar period. With the latter sense of urgency, some began to raise the possibility that such a policy might be an effective method, particularly in relation to black employment. However, the hopes and fears of postwar liberal thought influenced policy makers, ensuring that quota-based remedies were not seriously considered. As a "hearts and minds" issue, racial discrimination would not be dealt with effectively by edicts; with the experience of Prohibition no doubt still in their minds, policy makers felt that stringent requirements might backfire. There was also a patent fear of the white working class still present in the minds of those who remembered the rise of Hitler and had the threat of Communism on their minds. When the main threat to democracy seemed to come from the "masses," policies that might cause blue-collar resentment did not seem prudent. Democrats wished, too, to accentuate the positive aspects of race relations and hoped that employment discrimination would disappear along with a host of other problems with education, increased contact, and increased African-American power through voting. All civil rights efforts by the federal government in this period concerned removing barriers to equality rather than directly engineering it.

Notes

1. Nicholas Lemann, "Taking Affirmative Action Apart," in Francis J. Beckwith and Todd E. Jones, *Affirmative Action: Social Justice or Reverse Discrimination?* (Amherst, NY: Prometheus Books, 1997), 34–55, esp. 39. Nearly all observers reach a similar conclusion. See Hugh Davis Graham, *The Civil Rights Era: Origins and Development of National Policy 1960–1972* (New York: Oxford University Press, 1990), 457; John Skrentny, *The Ironies of Affirmative Action: Politics, Culture, and Justice in America* (London: University of Chicago Press, 1996), 6; Niclaus Mills in the introduction to Niclaus Mills, ed., *Debating Affirmative Action, Race, Gender, Ethnicity and the Politics of Inclusion* (New York: Delta, 1994), 4–18, esp. 5; and Seymour Martin Lipset, *American Exceptionalism: A Double-Edged Sword* (London: W.W. Norton and Co., 1996), 118–20.

2. Editorial, "Our System of Legislation," *The Nation*, May 15, 1866, 617.

3. See, for example, Frank J. Goodnow, "State Taxation of Interstate Commerce," Publications of the American Economic Association, 3rd series, vol. 5, no. 2, Papers

and Proceedings of the Sixteenth Annual Meeting, Part II. New Orleans, LA, December 29–31, 1903.

4. William F. Willoughby, "The Philosophy of Labor Legislation: Presidential Address, American Association for Labor Legislation," *The American Political Science Review* 8, no. 1. (February 1914): 14–24, esp. 20–21. Italics added.

5. Graham, *The Civil Rights Era*, 33.

6. Inter-American Juridical Committee: Draft Declaration of the International Rights and Duties of Man and Accompanying Report, *American Journal of International Law* 40, no. 3, Supplement: Official Documents (July 1946), 93–116, esp. 106, 109.

7. Cited in Andrew Edmund Kersten, *Race, Jobs, and the War: The FEPC in the Midwest, 1941–1946* (Chicago: University of Illinois Press, 2000), 123.

8. See *Equal Economic Opportunity: A Report by the President's Committee on Government Contract Compliance,* (Washington, D.C.: U.S. GPO, January 16, 1953). Hardly ever cited, this report fails to get any mention at all in *Five Years of Progress, 1953–1958: A Report to President Eisenhower by the President's Committee on Government Contracts* (Washington, D.C.: U.S. GPO, 1958).

9. Final Report of the Committee and Related Working Papers 1952–1953, box no. 3, entry 12, Records of the CGCC: RG325, NARA. The published version omits this reference.

10. "Equality of Opportunity: The Right to Work"—A Report by the PCGCC, December 1952, box no. 3, entry 12, Records of the CGCC: RG325, NARA.

11. See, for example, Otis W. Coan, "What One Visitor Discovered in the South," *The Crisis* 57, no. 2 (February 1950), 73–76, where "affirmative action" was used as a subject heading.

12. Paul D. Moreno, *From Direct Action to Affirmative Action: Fair Employment Law and Policy in America 1933–1972* (London: Louisiana State University Press, 1997), 58.

13. See Moreno, *From Direct Action to Affirmative Action,* 57–65. Moreno admits that "the quotas were grants of immunity—and this may explain why they were never challenged by contractors. Usually the quotas were exceeded, so black groups did not try to sue for enforcement." Ibid., 58. A similar point is made by Michael S. Holmes, "The New Deal and Georgia's Black Youth," *The Journal of Southern History* 38, no. 3. (August 1972), 443–60.

14. "Nixon Broadcasts On Job Discrimination," Press Release of the Conference on Equal Job Opportunity, Sponsored by the President's Committee on Government Contract Compliance (CGCC), held October 25, 1955, Washington, D.C., box no. 4, entry 12, Records of the CGCC: RG325, NARA.

15. Unsigned letter headed "The President's Committee on Government Contract Compliance", no date, *Final Report of the Committee and Related Working Papers 1952–1953,* Copies of Letters Sent to Agency Heads and Private Persons by the Executive Director of the Committee, April 18, 1952–May 29, 1953, box no. 1, entry 12, Records of the CGCC: RG325, NARA.

16. *Equal Economic Opportunity: A Report by the President's Committee on Government Contract Compliance,* January 16, 1953, 73.

17. Gunnar Myrdal, *An American Dilemma: The Negro Problem and American Democracy* (London: Harper and Brothers Publishers, 1944), 394.

18. The President's Committee on Government Employment Policy, *Some Questions and Answers on the Non-Discrimination Policy of the Federal Government* (Washington, D.C.: U.S. GPO, 1955).

19. *Hughes v. Superior Court* 339 US460 (1950), cited in James E. Jones, Jr., "The Bugaboo of Employment Quotas," *Wisconsin Law Review* 27 (1970): 341–403, esp. 378. Moreno, *From Direct Action to Affirmative Action*, 92.

20. *Pattern for Progress: Final Report to President Eisenhower from the President's Committee on Government Contracts* (Washington, D.C.: U.S. GPO, 1960).

21. See Martin Luther King, Jr., *Why We Can't Wait* (New York: Harper & Row, 1963).

22. Moreno, *From Direct Action to Affirmative Action*, 132.

23. *Pattern for Progress*, 14.

24. Richard P. Nathan, *Jobs and Civil Rights: The Role of the Federal Government in Promoting Equal Opportunities in Employment and Training* (Washington, D.C.: USCRC Clearinghouse Publication by the Brookings Institution, April 1969), 91. Subsequent Civil Rights Commission Reports, however, denied that any debarments or cancellations had taken place up until the 1970s. See, for example, the Civil Rights Commission's *The Federal Civil Rights Effort: Seven Months Later* (Washington, D.C.: U.S. GPO, May 1971), 18.

25. The PCEEO did break new administrative ground in that it oversaw the enforcement efforts of other agencies who were often unwilling to jeopardize close relationships with their contractors. See Skrentny, *Ironies of Affirmative Action*, 114.

26. *The Administration of the Non-Discrimination Requirements in Government Contacts*, prepared by Dept. of Labor, October 1952, *Interim Report* of October 8, 1952 (not released), folder marked "Final Report," Records of the CGCC: RG325, NARA.

27. *Service to Minority Groups*, U.S. Department of Labor Employment Office Training Program: Instructor's Guide, December 1951.

28. Ibid.

29. *Equality of Opportunity: The Right to Work*, A Report by the President's CGCC, December 1952, folder labeled "Equality of Opportunity: The Right to Work," box no. 3, entry 12, Records of the CGCC, NARA. Nixon warned businessmen to adopt affirmative action (then termed nondiscriminatory) policies before they were made mandatory. See "Nixon Broadcasts On Job Discrimination."

30. *Equality of Opportunity: The Right to Work*, A Report by the CGCC, December 1952, folder entitled Equality of Opportunity: The Right to Work, box no. 3, entry 12, Records of the CGCC, NARA.

31. Letter from Durward V. Sandifer, Acting Assistant Secretary for United Nations Affairs, to Robert Granville, August 22, 1952, folder labeled "Final Report," box no. 2, entry 12, Records of the CGCC: RG325, NARA.

32. Walter A. Jackson "White Intellectuals and Civil Rights," in *Martin Luther King and the Making of the Civil Rights Movement*, ed. Brian Ward and Tony Badger (Basingstoke: Macmillan, 1995), 96–114, esp. 99.

33. A good history of these organizations and the people within them is contained in Linda Reed's *Simple Decency and Common Sense: The Southern Conference Movement, 1938–1963* (Indianapolis: Indiana University Press, 1991).

34. Paul Jacobs, "The NAACP's New Direction," *New Republic* 135 (July 16, 1956): 9–11.

35. "Moderates and Militants," Benjamin Muse (Virginia State Senator) v. Thurgood Marshall, *New Republic* 134 (April 2, 1956): 8–10. See also "Negroes on Southern Campuses: What the Editors of Six College Newspapers in the South Think about Desegregation," *New Republic* 133 (February 27, 1956): 11–13.

36. Cited in Dean Kotlowski, *Nixon's Civil Rights: Politics, Principle, and Policy* (London: Harvard University Press, 2001), 72.

37. Cited in Stephen Rousseas and James Farganis, "Retreat of the Idealists," *The Nation* 196, no. 12 (March 23, 1963): 7–10. Emphasis in original.

38. Editorial in *Liberation* 9, no. 6 (August 1964), 4.

39. Loren Miller was the California NAACP Vice President and a black newspaper owner. Loren Miller, "Farewell to the Liberals: A Negro View," *The Nation* 195, no. 12 (October 20, 1962): 235–38, esp. 235.

40. Harry McPherson, *A Political Education* (Boston: Houghton Miflin Co., 1988), 142.

41. Jackson, "White Intellectuals and Civil Rights," 98.

42. Harold C. Fleming, "The Federal Executive and Civil Rights: 1961–1965," in *The Negro American*, ed. Talcott Parsons and Kenneth B. Clarke (Boston: Beacon Press, 1966), 371–400, esp. 371.

43. Herbert Hill, whom Carl Brauer says was friendly with liberal Republicans, denounced Plans for Progress as "one of the great phonies of the Kennedy administration's civil rights program." Carl M. Brauer, *John F. Kennedy and the Second Reconstruction*, (New York: Columbia University Press, 1977), 149. Martin Luther King, Jr.'s reaction was similar. See Moreno, *From Direct Action to Affirmative Action*, 191–94.

44. Cited in Graham, *The Civil Rights Era*, 106. For a useful discussion of the issue of quotas during Kennedy's time, see Graham, *The Civil Rights Era*, 100–120.

45. Moreno, *From Direct Action to Affirmative Action*, 205–6.

46. Cited in Moreno, *From Direct Action to Affirmative Action*, 215.

47. *The Civil Rights Act of 1964* (Washington, D.C.: Bureau of National Affairs, 1964), 335, 336, 338.

48. Cited in *Congressional Record (CR)*, 91st Congress, vol. 115, 39965.

49. *CR*, 88th Congress, vol. 110, 7218.

50. Alexander Bickell, *The Least Dangerous Branch: The Supreme Court at the Bar of Politics* (New York: Bobbs-Merrill Co., Inc., 1962), 65.

51. *A Report on the 1966 Plans for Progress, Fourth National Conference*, held at the Washington Hilton Hotel on January 24–25, 1966 (Washington, D.C.: U.S. GPO, 1966), 36.

52. Cited in Dan T. Carter, *The Politics of Rage: George Wallace, The Origins of the New Conservatism, and the Transformation of American Politics* (London: Simon and Schuster, 1995), 213.

3

The Liberal Crisis, 1965–1969

L YNDON JOHNSON, in his celebrated Howard University speech in May of 1965, promised that a White House Conference on Civil Rights would be held to determine the future of civil rights after the passage of the 1964 Civil Rights Act and the Voting Rights Act were signed into law. Johnson neglected, however, to mention this conference, which was to be the launching platform of his administration's post-1965 civil rights efforts, in his memoirs. No wonder. After the shock of the Watts riot in August and the furor over Daniel Patrick Moynihan's semi-public pamphlet, entitled *The Negro Family: The Case for National Action*, the pre-conference discussions descended into arguments and bitter recriminations.

Accordingly, the conference was rescheduled and a "planning conference" with 250 delegates took place in November 1965 (the full conference, tightly controlled and far less interesting than the planning conference, was held in May 1966). Amidst the rancor and confusion, the conference transcripts expose the central problems for liberals dealing with racial issues at the time. First, no consensus about how to proceed existed among "the coalition which staged the March on Washington, passed the Civil Rights Act, and laid the basis for the Johnson landslide—Negroes, trade unionists, liberals, and religious groups."[1] Second, no matter how much sense preferential treatment for African Americans made in relation to specific problems, it contradicted too many of the essential values and principles of the Myrdalian paradigm. To admit the need for affirmative action flew in the face of the beliefs that had inspired liberals for a decade.

This chapter shows how this crisis, in the true sense of the word, formed the backdrop of nearly every consideration of race issues in the latter half of the 1960s. Even before the long, hot summers of rioting, liberal defensiveness on racial questions meant an interrogation of the Myrdalian paradigm accompanied by an ever more shrill and insistent defense. One by one the barriers preventing affirmative action detailed in the last chapters fell. But, even by the end of the decade, few Americans would consider affirmative action regulations. Liberals would not countenance giving up their belief in the general soundness of American institutions and radicalized civil rights proponents, who would, simply refused to think that small. In fact, as later chapters will show, it was conservatives who first began to seriously suggest quotas.

The White House Conference on Civil Rights

Johnson had hoped that the White House Conference on Civil Rights would recreate the political consensus around civil rights. The consideration, therefore, was to line up the political forces that could deliver a mandate to solve the problem. Watts, however, created splits in the civil rights movement, beset as it was by confusion and increasing hostility toward liberal politics, and within the liberal camp itself before the Vietnam War became a divisive political issue.

The conference transcripts reflect disorientation of nearly all those attending. Splits occurred not only between liberals and the civil rights movement but within both camps as well. Vivian W. Henderson, who was forced to sum up the session on jobs, admitted in a memorandum to Carl Holman in December 1965: "Virtually no recommendations came out of the panel on jobs to get at the problem of race relations in employment. . . . (This is) in spite of the fact that considerable discussion was devoted to Title VII of the 1964 Civil Rights Act."[2] Even the subgroups of the conference became increasingly divided. Very few issues created a united front. Within the NAACP, for example, Dr. Morsell in Panel VII argued strenuously for "racially-conscious" statistics—in other words, statistics based on race—whereas, when the same question was brought up in Panel IV, Clarence Laws, the NAACP representative, objected that "this is the very thing we have been fighting against."[3] Herbert Hill, the NAACP labor spokesman, stated bluntly that "We are opposed to the keeping of such records."[4]

An important indication of the shared fears about the future of various institutions in the aftermath of Watts can be found within the transcripts. The implications for the whole post-war pattern of politics seemed serious to many at the conference. The preliminary report to Panel 1-A suggests that "the old basis for such (political) organization—the ward clubhouse and the organization of job-holders—is decaying or eliminated" and called for a discussion on the psychological dimensions of citizenship.[5] Above all, discussion in the panel addressed the problem of black political participation. Another preliminary report warned that "the concentration of Negroes in overcrowded areas decreases their political representation in city councils. This, in turn, reduces patronage posts and the exclusion from a fair share of the 'spoils system' discourages participation in ward organization." The same report went on to suggest that besides the danger of riot is the danger that nonparticipation of blacks in the electoral process will "deal a serious blow to effective government in the urban North."[6] Another panel expressed the anxiety of liberals faced with segregated schools: "Public education—the public schools and colleges— are (sic) the basic social institutions designed to make real, vitalize and strengthen American democracy. . . . Racially segregated schools . . . contribute to social instability and community pathology. They weaken the foundations of the American system of government."[7]

The Intellectual Crisis Foreshadows Watts

In fact, the much more public recriminations of the White House Conference had been rehearsed before the Watts riot in a more intellectual setting indicating, among other things, that the crisis was implicit in postwar liberalism rather than, as sometimes imagined, a result of rioting and disorder.[8] In an extraordinary roundtable discussion held by the liberal journal *Commentary* in 1964, academics Sidney Hook and Nathan Glazer, Gunnar Myrdal, and black author James Baldwin debated the implications of the "Negro revolution" on liberal thought. Nathan Glazer neatly introduced the discussion with a précis of the problem for liberal assumptions about political incorporation.

> Traditionally, there have always been ways of dealing with this problem, and these ways have worked well enough to prevent ethnic and race wars from breaking out. One of them has been the provision of formal equality itself: formally we take no cognizance of differences among groups. Informally, however, cognizance has always been taken of these differences. We set up 'balanced' tickets, we make sure that different groups are represented on boards, commissions, and so on.[9]

The discussion quickly polarized between James Baldwin and the others. Baldwin, while not denying the efficacy of the American Creed, insisted that a reconstitution of American democracy was necessary for African Americans to take their rightful place within it: "I might even be perfectly willing to wait ten years or a generation to be fitted into American civilization, or American society, if I really felt that I *could* be fitted into it as it now is, as it's now constituted." Baldwin made the point that American racism was a "white people's problem."[10]

Though this same point was made by Myrdal in 1944, the context had changed enough to make the others nervous and defensive. The argument went back and forth between Baldwin's assertion that something fundamental was missing from the values of American society and the others' insistence that the treatment of blacks was an anomaly in an otherwise basically healthy system of values held by Americans. Sidney Hook insisted that things were basically going along the right track in terms of racial justice and that the "ethical principles" so vital to the Creed and to liberals' belief in their own legitimacy still represented the best hope of further progress: "We certainly can say we made *some* progress—not enough . . . but progress nevertheless—by virtue of the extension of our ethical principles to institutional life." Hook declared that any progress over the past twenty years was, at least in part, a result of "our commitment to democracy, imperfect as it may be."[11]

Myrdal insisted, as he had twenty years previously, that liberal institutions contained the solution within themselves but that they must be morally pressured in order to draw out the inherent equalizing tendencies: "So what the Negroes have to rely upon in the end is that America *is* its institutions, and that the highest of these institutions will act when they come under pressure. And when they act, they will act according to certain principles, which, like Professor Hook, I call ethical." A point made by Glazer provides an interesting insight into the way liberals still viewed the issue of race, primarily as a contest between the enlightened few and the venal many: "Down below hardly anyone wants equality or is in favor of civil liberties. But up above they remember the American Creed. And the system works because there's enough power at the top to keep it going. Is that progress? I don't know. But I think that's the way things work in America."[12]

The roundtable discussion stands out for the defensiveness with which those representing, broadly, postwar liberalism approached the challenges laid out by James Baldwin. Before widespread rioting and with a huge consensus behind civil rights, liberal thinkers worried about the effectiveness of existing institutions and methods for achieving equality and, thus, the basis of their own legitimacy. Tension between concern about the viability and legitimacy of American institutions and the pursuit of civil rights made up the background of nearly all discussions of civil rights in the early 1960s.

The operational optimism and philosophic pessimism that characterized postwar liberalism in many ways affected the later course of affirmative action. The view that only a few free institutions stood as a bulwark between America and the darkness of communism and fascism amplified any dissent within the fortress. Mass political campaigns to oppose racism were considered inherently dangerous with perhaps the opposite effect (Sidney Hook's sharp delineation between those "up above" and "down below" should serve to remind us that the specter of the "masses" haunted liberal thinking at this time) and only institutions held out the promise of peaceful change. Thus, responses to the civil rights movement's pressure included ever-more shrill declarations that the existing machinery was in place, louder calls to get it moving, and quieter appeals for patience among civil rights dissenters. The sort of flexibility within a system borne of confidence in its future did not exist at that time.

The roundtable discussion represented existing sentiment amongst articulate liberals. Tilman C. Cothran wrote in 1965 that the most obvious consequence of civil rights demonstrations was "the validation of Myrdal's hypothesis" that race was "a problem in the minds of white people."[13] Loren Miller observed the differences between blacks and liberals in approach: "The liberal sees 'both sides' of the issue: the force of the Negro's constitutional argument and the existence of customs, sometimes gelled into law, that justify the gradualist approach. He is impatient with 'extremists on both sides.'" However, as Miller noted, "every civil rights victory adds to the Negro's intransigence." Miller concluded somberly that "(t)he middle ground on which the traditional liberal has taken his stand is being cut from beneath him."[14] James Baldwin stated in 1962 that Negroes "twenty years younger than I don't believe in liberals at all."[15]

Some Myrdalian precepts came in for early interrogation. In the early 1960s in the journal *Social Forces*, several correspondents tested key Myrdalian concepts, such as his "rank order of discrimination" and his assessment of the primary problem as moral. One of the greatest challenges to Myrdal's rosy picture of the future of black–white relations in the United States came from the pen of journalist Charles E. Silberman in 1964. *Crisis in Black and White* declared that "what we are discovering, in short, is that the United States—all of it, North as well as South, West as well as East—is a racist society in a sense and to a degree that we have refused so far to admit, much less face."[16] In other words, Myrdal had concentrated on the South as the source of the problem but in the North, too, pervasive racism had been found to exist. Silberman doubted Myrdal's optimistic assertion that American whites simply had to divest themselves of outmoded beliefs in the inferiority of blacks. The timing was, of course, important. By 1964 the racial crisis appeared much more serious than it had in 1962 or, for that matter, at any time since the Detroit race riot of 1943.

Silberman had already written a provocative article in *Fortune* magazine that appeared in September 1963. In it he suggested, in alarmist tones, that African Americans were becoming "increasingly intolerant of 'moderation,' and the poor, in particular, are contemptuous of the doctrine of nonviolence that has dominated the struggle so far." He noted that within a single week, Martin Luther King, Jr. was pelted with eggs in Harlem and Alabama activist James Meredith was publicly rebuked for being a "moderate." He then suggested that businessmen adopt "positive discrimination," implying that the cost for business would be less than the "cost to the community of racial violence." "Executives can be expected to be attacked from both sides," he warned. "(T)hey will need all the political art they can muster to persuade white employees that 'reverse discrimination' is socially necessary and for the greater good." These arguments, though they stopped short of calling for government-enforced affirmative action, showed the availability of affirmative action as a solution, especially to business, and connected it with the threat of racial violence.[17] Interestingly, Silberman worried not about the fairness of affirmative action but, as liberals did at the time, about the "backlash" from white workers (the changing basis for opposition to affirmative action will be explored in later chapters).

Intellectuals increasingly ran into the same problems that professionals in the Committee on Government Contract Compliance and Eisenhower's Contract Compliance committee had (albeit in a much less pressurized environment) some ten years earlier. At the first of two *Daedalus* conferences on the Negro in America in April 1964, "(t)he participants all agreed that the situation of Negro Americans required preferential treatment, but they were very unclear as to how this could be rationalized in traditional political rhetoric." The conference also highlighted the need for "equality of results," which Lyndon Johnson would later use to great effect in his celebrated Howard University speech.[18]

At first, many insisted that black protest meant that Myrdal's analysis was vindicated. Daniel C. Thompson wrote in January 1965, "(t)he Negro protest is, itself, a clear endorsement of the 'American Creed' and a reaffirmation of the faith Negroes have in the democratic process."[19] Martin Luther King, Jr. defined the issue as moral, skilfully forcing liberal opinion on the side of civil rights protest. As King said in an address to the National Press Club in 1962: "We feel that we are the conscience of America—we are its troubled soul—we will continue to insist that right be done because both God's will and the heritage of our nation speak through our echoing demands."[20]

In King's 1963 publication, *Why We Can't Wait*, he continued this theme but also began to ask that black problems be addressed in more immediate terms. In the end section of the book he discussed the issue of preferential treatment in a way redolent of Vice President Nixon's earlier veiled threat to business: "Whenever this issue of compensatory or preferential treatment for the Negro is raised, some of our friends recoil in horror." King then raised the issue of the quota-based system in India, whereby those from the untouchable caste received preferential treatment in college places, approvingly. King, however, was careful not to insist on quotas or any sort of preferential treatment. In line with most liberal thinking at the time, he simply wished to emphasize the urgency of the task and the effort needed to overcome black inequality.[21]

But it was not that the liberal imagination could simply not countenance affirmative action. Instead, there was an appreciation that affirmative action might jeopardize particular goals and values. Even more, liberals and civil rights rejected affirmative action in its modern sense as needlessly small-minded and limiting. It is important to emphasize that, at this stage, there were no limits to the liberal imagination in its response to social problems. Giving some indication of the experimentalism of the time, an obscure civil rights task force from the Bureau of the Budget, set up after Johnson's Great Society Speech on May 22, 1964, worked on prescriptions for race relations problems. Captured in their suggestions are both the expansive confidence and the naivety of the 1960s. They called for federally-sponsored model new cities on the urban periphery that *required* integration by both race and economic class, federal sponsorship of "voluntary 'bridge' organizations where people would sign up to go to church together, exchange visits at home, and play together." New federal programs might reduce the geographic concentration of blacks ("Quotas? Housing requirements? Relocation allowances?") Perhaps a joint, federal-state foster-care program could encourage whites to adopt black children.[22] These suggestions, while almost laughably unworkable from today's standpoint, at least spoke of a more positive, optimistic social order. Nor were they restricted to bureaucrats. One of the more (albeit out of very few) touching experiences of researching the archives of this period was reading the huge numbers of letters to the American president, each of them earnestly putting forward a "solution," usually hare-brained, to the problem of race.

Johnson, the heir of Kennedy's muscular liberalism, raised the stakes in 1965 by speeding up civil rights reforms in an attempt to preempt the civil rights movement. In doing so, he altered the usual way that the government did business with interest groups by taking the initiative himself. To some extent, Johnson was preparing the ground for affirmative action by creating a new role for the federal government in initiating federal action on civil rights. John D. Pomfret, writing in the *New York Times*, noted the unusual manner that the initiatives contained in a then-obscure report entitled "The Negro Family: The Case for National Action" (later known as the Moynihan Report) emerged. "Ordinarily, legislative proposals are put forward by pressure groups and the government acts as a sort of broker working out a politically feasible compromise between these groups." This time, however, "the initiative so far has come largely from the administration" apparently because "the problem and the need for fast action are so great that it must take the lead."[23] This preemptive style of government had the effect of undermining the very institutions it sought to aid, as later chapters detail.

Voluntary action, part of the Kennedy plans for revitalizing American democracy, became an acceptable fact of quotas, though it aligned business and civil rights activists against the unions. The aforementioned *Plans for Progress*, organized by Bobby Troutman, a businessman who had caught the ear of John F. Kennedy, was designed to induce prominent government contractors to devise their own plans for increasing minority group hiring and employment mobility. By 1966 it included 317 of the country's largest businesses, employing some 8.6 million employees. It embodied the still-popular sentiment that business should lead efforts to create racial equality. Its purpose was to "provide leadership in bringing more Americans into fuller participation in the economy." Franklin Roosevelt, Jr. told delegates to a Plans for Progress Conference in 1966 that "it is time that you get into the school system, you participate in working up the curriculum, you participate in the remedial educational programs of the city school system. . . . Whatever your obstacles, you are in a better position to overcome them than Uncle Sam is."[24]

Black entrepreneur and Johnson ally Hobart Taylor, speaking at the same conference, encapsulated the still-hopeful perception in early 1966 that, whatever recent difficulties, "the institutions created by our forefathers have proved their viability and the ability to adapt to new conditions." He said that the period since Plans for Progress had been "an exceptional period morally and socially—one in which the American people picked up the American Dream, brushed it off, and put it to work for the whole country."[25] Implicit within Taylor's prose is both the idea that the American Dream had fallen from its plinth but also the conviction that American institutions might yet overcome these severe difficulties.

In May 1965 Johnson made his Howard University speech, launching the "next and the more profound stage of the battle for civil rights." Johnson biographer Robert Dallek, echoing many other accounts, called the speech "the beginnings of a campaign for affirmative action."[26] The main effect of the speech was not so much to start affirmative action, much less to create a campaign for it (a point that will be discussed later). Instead, it effectively indicted equality of opportunity—an important American symbol of fairness and economic justice—as inadequate in creating racial equality. Johnson no doubt intended equality of opportunity and equality as a fact to coexist but, as problems remained, it looked very much like equality of opportunity was a myth and that the president had said so.

But the Howard speech may also be viewed as another cajoling effort by the Johnson administration, well within the boundaries of what Gareth Davies refers to as the "individualist ethos."[27] It aimed at convincing businessmen and other Americans that they must be committed to equal opportunities and must indicate their commitment with results. No new definition of affirmative action emerged because of the distinction between equality as a right and equality as a fact. Johnson was simply announcing that affirmative action (at its most basic meaning of "positive action") must augment the Civil Rights Act in order for real equality of opportunity to exist. He expressed a sentiment that had been heard many times before, if not, perhaps, with the same urgency or from the same office. Had Johnson's cajoling and legislative action brought about real change for African Americans, had liberalism successfully integrated blacks, the speech would be seen as the hiatus of the existing campaigns, not the beginning of a new one.

John D. Skrentny points out that a moment of at least equal importance, but less noticed, was in March 1966, when EEO-1 forms were sent out to every employer contracted with the federal government requiring employers to keep track of the race of every employee, contradicting the federal color-blindness called for by Truman. This, however, marked the extent of Johnson's willingness to enforce the affirmative action he had called for at Howard University. Instead, Johnson pushed voluntaristic affirmative action programs such as the Plans for Progress harder. He gambled that American employers and employees, like many Southerners, could be cajoled and bullied into accepting black employees without any real force being applied. The EEO-1 forms would be yet another application of pressure to hire blacks.

Watts

On a hot August night, the Watts area of Los Angeles erupted into the worst racial violence since the 1943 Detroit race riot. It continued for six days, with over forty million dollars in property destroyed, over one thousand injuries, four thousand arrests made, and thirty-four persons killed. Its biggest effect, however, was to bring attention to the failure of liberal society outside the South to deal effectively with racial problems. It served to confuse and disorient liberals. Joseph Califano remembered the effect of news of the Watts riot on his boss:

What came through to me was how much Watts had depressed him. . . . On civil rights matters he was at his most demanding. He knew it was essential to arouse the oppressed, and that, once aroused, their clock ticked impatiently. I began to grasp how acutely Johnson feared that the reforms to which he had dedicated his presidency were in mortal danger, not only from those who opposed him, but from those he was trying to help.[28]

Liberal policy makers—especially Johnson—had succeeded in raising the stakes for the American Creed and American institutions so high that they risked losing all. The institutions that Myrdal insisted were to lead Americans from their individualized prejudices were now held up under a harsh light, revealing problems that appeared to be more and more intractable. Johnson had inadvertently exacerbated the crisis by attempting to match the activism of the civil rights movement with executive action on civil rights. He had little choice. The civil rights movement managed to show how little the institution of law meant to Southern segregationists. The response of the Kennedy administration, fulfilled by Johnson, was to prepare the 1964 and 1965 civil rights bills, which would prevent any agency from administering unequal treatment on the basis of race, creed, color, or sex. Now, with their passage, justice might finally be done for the Negro. Johnson believed that a process toward racial equality, once the formal apparatus of oppression had been dismantled, had been initiated and would spread from the South into the ghettos in northern cities, where many blacks watched the events in the South eagerly. Johnson's "second-rate mind," as his aide Harry McPherson once pointed out, was relatively untouched by the skepticism of the intelligentsia up until the first of the long, hot summers. But Watts served for him, as it must have for many Americans, as an indication of the complexity of the racial crisis in the United States.

The Coleman and Kerner Reports

Though Watts may not have been so revelatory for liberal intellectuals and race relations experts, it certainly focused their attention to the problems of race relations and confirmed their pessimistic impulses. Two reports initiated by the federal government undermined the existing analysis of the problem of black inequality and suggested that existing efforts were misplaced. In 1966, the *Coleman Report* pulled the rug out from the under the theory that, with desegregated schools, blacks could achieve equality. Kennedy came to power promising "to help equalize educational opportunity throughout the country."[29] Education had been highlighted both as a means to bring African Americans into the mainstream by better preparing them for job opportunities and also by lessening prejudice in whites through Gordon Allport's contact theory.

The *Coleman Report* had been called for by the 1964 Civil Rights Act. It addressed itself to four major questions: (1) How segregated are school children? (2) Do different schools offer equal educational opportunity? (3) How much

. In fact, it did call for affirmative action, though the notion of th[e]
the report is very different than today's affirmative action. Specifically
for efforts "(l)inking enforcement efforts with training and other aid[s]
[empl]oyers and unions, so that affirmative action to hire and promote may
[enc]oraged in connection with investigations of individual complaints and
[of] broad patterns of discriminations."42 The word "encouraged" is, of
[di]fferent in its implications than "enforced." The voluntarist perspec-
[ve]ry much alive, though other elements of liberals' perspectives on
[pe]rished.

[I]ts outlandish-sounding proposals costing huge amounts of money,
[read carefully, is more a call to redouble existing efforts than a call
[effo]rts:

[serv]es to underscore our basic conclusion: the need is not so much for the
[...] to design new programs as it is for the nation to generate new will.
[ente]rprise, labor unions, the churches, the foundations, the universities—
[...] institutions—must deepen their involvement in the life of the city
[com]mitment to its revival and welfare.43

[a]ssumed that the problem of black unemployment was seen as
[of] coordination. Many reasoned that the migration of Southern
[wit]h no employment skills and little education meant that, in an
[...]d, employers simply could not use black labor. The term "un-
[...]" (tellingly, it was referred to at this time as "underutiliza-
[...]ted this understanding of the problem. In order to stem the
[trai]ning programs became the focus of federal civil rights efforts

[...] Development and Training Act of 1962 set up the Man-
[...]opment and Training Program, which set a target of
[...]ver three years. In its second year, projects were approved
[...]es, of which 27,000 completed the training and about
[...]in jobs. About a quarter of the trainees were black.44 In
[...]nts to the Manpower Development and Training Act,
[...]icit cognizance for the first time of the fact that inade-
[...]eparation might be the major barrier to employability
[...]e Vocational Education Act of 1963, the Vocational Re-
[...] and the several manpower components of the Eco-
[...]ct were all directed toward providing training oppor-
[...]ged youth. The Job Corps was established by the 1964
[...]y Act to benefit low-income youths between fourteen
[...]old who required remedial education, occupational
[...]rvices to gain employment. Federal expenditures for

do different children learn as measured by their performance on standardized achievement tests? (4) What are the possible relationships between students' achievement and the kind of schools they attend? First, the report found that "when measured by that yardstick [1954 decision], American public education remains largely unequal in most regions of the country." Twelve years after the *Brown* decision, there had been no change. Much more disturbing, however, was the finding that the success of children was determined *before* they attended school and was related to socio-economic background rather than unequal educational opportunities. As it stated: "For most minority groups, then and most particularly the Negro, schools provide no opportunity at all for them to overcome this initial deficiency; in fact they fall farther behind the white majority in the development of several skills which are critical to making a living and participating fully in modern society." This implied that efforts to desegregate schools, while desirable for many reasons, would not improve the life-chances for African-American children and would thus have little effect on black inequality, even in the long-term.30

Even as it appeared to damn liberal efforts at desegregating schools, the report refused to give up on them, insisting that "in the long run, integration should be expected to have a positive effect on Negro achievement as well."31 The negative points were little noticed or acknowledged at the time the report was published. As Daniel Bell later noted, the *Coleman Report* findings "dismayed the educational bureaucracy, and at first, received little attention"; it was reported neither in the *New York Times* nor in the news weeklies.32 But, to those who did read the report, it emphasized that the racial divide was a far less tractable problem than it had been in previous understanding. The theories relying on education as a means of integrating African Americans into the mainstream received a blow. So did those theories relying on black and white contact to alleviate white racism; the differences between black and white children might be emphasized rather than lessened by integrated education. However, the fact it was widely ignored is an indication of the strength of liberal confidence (and, perhaps, intellectual investment) in the benefits of integrated education.

Far more public and, perhaps more importantly, with a political agenda equally ambivalent in its assessment of current race relations efforts, was the *Report of the National Advisory Commission on Civil Disorders*, or Kerner Commission Report, as it is more commonly known. Set up by Johnson after the third consecutive summer of serious rioting in 1967, the Kerner Commission released its report in 1968 with great fanfare. The commission, governed ostensibly by trusted Johnson deputy Otto Kerner, but in reality manipulated by Mayor John Lindsay of New York, was published in March 1968 with a print run of 30,000 but was sold out in three days.33 It sold another 1.6 million between March and June 1968.[34] The report turned out very differently than Johnson had imagined. Its impact was immediate. It rejected the idea that there had been any conspiracy involved. Its keynote theme was that "white racism is essentially responsible for the explosive mixture which has been accumulating in our cities since the end of World War II."[35]

To appreciate the impact upon the hopes of racial liberalism, one only has to compare the oft-cited line at the beginning of the report, "our nation is moving toward two societies, one black, one white—separate and unequal," to *Pravda*'s assessment of the American race riots of the 1960s. It observed in the riots "two Americas which are at war with each other—that of the rich and strong and that of the poor and humiliated, of whom the majority are Negroes."[36] In essence, American liberalism had admitted to all the accusations made by Soviet propaganda on racial issues heard since the beginning of the Cold War.

The most important conclusion of the report was that the federal government could not "continue its present failing efforts towards an integrated society."[37] The institutions that had been championed by Myrdal and other liberals through to Lyndon Johnson were condemned: "[W]hite society is deeply implicated in the ghetto. White institutions created it, white institutions maintain it, and white society condones it."[38] In other words, instead of institutions correcting the sometimes-irrational proclivities of white citizens, the (white) institutions *created* a system whereby racism, latent or otherwise, within (white) individuals came to the surface. Though the report, in some ways, was pure Myrdal in its assessment that the problems of black Americans lay on the white side of the equation, it came as an indictment of democratic institutions, of the American Creed itself.

After such a broadside against them, the report expressed concern for the survival of American institutions, indicating that, whatever their problems, liberal institutions—as opposed to a political campaign among white Americans—continued to be the greatest hope for racial progress. Despite its radical way of framing the question, aspects of the report might strike the present-day reader as moderate. It reflected in its recommendations the divisions between members of the commission over how to overcome the problems of black riots. For instance, in the then-current debate about whether to destroy the ghettos and integrate black Americans within white suburbs or to enrich life in the ghettos, the report compromised. Many of its recommendations show that contentious issues were avoided; the report continually emphasised that the programmatic suggestions would benefit poor whites as well as blacks, perhaps an indication that the commission still saw the need to get white Americans behind civil rights efforts.

Like Johnson's Howard University speech, the Kerner Commission Report appears damning of the Great Society only after Johnson's reforms no longer

looked viable. Evident also was its incredible optimi
dented resources to be dedicated to resolving the
tragic events to light, it was hoped that the probl
Despite superficial similarities of the report's ana
no return to blaming the inequities of capitalism
sion of the nation's black citizens. "This report is
of government and to the conscience of the nati
the minds and hearts of each citizen. The res
never more clearly demanded in the history o
Again, the report can be seen either as the h
in its coffin.

The Kerner Commission Report repeate
Dilemma that all whites, rather than just th
implicated. However, now the leaders an
a solution were condemned. Though
contained some conservative implicatio
ingly pessimistic intelligentsia. By ext
white institutions, it underlined the i
a permanent feature that would hav
completely. Effectively, blame for th
all whites, from the chiefs of corpo
ton bureaucrats to Montana ranc
about riot commissions published
Report, concluded that its researc
"to demand changes and advoca
The problem is identified and
sponsible, and no one is blam
ently."[40] Put another way, as
would press quite heavily or
durable when divided amor

The Kerner Commissio
justice was a moral probl
dicted Myrdal's hope that
away from their racism.
cension of the affirmati

Why was affirmativ
sion Report? Cert

manpower development and training increased from less that $60 million in 1963 to $1.6 billion in 1968.[45]

The training programs had two official raisons d'étre. "The manpower programs have as basic goals increasing national production (the efficiency goal) and increasing the employment and earnings of particular groups of workers (the equity goal)," observed Michael E. Borus and Charles E. Buntz in 1972. Today the efficiency goal has effectively been dropped from training programs, as will be discussed in later chapters. But in the 1960s little progress on black unemployment was possible, it was felt, unless there was full employment. On this, most observers—everyone from the Black Panthers to the most centrist liberals—agreed. At this stage, the goal of full employment removed focus from distribution onto production. As economist James Tobin noted:

> In a slack labor market, employers can pick and choose, both in recruiting and in promoting. They exaggerate the skill, education, and experience requirements of their jobs. They use diplomas, or color, or personal histories as convenient screening devices. . . . A slack labor market probably accentuates the discriminatory and protectionist proclivities of certain crafts and unions. When jobs are scarce, opening the door to Negroes is a real threat. Of course, prosperity will not automatically dissolve the barriers, but it will make it more difficult to oppose efforts to do so.[46]

Tobin summed up: "I conclude that the single most important step the nation could take to improve the economic position of the Negro is to operate the economy steadily at a low rate of unemployment."[47] Oscar Handlin, a liberal academic, noted: "In the last analysis, the welfare of the Negroes depends upon the health of the whole economy and its capacity to produce and distribute goods according to an acceptable pattern."[48] Similarly, the Black Panther Party made full employment the second demand of their party platform when they organized themselves into a political party in October 1966.[49]

Such perspectives—from radical, liberals, and conservatives alike, it should be noted—serve to remind us that the 1960s knew none of the limits that subsequent decades have imposed. The attack on growth, as later chapters will discuss, was an important determinant of an affirmative action that, when the Kerner Commission Report came out, had not yet fully formed. In this climate, few liberals could envisage white Americans assenting easily to demands that they share out limited numbers of jobs with black Americans without the sort of strife feared by liberals. Nor could they imagine forcing employers to hire and promote the necessary numbers of African Americans without offering substantial pecuniary rewards for doing so. Even though the Kerner Commission Report was willing to condemn all white society, it remained true to the postwar emphasis on full employment. Under "Goals and Objectives" the report lists nine topics, the first of which mentions growth and job creation "so that there will be jobs available to those who are newly trained, *without displacing those already employed*."[50]

Conclusion

As Thomas Sugrue shows, there was an active campaign in cities like Philadelphia to integrate various industries that met with some success.[51] Yet it was pointedly dropped from demands by national civil rights leaders by late 1963. Why? Beside the objections indicated in earlier chapters, they had bigger fish to fry. Affirmative action was at best a small part of a campaign for comprehensive change in the United States. As indicated above, this tiny and localized demand was dwarfed by what liberals and civil rights leaders still felt was possible. The dream of racial integration had yet to recede into an indefinite future. Among the giant demands of the Kerner Commission—that a million new jobs be created in three years, for instance—a demand that a few African Americans be hired on building sites in specified cities would have appeared paltry indeed.[52]

As the liberal consensus fragmented, the elite's concern for the future of the institutions that would deliver black equality began to eclipse its commitment to black equality itself. Trade unions, churches, businessmen, educational institutions, local and national political organizations—in short, "white institutions"—were all indicted as part of the problem rather than the solution. Rather than an excrescence upon an otherwise healthy American Creed moving the country toward equality, racial inequality was increasingly used as evidence of a systemic failure, of the moral decrepitude of the whole nation. Some action was needed to restore moral leadership to these American institutions. In this way, the developments of the second half of the 1960s heralded the appearance of affirmative action. However, it was the destruction of optimism about the ability of America to accomplish the far-reaching goals of the 1960s, a potent force in 1968 but almost entirely forsaken within a decade, that marked the true watershed for affirmative action.

Notes

1. Bayard Rustin, "From Protest to Politics: The Future of the Civil Rights Movement," *Commentary* 39 (February 1965): 25–31, esp. 25.

2. Memo to Carl Holman from Vivian W. Henderson, dated December 29 1965, Sylvester Papers, reel 2, part IV: Records of the White House Conference on Civil

Rights, 1965–1966, in *Civil Rights During the Johnson Administration, 1963–1969*, ed. Steven F. Lawson (hereafter "Records of the WHCCR").

3. Transcript to Panel No. 4, "Health and Welfare," November 18, 1965, 292, Planning Session Papers, reel 7, Records of the WHCCR.

4. Transcripts of Panel No. 1-B, "Jobs," November 18 1965, 290, Planning Session Papers, Records of the WHCCR. Transcript to Panel No. 4, "Health and Welfare," November 18, 1965, 292, Planning Session Papers, reel 6, Records of the WHCCR.

5. Memorandum from J. Q. Wilson and H. D. Price to "White House Conference on Civil Rights," dated November 3, 1965, Sylvester Papers, reel 5, Records of the WHCCR.

6. Memorandum from Sterling Tucker to Berl Bernhard, Harold Fleming, Carl Holman, Liz Drew, dated November 5, 1965 3, Sylvester Papers, reel 5, Records of the WHCCR.

7. Planning Session Agenda Paper on Education, p. 43, Sylvester Papers, reel 5, Records of the WHCCR.

8. "The seeds of crisis were sown by the crumbling of the American caste system; they germinated while governmental and political institutions failed to cope with the social evolution." Theodore Lowi, *The End of Liberalism: Ideology, Policy, and the Crisis of Public Authority* (New York: W.W. Norton & Company, Inc., 1969), xiv.

9. "Liberalism and the Negro: A Roundtable Discussion with James Baldwin, Nathan Glazer, Sidney Hook, and Gunnar Myrdal," *Commentary* 37, no. 3 (March 1964): 25–42, 26.

10. "Liberalism and the Negro: A Roundtable Discussion," 25.

11. "Liberalism and the Negro: A Roundtable Discussion," 40.

12. "Liberalism and the Negro: A Roundtable Discussion," 40.

13. Tilman C. Cothran, "The Negro Protest Against Segregation in the South," *The Annals of the American Academy of Political and Social Science* 357 (January 1965), 65–72.

14. Loren Miller, "Farewell to the Liberals: A Negro View," *The Nation* 195, issue 12 (October 20, 1962): 235–38, esp. 235. Miller also noted on the same page that "racial discrimination is becoming deeply rooted and institutionalized."

15. Cited in Miller, "Farewell to the Liberals," 235.

16. Cited in Stephen Steinberg, *Turning Back: The Retreat from Racial Justice in American Thought and Social Policy* (Boston: Beacon Press, 1995), 72.

17. Charles E. Silberman, "The Businessman and the Negro," *Fortune* (September 1963): 97–99, 184–94.

18. Cited in Lee Rainwater and William L. Yancey, *The Moynihan Report and the Politics of Controversy* (Cambridge, MA: The M.I.T. Press, 1967), 32.

19. Daniel C. Thompson, "The Rise of the Negro Protest" in *The Annals of the American Academy of Political and Social Science* 357 (January 1965): 18–29.

20. King in an address to the National Press Club, July 19, 1962, cited in David J. Garrow, *Bearing the Cross* (New York: William Morrow and Co., 1986), 13.

21. Martin Luther King, Jr., *Why We Can't Wait* (New York: Signet Books, 1964), 134–35, 140. King also used the running race metaphor here that Johnson later used in his Howard University speech.

22. Graham, *Civil Rights Era*, 155.

23. John D. Pomfret, "Drive For Renewed Negro Family Stability is Pressed by White House Panel," *New York Times*, July 19, 1965, 15.

24. Remarks by Franklin Delano Roosevelt, Jr., Chairman of EEOC, *A Report on the 1966 Plans for Progress Fourth National Conference*, Washington Hilton Hotel, January 24–25, 1966, 36.

25. "Remarks by Hobart Taylor, Vice Chairman of EEOC, A Report on the 1966 Plans for Progress," Fourth National Conference, Washington, D.C., 24–25 January 1966, 22.

26. Dallek, *Flawed Giant*, 222.

27. Gareth Davies, *From Opportunity to Entitlement: The Transformation and Decline of Great Society Liberalism* (Lawrence: University Press of Kansas, 1996), 68–72.

28. Califano, *The Triumph and Tragedy of Lyndon Johnson*, 62.

29. William Chafe, *The Unfinished Journey: America Since World War II* (New York: Oxford University Press, 1986), 193.

30. U.S. Department of Health, Education and Welfare, Office of Education, *Equality of Educational Opportunity* (Coleman Report), (Washington, D.C.: U.S. GPO, 1966), 20.

31. *Coleman Report*, 28.

32. Daniel Bell, "On Meritocracy and Equality," *The Public Interest* no. 29, (Fall 1972): 29–68, esp. 45.

33. See Gareth Davies, *From Opportunity to Entitlement*, 203–6. According to Nicholas Lemann, Lindsay preempted the report by prevailing on the commission at the last minute to include a dramatic executive summary written by his staff, including the line: "two societies—separate and unequal." He threatened the other commission members with publication of a minority report should they not include his summary. Nicholas Lemann, *The Promised Land: The Great Black Migration and How it Changed America* (London: Macmillan, 1991), 190.

34. Ellen Herman, *The Romance of American Psychology: Political Culture in the Age of Experts* (London: University of California Press, 1995), 216.

35. *Report of the National Advisory Commission on Civil Rights* (hereafter the Kerner Commission Report) (New York: New York Times Publications, 1968), 2.

36. John D. Skrentny, *The Ironies of Affirmative Action: Politics, Culture, and Justice in America* (London: University of Chicago Press, 1996), 99.

37. Tom Wicker, "Introduction" to the Kerner Commission Report, vii.

38. Kerner Commission Report, 2.

39. Kerner Commission Report, 34.

40. Cited in Ellen Herman, *The Romance of American Psychology*, 213.

41. Cited in Arthur M. Schlesinger, Jr., *The Vital Center: The Politics of Freedom* (Boston: The Riverside Press, 1949), 5.

42. Kerner Commission Report, 419.

43. Kerner Commission Report, 412.

44. William F. Brazziel, "Manpower Training and the Negro Worker," *Journal of Negro Education* 35, issue 1 (Winter 1966): 83–87, esp. 83–84.

45. Ginzberg, "The Changing Manpower Scene," 316, Kerner Commission Report, 414.

46. James Tobin, "On Improving the Economic Status of the Negro" in *The Negro American*, ed. Talcott Parsons and Kenneth B. Clarke (Boston: Beacon Press, 1966), 451–71, esp. 456.

47. Tobin, "On Improving the Economic Status of the Negro," 451–71, esp. 456.

48. Oscar Handlin, "The Goals of Integration," in *The Negro American*, ed. Talcott Parsons and Kenneth B. Clarke (Boston: Beacon Press, 1966), 659–77, esp. 671.

49. "2. We want full employment for our people. . . . We believe that if white businessmen will not give full employment, then the means of production would be taken from the businessman and placed in the community so that the people of the community can organize and employ all of its people and give a high standard of living." Black Panther Party Platform and Program, October 2, 1966, in *The Black Panthers Speak*, ed. Philip S. Foner (New York: J. B. Lippincott Company, 1970), 11.

50. Kerner Commission Report, chapter 17, "Recommendations For National Action," 414–15.

51. Thomas J. Sugrue, "Affirmative Action from Below: Civil Rights, the Building Trades, and the Politics of Racial Equality in the Urban North, 1945–1969," *The Journal of American History* 91, no. 1 (June 2004): 145–73.

52. Kerner Commission Report, 417.

4

Legitimation Crisis

THE SOLIDLY ESTABLISHMENT FIGURE of Irwin Miller, chief executive officer of
Cummins Engine Company, member of the steering committee of the
Urban Coalition, president of the National Council of Churches, among other
things, expressed some of the anxieties of the elite in 1969. Writing in the *Harvard Business Review*, he predicted ensuing social chaos and perhaps summed
up the feelings of many others: "Because of our new dependence on electric
power, communications, and transportation arteries, a small dedicated group
of men in each city could paralyze us. Alongside the opportunity there exist
men and women who might easily be motivated to seize it. These are the men
and women for whom this country does not work."[1] Such alarmist sentiments
were widespread in 1969 and alluded to the broad problem of alienation. Unlike Mr. Miller, clearly a "joiner," fewer and fewer Americans felt they were part
of the system.

There were two interrelated aspects of the crisis at the end of the 1960s that
the victor of the 1968 election would have faced. Both involved the authority
of existing institutions and both were related to the appearance of affirmative
action programs. The immediate danger came from the widespread chaos of
riots and the volatility of the cities and campuses across the country. As Doug
McAdam observed, "(i)t would not seem an overstatement to argue that the
level of open defiance of the established economic and political order was as
great during this period as during any other in this country's history, save the
Civil War."[2] Entire areas of central cities remained hostile to what was often
seen as an occupying force of the police (and, in the immediate aftermath of
the riots, the National Guard). Campuses were dominated and sometimes

occupied by those opposed to the "system." Some way of reaching out to these alienated groups had to be found and the latter part of Johnson's tenure and the earliest part of Nixon's focused on these primary problems. As chapter 7 will detail, the Philadelphia Plan may be understood as part of an immediate strategy to connect with black ghettos.

The second, deeper, and more problematic aspect of the crisis was the challenge to existing governing arrangements by the destruction of institutions. These institutions mediated between the federal government and its citizens. Besides imbuing citizens with patriotic ideals, providing them with an identity and a way to relate to other Americans, these institutions became a way of communicating, through organized political pressure, with Washington, D.C. Equally, they allowed Washington to gain some sense of the concerns of ordinary Americans, and allowed the political elite a way of reaching them and perhaps influencing their behavior, thereby enhancing their leadership. The destruction of the authority of these institutions led to what has been termed a legitimacy, or legitimation, crisis. Ultimately, this subtler but more profound crisis proved more important for the rise of affirmative action than the riots.

The Immediate Crisis

By 1968 the "acid weave" of left and right, to borrow Garry Wills's memorable phrase, began to bite. The issues of race and Vietnam revealed a deeply divided nation. On January 30, 1968 the Viet Cong and the North Vietnamese Army launched the Tet Offensive, a surprise attack that, despite the fact that the North Vietnamese and Viet Cong suffered heavy losses, convinced many Americans that the Vietnam War could not be won. American casualties climbed throughout the year, equalling in the first six months the total for the whole of 1967. In light of the apparent hollowness of Johnson's confident statements on Vietnam, discussions of the "credibility gap" became commonplace. As many Americans began questioning the correctness of the assumptions with which they had grown up, the authority of Johnson and his administration suffered. Many began to link the Vietnam War with the racial crisis, seeing the war as the annihilation of a people because of their difference from the mainstream.

On March 31, Johnson appeared on the nation's television screens to announce the scaling-down of the bombing of North Vietnam, adding to a surprised national audience that he would not be a candidate for re-election. When Dr. Martin Luther King, Jr. was assassinated less than a week later, blacks rioted in 168 cities and towns. Thirty-four blacks and five whites died in the violence. Robert Kennedy was shot in June as he campaigned to be Democratic presidential candidate. Violence erupted again in August at the Democratic National Convention in Chicago. However, it was protest about the Vietnam War that became the biggest worry for Nixon when he took office. This war, as Godfrey Hodgson observed, "became the organizing principle around which all the doubts and disillusionments of the years of crisis since 1963, and all the deeper discontents hidden under the glossy surface of the confident years, coalesced into one great rebellion."[3]

After four consecutive summers of serious rioting, there seemed little reason to think that the rioting would end. In 1968 and 1969 it moved to the campuses. At Columbia, one hundred black students armed with rifles and shotguns occupied the student union. In October three hundred Weathermen (a revolutionary splinter group) raced through Chicago smashing windows and attacking police officers in a rather pathetic attempt to incite armed class struggle. Between the beginning of the year and April 15, there were 8,000 bombings and threats of bombings. In the 1969–1970 academic year, 7,200 young people arrested for violent acts on campus, double that during 1968–1969. As Melvin Small observed, "(w)hatever legislative program the administration finally developed, the chief problem it faced in 1969 was the perception that the United States was coming apart at the seams. The nation was awash in unprecedented political and racial violence and a perceived rise in criminality that made many Americans insecure, even in middle-class neighborhoods and homes."[4]

Existing federal efforts to further civil rights progress were exposed as the urban rioting destroyed hope that progress was just around the corner. Each attempt to deal with the problem seemed to unearth another example of past failure to make any impact on the problems. Many were loath to give up the Myrdalian precept of "education, not regulation" when it came to discrimination in employment. As Alfred Blumrosen complained:

> This formula immobilized the agencies. The idea was that the law should not be enforced because it dealt with basic human motivations and attitudes. These attitudes could be corrected only by "education." But education was then defined to exclude enforcement of the law, despite a long history which has justified much law on the grounds of its deterrence or educational function.[5]

Blumrosen was indeed accurate regarding the immobilization of the agencies. In school desegregation cases, it was found that private sector actions in real-estate and home lending led to residential segregation that made school integration impossible. Busing between school districts became the favored remedy of the courts but created a very messy and costly solution. Additionally, it ran up against concerted opposition from parents who, for racial motives or otherwise, objected to busing.

The so-called "open housing" programs fared no better. In July 1967, Housing and Urban Development (HUD) revised its tenant selection policy, eliminated ineffective free choice plans and substituted a plan based on "first come, first served." In summarizing its experience under the free choice system, HUD said: "[F]or various reasons, such as the mores of the community, fear of reprisals, types of neighborhoods, inducement by Local Authority staff—whether by subtle suggestion, manipulation, persuasion, or otherwise—such freedom of choice plans did not provide applicants with actual freedom of access to, or full availability of, housing in all projects and locations."[6] The enforcement mechanisms provided for HUD—generally complaint processing through formal investigation and litigation initiated by individuals—according to the CRC report, "provide weak leverage because of their time-consuming and individualistic nature."[7]

Neither had other efforts been successful in lessening the gap between black and white Americans. The efforts at strengthening black communities through Community Action Projects and other experimental projects in the ghettos had also failed to make any ground. The Equal Employment Opportunities Commission (EEOC) could not be counted as a success at this stage. The number of cases successfully prosecuted emerged like the smallest of a set of Russian nesting dolls from the other relevant statistics. From an initial forty-four thousand charges reported to EEOC, twenty-seven thousand were recommended for investigation, reasonable cause found for seventeen thousand, conciliation was successful in less than eight thousand, and, of the nine thousand cases remaining, only nine hundred were even brought to court! As EEOC chairman William H. Brown complained, "All that an intransigent respondent has to fear is the unlikely possibility that whomever he has discriminated against will take him to court. This has happened in less than 10 percent of the cases where we found reasonable cause and attempts at conciliation were unsuccessful."[8]

When it came to contract compliance, officials still balked at the idea of forcing companies to comply with the conditions of the contract, not least because a useful working definition of "discrimination" that all contractors had foresworn remained elusive. Somewhat typical was the Allen-Bradley case. For the payroll period ending March 7, 1968, the company had 6,869 employees, 32 of whom were black. There was an official, written company policy giving preference to relatives and friends of employees. Between April 1964 and October 1968, there were four meetings and three letters exchanged between the federal government and Allen-Bradley. Neither the issues nor the attitude of the company changed. Nevertheless, four years passed before the company was formally notified in May 1968 that it was in noncompliance. After hearings, the Secretary of Labor ordered the company to "proceed immediately to attempt to agree on an appropriate program of affirmative action." No affirmative action plan had yet been agreed upon by June 1969.[9]

A survey appearing at the time was damning of the government's record in persuading companies that they needed to hire more African Americans. Of the fifty states, twenty-four (47 percent) showed increases in black employment of 1 percent or less in the five-year period 1962–1967. Of these, twenty-two had no increase or decreased—including Florida, Texas, Massachusetts, Mississippi, New Jersey, and West Virginia. Nearly one-fifth of all black federal employees in 1967 worked in Washington, D.C. (where only 11 percent of all federal employees worked). Most humiliating to Johnson, perhaps, was the spectacular failure of the high profile Plans for Progress program. A survey carried out by the President's Council on Equal Opportunity (PCEO) indicated that by 1968 companies in the program had worse records of hiring African Americans than the government contractors who were not in this preferred status and who had been lectured at by those in the program.[10] Edward C. Sylvester, the head of Johnson's Office of Federal Contract Compliance Programs (OFCC) complained in March 1967 of the government's equal employment programs, "[T]here is too much carrot and not enough stick."[11]

Of course, such surveys would have produced similar results had they been conducted earlier. At no time during the postwar period, based on available data, was there great cause for optimism about the effectiveness of government efforts at leading private business to employ more blacks. What changed was the increased receptivity of sections of the elite to the above criticisms. Those wielding the same figures five years previously would have been dismissed as hopeless Jeremiahs. By the end of the decade, figures pointing to successes were treated with suspicion.

The task of extending links into the black community thus became paramount. At a series of meetings in Boston in July 1967 after disturbances in the area, the lack of any sort of organization within which black demands might be channeled was repeated: "A recurring theme during the four days of meetings was the powerlessness of the Negro community."[12] An analysis of disturbances in Plainfield, New Jersey, also noted that "lack of coherent political organization" played a key role in the riot.[13]

These were by no means new problems. As the planning meeting of the White House Conference on Civil Rights (as well as the 1965 Voting Rights Act) indicated, efforts at creating participation within the black community existed before the most serious rioting. A report to the National Governors

Conference dated May 10, 1967 (and thus predating much of the rioting that year) by the "Advisory Committee on Federal-State-Local Relations" was entitled "Full Participation by All People in the Process of Government." In its second section were the steps for creating participation:

> Provide for participation by all citizens in the election process. . . .
>
> Foster dialogue between citizens and government: create and support human relations agencies or commissions at local and state levels; encourage dialogue between majority and minority groups. . . .
>
> Encourage community improvement groups. . . .
>
> Assure representation of all citizens. . . .[14]

When the Nixon administration took office, these were the uncompleted tasks awaiting it. The Kerner Commission Report focused much of its attention on this problem once the initial fear that the riots had somehow been orchestrated by Moscow no longer looked feasible. A letter from David Ginsburg, the executive director of the commission, stated at the outset that: "The basic theme of our work is that we must recognize and deal with the fact of deep political alienation in the ghetto."[15] The concern was that none of the institutions through which most Americans related to their government appeared to work—or even to exist—for black Americans. The authority of the police in ghetto areas hardly existed. Ginsburg continued: "What kinds of instruments (other than the police) are available for easing community tensions? For example, we are looking preliminarily at the role of Human Relations Commissions, the possibility of establishing new grievance machinery (perhaps modeled after labor mediation services); and the ombudsman idea."[16] In order to maintain some sort of control over ghetto areas, the Commission toyed with the fairly ludicrous idea of community policing roles for street gangs such as the "White Hats" in Tampa, Florida, the "Rebels with a Cause" in Washington, D.C., and the "Blackstone Rangers" in Chicago, Illinois. In Chicago and Tampa, these ideas were actually tried![17]

Not surprisingly, many of the solutions to these problems dealt with the lack of jobs within the ghettos. Some of the recommendations discussed by the Kerner Commission Report included in a section entitled "To expand and Improve Employment Opportunities":

> *Increase job opportunities:* recruit, train and hire slum area residents for public employment; provide tax incentives for industry and business to locate in blighted areas, provide neighborhood counselling to small business in urban areas; encourage industry and labor to expand job opportunities through across-the-board hiring of disadvantaged persons; promote and enforce equal employ-

ment practices in both public and private employment; use career fairs to pub-licize availability of jobs; utilize mobile employment units to bring employment information to the unemployed.[18]

Though these suggestions fall short of the kind of affirmative action con-tained in the Philadelphia Plan or in "set-asides" as per Section 8(a) of the Small Business Act (both discussed later), they at least point in the direction of black employment as a proximate issue. The riots themselves demonstrated graphically the inadequacy of existing policies. Clearly, new policies too radi-cal to be considered in previous years would have to be examined in the light of seemingly continuous rioting.

Early Calls for Affirmative Action

Before the Philadelphia Plan was rescued by the Nixon administration in 1969, some calls for affirmative action could be heard. However, they came from those outside of the still powerful liberal consensus on race issues. Early on, they emerged as demands from local, grassroots civil rights activists in northern cities and universities. These demands were looked at sympatheti-cally, especially after widespread rioting, as some of the most realistic within civil rights manifestos. Especially in universities, faculty and students could agree on better black representation. By the end of the decade, however, calls for affirmative action came from what some might consider a very unlikely source—business.

Most in the civil rights movement, like Martin Luther King, Jr., subscribed to the liberal view of the inevitable progress of the nation toward equality. They imagined that it was only a matter of time before blacks would take their place as equals in American society. At the time of Nixon's inauguration de-segregating Southern schools was still the biggest civil rights issue, with hous-ing desegregation a close second.

However, younger militants in the civil rights movement held a less rever-ential view of the American Creed. In 1962, Congress on Racial Equality (CORE) militants had won national endorsement of racial employment pref-erences. Sealtest Milk was forced by CORE, during the winter of 1962–1963, to give Negroes and Puerto Ricans "exclusive exposure" for at least a week when hiring its next fifty workers. This was in some ways more far-reaching than the Philadelphia Plan (to be discussed in chapter 7). Whitney Young, Jr., chief of the National Urban League (NUL), whose interest had long mirrored those of the business community, included a demand for preferential treat-ment in his "Marshall Plan" for black Americans. However, his demands were different from what affirmative action campaigners seek today. He called for preferential treatment within the context of a short-term, massive effort to equalize black and white Americans.

> For more than 300 years the white American has received special consideration, or 'preferential treatment,' if you will, over the Negro. What we ask now is that for a brief period there be a deliberate and massive effort to include the Negro citizen in the mainstream of American life. Furthermore, we are not asking for equal time; a major effort, honestly applied, need last only some 10 years.[19]

Both CORE's and the NUL's quota demands were dropped after requests from those pushing forward with the 1964 Civil Rights Act.

Many of the most militant cadre of the civil rights movement came from Northern universities and colleges. Returning to education after, perhaps, volunteering in the South, these students set about transforming their educational institutions, often radicalizing black and white students. Thus, in the turmoil on the campuses in the late 1960s, demands for more representation of minority students and staff could be heard. Quite early on, the elite universities made real attempts to increase black student, staff, and faculty representation. Richard P. McCormick, who has written a history of the black student movement at Rutgers University, identified the start of awareness at Rutgers as 1963, when a former student, then a civil rights activist, was arrested in Georgia. Professor Paul Tillet of the political science department led a self-constituted faculty group that pressed for the recruitment of black faculty and students and, in 1965, the Boehm Committee, formed in September 1963 just after the arrest, made its report. It suggested a plan for "talent hunts" for disadvantaged students and "revision of admission criteria to enhance minority enrollment," among other things. These efforts resulted in growth of black students from around 100 in 1965 to 266 in 1967, and 413 in 1968. A similar move to add more blacks to the faculty took place in 1966. The provost, the chief academic officer at Rutgers, made it known that some positions would be reserved for minority appointees.[20]

The addition of black students added a force that could lobby for more representation. The radicalization of white students over the issue of Vietnam and dissent on universities created another constituency sympathetic to the demands of black students for meaningful representation. By the late 1960s, protesting college students often adopted demands expressed by African-American students. Thus, the Ad Hoc Committee for Student Rights at Ohio State University (OSU) incorporated the demand by the Afro-American Student group ("Afro Am") that the university "recruit enough Black people to constitute 23% of the student body and that a proportionate number of slots should remain open to Indians, poor whites, Chicanos and Puerto Ricans." OSU Women's Liberation Demands included both "an end to restrictive quotas (based on sex) which apply to admission into any college or graduate school" and a demand that the university recruit and hire "more women Advisors, Administrators, and Faculty until 50% of the Academic employees at Ohio State are women."[21] Yale Law School initiated a system of quotas for the first year class of the fall of 1969 whereby forty-three black students were admitted, of whom five qualified under the regular standards and thirty-eight did not.[22]

There was little general discussion of the ramifications of the quotas called for by these groups (the lack of the sort of opposition to affirmative action heard today is discussed later). Calls for quotas from within the civil rights movement, broadly defined, were usually local and few called for affirmative action at a national level. Still, some worried about the implications of acknowledging racial divisions for liberal values, fearing that America would remain hopelessly divided along racial lines.

To the demands for preferential treatment heard in colleges and elsewhere, liberals answered that racial quotas might set an official seal of approval on segregation, shutting the door to any reform in the future. A debate of sorts occurred in legal journals during the second half of the decade regarding the legitimacy of preferential treatment in employment. Most observers, while recognizing the futility of current programs, rejected the idea of employment quotas. Part of the problem, they felt, was that it contradicted Myrdal's emphasis on the government as the head of an effort to educate Americans on racial equality. Thus, John Kaplan urged in 1966 that the "most important" objection to affirmative action was that it "weakens the government as an educative force."[23]

Ralph K. Winter argued along similar lines a year later that "preferential programs are fundamentally counter-educative on the basic issue of racial discrimination itself. Instead of helping to eliminate race from politics, they inject it. Instead of teaching tolerance and helping those forces seeking accommodation, they divide on a racial basis."[24] A government program based on racial divisions "would imply that there are important differences between the races, apparent if not real, and that those differences are sufficient to justify government action."[25]

However, fear of further politicizing the issue crept in (an issue that would be very relevant to Nixon). White backlash became part of the language in the 1964 election campaign primaries and continued to haunt the Democrats, especially after the 1966 midterm elections, in which the Republicans exceeded their expectations. It was invoked against arguments for preferential treatment, giving, perhaps, an indication of why quotas were suggested before the election in 1964 but almost universally rejected after it.

> Such programs tend to legitimate the backlash by providing it with much of the philosophic and moral base from which the civil rights movement itself began. . . .
> The costs of preferential programs, moreover, are far more certain than the gains. The very demands for such programs have already created a reaction along the lines described above. It would be a tragedy to pay all the costs of preferential treatment and to learn that it was not as effective as had been hoped. Certainly, such programs ought to be considered last resorts if not altogether too dangerous.[26]

Many of these legal academics understood that something fundamental in the relationship between government and citizen was implied by government-sanctioned preferential treatment. Government would then become an *arbiter* between groups in a racially divided society rather than a *leader* in a society striving toward racial equality. All traces of the moral leadership called for by Myrdal would disappear. Implicit in the discussion is a fear that, without this moral leadership, the government would struggle to legitimate itself.

The Wider Crisis of Legitimacy

Whatever the tumultuous events in the late 1960s, it was the context of a deeper disturbance involving the destruction of institutions and assumptions that gave them their real meaning.[27] Civic participation began a period of decline that has not yet abated from the mid-1960s. However, as the Harris Poll chart below shows, the most vertiginous decline in faith in institutions came during the last years of the 1960s (see table 4.1).

By the end of the decade, the problem was not simply one of alienated minorities failing to fit in with the American mainstream but of the mainstream

Table 4.1. Proportion of Americans Expressing a
"Great Deal of Confidence" in Leadership Institutions (Percent)[28]

Institution	1966	1971	1972	1973
Major companies	55	27	27	29
Organized labor	22	14	15	20
Higher education	61	27	33	44
Medicine	72	61	48	58
Organized religion	41	27	30	36

itself fragmenting into alienated minorities. Other polls back up Harris's contention. Business had been an important partner in the earlier postwar period and its participation was considered essential to any civil rights initiatives, as indicated by representation at the White House Conference on Civil Rights. Most Americans agreed that business, through its quest for profits, operated for the good of the whole of society. The Opinion Research Survey, which had been keeping track of American attitudes toward business, showed that the percentage of people agreeing with the statement "Large companies are essential for the nation's growth and expansion" increased from 60 percent in 1959 to 67 percent in 1965. However, the number of Americans agreeing that "the profits of large companies help make things better for everyone" dropped from 67 percent to 41 percent in 1975. As Seymour Martin Lipset noted: "The collapse of confidence in business appears to be quite broad; it applied to business in general and to every major part of the business community."[29]

Labor unions, identified by Myrdal as a molder and moderator of the opinions of individual union members, no longer maintained the importance that they had at their postwar zenith of 1955 (see chapter 10 for a discussion of this trend in relation to identity). Their influence had been profound. As Bayard Rustin commented in 1965: "The labor movement, despite its obvious faults, has been the largest single organized force in this country pushing for progressive social legislation."[30] Nathan Glazer and Daniel Patrick Moynihan indicated in a preface to their book, *Beyond the Melting Pot*, that they had both originally aspired to work for trade unions.[31] Its support was considered crucial for any civil rights initiative and played a huge role in getting the 1964 Act passed. But, indicted for being part of the problem, its influence declined, part of a long-term decline in membership. From 35 percent of the total workforce in the 1950s, union membership slid continuously to around 20 percent in 1980 and down to 13.5 percent in 2000. Gallup asked, "In general, do you approve or disapprove of trade unions?" Those who approved dropped continuously from 71 percent in 1965 to 55 percent in 1981.[32]

Churches, which had actively participated in the civil rights movement, part of the coalition credited by Bayard Rustin for passage of the 1964 Civil Rights Act, suffered blows to their moral authority in the wake of the riots. When James Foreman demanded five hundred million dollars from white churches and synagogues as "compensation" for their role in black oppression, the moral authority churches gained from being on the "right" side of the civil rights question virtually disappeared. Instead, the issue served to divide clergy and lay men and women. As the *Religious Congregation and Membership 2000* survey found, liberal churches declined in the United States even as conservative churches grew in membership.

Nor were other institutions able to escape the wholesale destruction of an essential part of what German social theorist Jürgen Habermas referred to as the "public sphere," that hinterland between the private family sphere and the state.[33] Pollster Daniel Yankelovich noted in 1977:

> We have seen a steady rise of mistrust in our national institutions. . . . Trust in government declined dramatically from almost 80% in the late 1950s to around 33% in 1976. . . . More than 61% of the electorate believe that there is something morally wrong in the country. More than 80% of voters say they do not trust those in positions of leadership as much as they used to. In the mid-60s a one-third minority reported feeling isolated and distant from the political process; by the mid-70s a two-thirds majority felt that what they think "really doesn't count." . . . [F]ewer than one out of five feels that congressional leaders can be believed. . . . The change is simply massive. Within a ten- to fifteen-year period, trust in institutions has plunged down and down, from an almost consensual majority, two-thirds or more, to minority segments of the American public.[34]

This was not simply a crisis in race relations but a broader crisis that loosened the tie between citizen and government. The importance of the nature of the problem is important in understanding the role affirmative action later played—beyond race relations—in providing some sort of bridge between citizens and the federal government in the ensuing years.

In the postwar period, Americans related to the federal government through institutions. Not only would the education of its citizens filter through organizations, as Myrdal imagined, but the power of citizens to effect changes also worked through local organizations. Trade unions put pressure on government to act. Local wards and ethnic organizations dealt with politicians, gaining favors and promising votes. Local political parties ensured that the particular voices in that locality were heard. Elks and Shriners took up specific causes of interest to their members and promoted patriotism and various government campaigns to their members. Churches preached anti-communism as well as the Bible to their congregations and influenced national politics on crucial issues. Without these institutions, government lost an important legitimizing tool and citizens became disconnected from government and from each other.

The Crisis of Political Organizations

The political class experienced this deepening crisis as primarily the alienation of voters from the two-party system. The Democratic Party, hitherto the political gathering point for civil rights liberals, appeared on the verge of collapse after the Chicago convention. A delegate told the audience in Chicago: "To an extent not matched since the turn of the century, events in 1968 have called into question the integrity of the convention system for nominating presidential candidates. Recent developments have put the future of the two-party system into serious jeopardy."[35]

But it was not simply the Democrats who saw a crisis emerging. Elliot Richardson, who would replace Bob Finch as Nixon's secretary of Health, Education, and Welfare, pontificated in 1967 about "[A] new and potentially disastrous development [that] threatens us: the growing loss, by millions of Americans of their sense of purpose and identity." He blamed the Johnson administration for the debacle, not entirely surprising, given that he spoke to the Republican Ripon Society.[36] Conservatives galvanized their constituents by spreading panic about the perceived (and often very real) lack of law and order in American society. "Crime and violence, disregard of law and disrespect for authority, immorality and irresponsibility are on the rise," one report exclaimed brightly to the Republican National Conference in Miami in 1968.[37] "Rising crime rates and a series of major riots and civil disorders have left a trail of victims, both Negro and white, and have created an atmosphere of fear, alarm, mistrust and apprehension all across the country," chimed in another.[38] Nixon, not to be outdone by his Republican colleagues, topped the hyperbole stakes in speeches around the country. "The violence being threatened for this summer is more in the nature of a war than a riot. A riot, by definition, is a spontaneous outburst. A war is subject to advance planning."[39] Later, he warmed to the "war" descriptor for domestic violence. "The war in Asia is a limited one with limited means and limited goals. The war at home is a war for survival of a free society."[40]

The Republicans themselves had been in crisis for some time. An interesting report entitled *Where the Votes Are* published in 1966 indicated the extent of the rot. In 1940, 38 percent of American voters considered themselves regularly affiliated with the GOP. By 1950, 33 percent of the American population still affiliated themselves with the GOP. In 1960, the number dropped to 30 percent, in 1962, 28 percent, and by 1964, only 25 percent of the population called themselves Republicans. Meanwhile, Democratic party affiliations rose to over 50 percent and those who called themselves Independents remained between 20 and 24 percent between 1940 and 1966. Party affiliation was at its weakest among voters in their early and middle twenties. Despite the report's suggestion that its implications were of an "enormous opportunity," the statistics were clearly gloomy reading for Republican officials.[41]

Habermas's "Legitimation Crisis"

Specifically how this crisis would affect the incoming administration in 1969 can be shown by using the model devised by German social theorist Jürgen Habermas in *Legitimation Crisis*. Though sometimes opaque in his language, the model created by Habermas is perhaps the most useful in understanding the dynamic behind rapidly expanding affirmative action programs:

> Because a class compromise has been made the foundation of reproduction, the state apparatus must fulfill its tasks in the economic system under the limiting condition that mass loyalty be simultaneously secured within the framework of a formal democracy and in accord with ruling universalistic value systems. These pressures of legitimation can be mitigated only through structures of a depoliticized public realm.[42]

Legitimation, which in the past referred to the act of making lawful a child born out of wedlock, indicated that the problem lay within the action of the state in making itself legitimate. Habermas's theory thus both pinpointed the specific legitimacy problems and indicated how the response of the authorities to questions over their legitimacy added to the dynamic behind the legitimacy crisis, doubtless his most important contribution and of key importance in understanding why affirmative action expanded so rapidly.

The term "legitimacy"—virtually unknown before 1950—became a widely-discussed subject in the late 1960s. Seymour Martin Lipset provided an early rehearsal of the discussion in a work first published in 1959:

> The stability of any given democracy depends not only on economic development but also upon the effectiveness and the legitimacy of its political system. . . . Legitimacy involves the capacity of the system to engender and maintain the belief that the existing political institutions are the most appropriate ones for the society.[43]

Many others described the legitimacy crisis in the late 1960s and, especially, during the 1970s, in progressively pessimistic terms.[44] However, Habermas showed that the legitimacy crisis was in fact a legitimation crisis. In other words, it was the *response* to the legitimacy crisis, the attempt at legitimation, that created the crux of the problem. Habermas described accurately the process whereby the State extends its activities into realms previously organized spontaneously and on a local, informal, and private basis. The process is triggered by fears within the establishment that the legitimizing political system—the specific set of institutions—does not succeed in maintaining the requisite level of mass loyalty (and thus its own authority). This threatens the informal arrangement within advanced capitalist democracies whereby, as Gabriel A. Almond and Sydney Verba put it, the democratic citizen is "active, yet passive; involved, yet not too involved; influential, yet deferential."[45] The process continues inexorably after initial government intervention undermines remaining institutions, creating the perceived need for another round of intervention.

The problem is then twofold. First, because of lower economic growth and the fact that the state must extend itself into many new areas, it becomes unable to generate the requisite financial resources.[46] Second, because the state steps into areas formerly administered informally and reified automatically, its action in replacing the administration tends to throw other areas into question, undermining more institutions and thus creating the need, in the consciousness of the ruling elite, for more intervention. This sort of a crisis, Habermas insisted, was not a constant phenomenon within advanced capitalist societies where a legitimation *deficit* might occur as the State assumed aspects that had formerly been dealt with by the market. Instead:

> [O]nly when members of a society experience structural alterations as critical for continued existence and feel their social identity threatened can we speak of crises. Disturbances of system integration endanger continued existence only to the extent that *social integration* is at stake, that is, when the consensual foundations of normative structures are so much impaired that the society becomes anomic. Crisis states assume the form of a disintegration of social institutions.[47]

Thus, the subjective sense of the crisis is paramount. It is no doubt in the efficacy of the system that distinguished what happened in the late 1960s from other strictly objective difficulties. Then, the perception was that social institutions were certainly disintegrating. Government intervention is the state's answer to the crumbling of the threatened semi-private institutions. If we view the issue of affirmative action within the context of Habermas's theory, involving officials of both Johnson and Nixon administrations, members of the permanent bureaucracy, and politicians toward more government intervention becomes easier to understand.

Affirmative action on a voluntary level was meant to harness the energy and determination of various private and semi-private institutions in order to include African Americans. There was little attempt—despite the rhetoric—by government at any level to forcibly reform the racial status quo in these institutions; instead, the federal government hoped to lead these organizations which would in turn lead their members away from racial attitudes. However, the progressive failure of these institutions to integrate African Americans and the charge that they were "institutionally racist" implied that they were failing in their Myrdalian role and opened them to question. Even those—like some universities—that did successfully implement some form of quota were condemned for making too little effort. The Philadelphia Plan sought to break the deadlock within building unions by creating numbers and targets. Other plans involving government intervention, as chapter 8 describes, were put in place at around the same time. Though the purpose of the intervention was to shore up the institutions by removing barriers to black participation within them, to make the institutions good enough for African Americans to be integrated, the implied inadequacy of existing semi-private ways of allocating jobs or college places threw the informal nature of all allocation systems into doubt.

Habermas noted the ominous implications for democratic structures and traditions. The effect of government involvement in a sphere that was previously governed by informal local traditions has the effect of undermining those traditions: "It . . . results from the fact that the fulfilment of governmental planning tasks places in question the structure of the depoliticized public realm and, thereby, the formally democratic securing of private autonomous disposition of the means of production."[48] Part of the difficulty came because areas that had not previously been subject to political debate became, because of state intervention, politicized. The scope of politics, though widened because of new areas the State dealt with, also narrowed as activity in these areas could only reinforce the perception that there was little alternative. In other words, intervention in these new areas, where no real political alternatives existed, contributed to the perception that politics was simply a managerial, administrative issue.

With politicizing these new areas comes the need to justify what had formerly been accomplished almost automatically through private institutions. These new areas are also subject to political pressures. The purposes for acquiring these new realms must be justified. Why should the State be active here, to what end, and by what guiding philosophies?[49] With the encroachment of the State into the realm of job allocation, for instance—previously negotiated between employers and organized labor—the State declared that the goal of African-American participation in the labor movement and hence in the mainstream of American life was the reason for the intervention. The prior economic self-interest of union members and the need for efficiency were laid open to question and debate and were, by implication, declared part of the problem or even racist. By opening these areas up to scrutiny, the finger was pointed at all *other* systems of allocating jobs or college places. In turn, the publicly-stated goal of African-American labor force participation became open to challenge from other groups who could also claim underparticipation.

Once the unquestionable character of traditions is destroyed, more areas within the private sphere come under scrutiny. The collapsing nature of the phenomenon sheds light on a problem explored in some of the literature on affirmative action. Why did affirmative action—obviously first implemented with the specific problems of African Americans in mind—expand so rapidly and effortlessly even as the threat of riots receded? Within a matter of two years, Spanish-surnamed Americans, Indians (Native Americans), Eskimos, Aleuts, and women were included as "protected categories," despite, as John D. Skrentny points out, a lack of campaigning on the part of these other categories. A legitimation crisis suggests that the sudden collapse of institutional authority and the ensuing attempts to correct it made government officials seek to replace previous ways of relating to citizens before the citizens themselves actually called for them. The inadequacy of the way the State previously dealt with black civil rights issues suggested to government officials that the way it dealt with other citizens might be inadequate, too. Though Skrentny alludes to Habermas's legitimation theory in his book on affirmative action, he does not follow through the logic of the theory in explaining why affirmative action categories grew, especially in the early 1970s.[50] Similarly, it answers the question of why the Philadelphia Plan—a limited and unnoticed program—prefaced an explosion of affirmative action plans within and without government. Again, once the informal systems governing hiring, firing, and promoting were deemed inadequate, *all* systems not employing affirmative action were *ipso facto* inadequate if not racist. Like a Supreme Court decision, affirmative action struck down all previous ways of hiring, firing, and promotion. Many authors have looked at the expansion of affirmative action as a result of pressure from civil rights activists inside or outside the government. As Skrentny has pointed out, that pressure simply was not there.[51] Understood as the collapse of previous informal (or, in the case of labor relations, semi-formal[52]) institutions after the Nixon administration, by putting in place the Philadelphia Plan, effectively put hiring, firing, or promotion on merit in the dock, the expansion of affirmative action makes sense.

If we apply Habermas's analysis to the problem, we can see that the implicit indictment of existing justifications for employment decisions laid them completely open to question. Once judged unjust, as the low numbers of African Americans employed were seen as the result of institutional racism, any low number of numerous other categories would be seen as the result of injustice also. The destruction of the traditions and informal regulations set off a panicked reaction by the authorities as there appeared to be a lack of controls and rules governing the whole sphere. Habermas warned that the entire private sphere was in danger of being destroyed through this process.[53] Alan Wolfe expressed the problem in a slightly different fashion, showing that options close with the enactment of the whole process:

> The activity of the state has increased to the point where it has become a major producer and certainly the major consumer, but often forgotten is that the growth in potential power of the state is matched by a decline in the options that the state has at its command. For this reason, the increased activity of the state reflects, not an expansion of alternatives, but an exhaustion of them.[54]

Johnson's civil rights actions aimed to, as Habermas put it, "ward off system crisis" by focusing "all forces of social integration at the point of the structurally most probable conflict [civil rights]—in order all the more effectively to keep it latent."[55] Affirmative action measures differed, however, from previous civil rights initiatives in that they no longer simply exhorted American citizens at all levels to adjust their behavior in order to include African Americans within the economic and social life of the country. The crisis that created the need for affirmative action sprang from the examination in light of the racial crisis of the 1960s of the (generally private) institutions that ostensibly created the basis of equal opportunity. They were found wanting. Existing mechanisms that should have created the basis of equal opportunity in both public and private employment, higher education and traditional contracting arrangements simply did not work for blacks. Affirmative action broke new ground in that it attempted to replace these traditional structures that had proved inadequate to the inclusion of black Americans within American life with a specific regulatory structure. It responded to a legitimation crisis initially within the African-American community that, by the time Nixon took power, extended way beyond.

Yet one other aspect related to Habermas's model stands out. A lack of philosophical justification for or coherence about early affirmative action measures reflected a general turmoil about the legitimacy of socio-cultural traditions and the legitimacy of the motivations behind new administrative procedures. Early affirmative action measures could not be and were not defended confidently, especially after the initial justifications—the need to extend civil rights and to stem the threat of rioting—lost resonance, despite the destruction of socio-cultural traditions that stood in the way of affirmative action measures. Instead, some new basis of authority had to be created that would provide the groundwork for the widespread adoption of these measures. Here was a motivation crisis, created by the need for motivation by the state and the educational system, and the motivation behind the existing socio-political system.

Conclusion

Some reforms, remnants of the previous, more hopeful era, survived into the 1970s. The school desegregation campaign extended into northern areas continuing to hope that black and white children, at least, might be able to break down some of the barriers between them. Here, at least, was a shadow of the "contact theory" of Gordon Allport. Housing desegregation, too, continued for some time. But, without the basic belief that the wall of prejudice within white Americans would soon be breached, without the promise that integration would take place soon, the energy behind these campaigns disappeared.

Much had occurred that removed the barriers to affirmative action. The riots certainly supplanted the liberal fear of instability among whites might result from the imposition of quotas. The optimism with which liberal policymakers launched programs designed to eradicate racism began to desert them. The crusades to integrate education and housing had only just begun when doubts clouded their future.

The doubts ultimately gathered at the door of the U.S. federal government. Some action had to be attempted to restore the chain of command that linked Americans to their government. Early affirmative action programs experimented with enabling African Americans to participate in areas where they had not traditionally been included. But, in stamping their imprimatur only on contractors with affirmative action programs, the government opened to question all other hitherto-informally governed systems of hiring, contract awards, and student admissions. As Habermas showed, a legitimation crisis occurred, requiring the state to be active in more and more spheres. That affirmative action backed into existence and that it expanded at a huge rate in the 1970s with little direct pressure is at least partially explained using Habermas's theory.

Notes

1. Irwin Miller, "Business Has a War to Win," *Harvard Business Review* 47, no. 2 (March/April 1969): 4–12 (continued on 164–68), esp. 6–7.

2. Cited in John D. Skrentny, *The Ironies of Affirmative Action: Politics, Culture, and Justice in America* (London: University of Chicago Press, 1996), 68.

3. Godfrey Hodgson, *In Our Time: America from World War II to Nixon* (London: Macmillan, 1976), 275.

4. Melvin Small, *The Presidency of Richard Nixon* (Lawrence: Kansas University Press, 1999), 70, 157.

5. Alfred Blumrosen, *Black Employment and the Law* (New Brunswick, NJ: Rutgers University Press, 1971), 14.

6. "[Civil Rights] Background Material for *The Reluctant Guardians: A Survey of the Enforcement of Federal Civil Rights Laws* by Barney Sellers" (note: it appears that this book was never published). [CFOA 908], box 61, WHSF: SMOF: Garment, NPMP, 1-68.

7. Civil Rights Study Paper Draft, Housing, 1/5/71, Civil Rights—Garment-Nathan Study Committee [CFOA 908], box 59, WHSF: SMOF: Garment, NPMP.

8. Statement of William H. Brown, III, Chairman, Equal Employment Opportunity Commission, to the House General Subcommittee on Labor, December 1, 1969, EEOC 1969 [2 of 4] [CFOA 7730], box 84, WHCF: SMOF: Garment, NPMP.

9. "Background Material for *The Reluctant Guardians,*" 1–29.

10. "Background Material for *The Reluctant Guardians,*" i.53, i.68, esp. ii.8.

11. Cited in Hugh Davis Graham, *The Civil Rights Era: Origins and Development of National Policy 1960–1972* (New York: Oxford University Press, 1990), 286.

12. "Voice of the Ghetto: Report on Two Boston Neighborhood Meetings," by the Massachusetts State Advisory Commission to the United States Commission on Civil Rights, July 1967, Civil Rights: Massachusetts State Advisory Committee to the U.S. Commission on Civil Rights, box 422, Brooke Papers.

13. Analysis of Plainfield, NJ Disturbance, Office of the Assistant Deputy Director for Research, Staff Paper no. 3 draft, October 29, 1967, box 464, Brooke Papers.

14. Memo to Honorable Otto Kerner, Chairman, National Advisory Commission on Civil Disorders with Attached "Call and Commitment: Action to Alleviate Civil Disorder and Eliminate Social and Economic Injustice," National Governor's Conference, Advisory Committee on Federal-State-Local Relations (draft) May 10, 1967, box 465, Brooke Papers.

15. Memo to the Commission from David Ginsburg, executive director, The National Advisory Commission on Civil Disorders, Nov 7, 1967 plus attached "Survey Paper on Short-Term Domestic Program Options," no date, National Advisory Commission on Civil Disorders—Records, November 1967, box 465, Brooke Papers.

16. Ibid.

17. Ibid. According to the Senate permanent investigations subcommittee headed by John McClellan of Arkansas, Blackstone Rangers' leaders stole from a $927,000 Office of Economic Opportunity (OEO) kitty to buy cars and drugs and to consolidate their control on ghetto areas. Edward P. Morgan, "Political Retreat from the Poverty War," in *Poverty in Affluence: The Social, Political, and Economic Dimensions of Poverty in the United States,* ed. Robert E. Will and Harold G. Vatter (New York: Harcourt, Brace & World, Inc., 1970), 221–223.

18. "Call and Commitment: Action to Alleviate Civil Disorder and Eliminate Social and Economic Injustice," National Governor's Conference, Advisory Committee on Federal-State-Local Relations (draft) May 10, 1967, box 465, Brooke Papers.

19. Cited in Gabriel Chin, "Series Introduction," *Affirmative Action Before Constitutional Law, 1964-1977* (London: Garland Publishing, Inc., 1998), x.

20. Richard P. McCormick, *The Black Student Protest Movement at Rutgers* (London: Rutgers University Press, 1990), 13–14.

21. Original documents available at http://history.ohio-state.edu/osuhist/1970riot /demand2.htm and http://history.ohio-state.edu/osuhist/1970riot/women.htm (accessed 04/02/03).

22. Macklin Fleming, Louis Pollak, "The Black Quota at Yale Law School," *The Public Interest* no. 19 (Spring 1970): 44–52.

23. John Kaplan, "Unequal Justice in an Unequal World: Equality for the Negro—the Problem of Special Treatment," *Northwestern University Law Review* 63, no. 3 (July–August 1966): 363–410, esp. 392.

24. Ralph K. Winter, "Improving the Economic Status of Negroes Through Laws Against Discrimination: A Reply to Professor Sovern," *University of Chicago Law Review* 34 (1966–1967): 817–55, esp. 854. Moreno felt that Winter argued in favor of quotas. As the above passage shows, however, Winter presented important arguments against quotas.

25. Norman Vieira, "Racial Imbalance, Black Separatism and Permissible Classification by Race," *Michigan Law Review* 67 (June 1969): 1523–1625, esp. 1615.

26. Winter, "Improving the Economic Status of Negroes Through Laws Against Discrimination," 854.

27. Compare, for instance, the relative lack of long-term impact of the worst racial riot in United States history—the 1992 Los Angeles riot—with the lesser, if more widespread, riots of the 1960s.

28. Chart reproduced from Alan Wolfe, *The Limits of Legitimacy: Political Contradictions of Contemporary Capitalism* (New York: The Free Press, 1977), 310.

29. Seymour Martin Lipset and William Schneider, "The Decline of Confidence in American Institutions," *Political Science Quarterly* 98, issue 3 (Autumn 1983), 379–402.

30. Bayard Rustin, "From Protest to Politics: The Future of the Civil Rights Movement," *Commentary* 39 (February 1965): 25–31, esp. 25.

31. Nathan Glazer and Daniel Patrick Moynihan *Beyond the Melting Pot* (London: The M.I.T. Press, 1970 [1963]), xxxiv.

32. Steven Greenhouse, "Fewer Workers Belong to Unions," *New York Times*, January 22, 2001.

33. The public sphere, in some ways, played a similar role to the *polis* of antiquity, distinct from the state. See Nancy Fraser, "Rethinking the Public Sphere: A Contribution to the Critique of Actually Existing Democracy" in *Habermas and the Public Sphere*, ed. Craig Calhoun (Cambridge, MA: The M.I.T. Press, 1992), 109–20, esp. 110.

34. Cited in Lipset and Schneider, "The Decline of Confidence in American Institutions," 380.

35. Cited in Byron E. Shafer, *Quiet Revolution: The Struggle for the Democratic Party and the Shaping of Post-Reform Politics* (New York: Russell Sage Foundation, 1983), 25.

36. Ibid.

37. Cited in *The Republican* 3, no. 2 (February 10, 1967), "The Republican," RNC Publications, box 99, RNC Records.

38. "New Directions for Urban America," draft dated 19 March 1968, folder marked "Human Needs," box 60, 1968 Republican National Convention, RNC Records.

39. A statement by Richard M. Nixon: NBC Radio Network, March 7, 1968, 1968 Presidential Campaign: RNC news releases 8/23/68–9/25/68, comment 8/26/68–11/4/68, Nixon speeches 10/67–9/25/68, 1968 Nixon Campaign: Press Releases and Nixon Speeches, box 5, RNC Records.

40. An address by Richard M. Nixon at the 72nd Congress of American Industry of the NAM Annual Dinner, Waldorf-Astoria, New York, December 8, 1967, 1968 Presidential Campaign: RNC news releases 8/23/68–9/25/68, comment 8/26/68–11/4/68, Nixon speeches 10/67–9/25/68, 1968 Nixon Campaign: Press Releases and Nixon Speeches, box 5, RNC Records.

41. *Where the Votes Are*, prepared by the staff of the U.S. Senate Republican Policy Committee, July 10, 1966, RNC Publications, box 99, RNC Records.

42. Jürgen Habermas, *Legitimation Crisis*, translated by Thomas McCarthy (Boston: Beacon Press, 1975, [1969]), 58, cf. Alan Wolfe, *The Limits of Legitimacy: Political Contradictions of Contemporary Capitalism* (New York: The Free Press, 1977), 295.

43. Seymour Martin Lipset, *Political Man: The Social Bases of Politics* (Baltimore: The Johns Hopkins University Press, 1981 [1959]), 64.

44. Perhaps the most pessimistic treatise produced around this time dealing with the legitimation or legitimacy crisis is Robert Nisbet's *Twilight of Authority* (London: Heineman, 1976).

45. Cited in Habermas, *Legitimation Crisis*, 77.

46. This point is elaborated in Dieter Fuchs and Hans-Dieter Klingemann, "Citizens and the State: A Changing Relationship?" In *Citizens and the State*, ed. Hans-Dieter Klingemann and Dieter Fuchs (Oxford: Oxford University Press, 1995), 1–23, esp. 6–7.

47. Habermas, *Legitimation Crisis*, 4.

48. Habermas, *Legitimation Crisis*, 46.

49. Habermas, *Legitimation Crisis*, 70–71. Habermas was careful to delineate between a *rationality crisis*, in which the administrative system does not succeed in reconciling and fulfilling the imperatives received from the economic system, and a *legitimation crisis*, whereby the legitimizing system does not succeed in maintaining the requisite level of mass loyalty while the steering imperatives taken over from the economic system are carried through. See Habermas, *Legitimation Crisis*, 46.

50. Skrentny, *The Ironies of Affirmative Action* and Skrentny, *The Minority Rights Revolution* (Cambridge, MA: The Belknap Press of Harvard University Press, 2002). Part of the question Skrentny begins with in the latter book is why the minority revolution spread.

51. Skrentny, *The Minority Rights Revolution*: "From the perspective of rationalist studies of policy development, the minority rights revolution also presents a mystery," 6.

52. The Wagner Act, of course, put into place organizations made up of employers, union and government representatives as well as arbitration machinery that can not be placed within what Habermas referred to as the "privatized public realm."

53. Habermas, *Legitimation Crisis*, 72.

54. Alan Wolfe, *Limits of Legitimacy: Political Contradictions of Contemporary Capitalism* (New York: Free Press, 1977), 258.

55. Habermas, *Legitimation Crisis*, 37–38.

5

Affirmative Action:
The Conservative Option

O NE OF THE MANY IRONIES OF AFFIRMATIVE ACTION is that conservatives, rather than liberals, who were notably reticent about it, were the first advocates of government-enforced affirmative action. A good example of this occurred when the provocative conservative columnist William F. Buckley, who backed Nixon in 1968, came out in favor of quotas. In a column in 1969 on jobs, he stated: "We must in fact encourage a pro-Negro discrimination."[1]

The most conservative elements, of course, supported affirmative action for different reasons than those who defend affirmative action programs today. These forces adopted affirmative action not out of a moral commitment to the betterment of African Americans or any other group but for defensive reasons. They shared the immediate concern for the implications of the destruction of authority from large areas in American cities. Thus, as Skrentny and others have pointed out, quotas, especially highly visible ones in the black areas of central cities, might serve to blunt the anger of potential rioters and the kind of urban guerrillas that kept the aforementioned Irwin Miller awake nights. Such measures might, in the longer term, integrate those most alienated from American life and give them some stake in the system, as Nixon termed it.

On another level, the elite, "who had inherited, or acquired, a sense of entitlement mixed with civic responsibility that in another time or place might be called *noblesse oblige*," might regain some moral authority by implementing or at least advocating these measures.[2] Compared with the extremely ambitious recommendations of the Kerner Report and the radical demands of African-American groups, affirmative action was, as Skrentny put it, "cheap, easy, and available."[3] It was not important whether or not the measures worked; as long as they could be easily and cheaply implemented and counter the constant question, "What is your solution?" that must have been shouted by angry liberals, their primary purpose for conservatives was answered.

It could also be argued, however, that the origin of business's openness to quotas lay in the "human relations" management revolution of the 1950s. By focusing on broader human relations goals within a work environment rather than on micromanaging production targets, some management theorists concluded, overall production levels at a business concern would rise.[4] Harmonious relations between employees became a new business imperative in the postwar period; affirmative action, with its goals and targets attempting to manipulate inter-employee relations, might be seen as a development of these earlier theories.

Affirmative Action's Surprising Proponents

Business, along with unions, had reason to oppose any effort to interfere with its prerogative to hire, fire, and promote whom it saw fit. Certainly, the pre-Depression perspective of business was laissez-faire and usually shunned attempts by the government to interfere in its business. From the Depression-era onward, however, many of the mechanisms of government were dedicated to the smooth running of the accumulation of capital. Companies became increasingly dependent on what Habermas called "steering imperatives" of the government, and a business-government interdependence grew. During World War II and in the midst of the Cold War, defense spending bound government and business even further.

However, the extraordinary merging of business and government, both economically and ideologically, occurring in the United States in the postwar years ensured that business was an early advocate of affirmative action. Business, like the state, suffered a subjective legitimacy crisis. By 1969, however, the importance of merit as a business principle had been eclipsed by concern about the preservation of social order. Support in 1969 for affirmative action could be found, not in the pages of *Ramparts* or other liberal periodicals, but in the *Harvard Business Review* and *Fortune*. Having more to lose from riot and disorder than most, business also had less to lose from employing quotas.

As Whitney Young pointed out at the time, some businesses in the early 1960s were turning to racially preferential hiring policies while officially denying it. The CEO of Pitney-Bowes of Stamford, Connecticut, announced that the company would adopt a formal policy of preferential hiring within days of Kennedy's assassination.[5] As rioting spread through major cities across the

United States, businessmen stepped up their efforts. The organization Freedom, Independence, God, Honor, Today (FIGHT), created by Chicago activist Saul Alinsky, demanded in 1965 that Eastman Kodak, Rochester's biggest employer, hire six hundred hard-core unemployed within eighteen months—with FIGHT picking the new workers. Eastman proposed instead "a community-wide quota of fifteen hundred hard-core jobs in eighteen months, with participation by all Rochester's employers and agencies that deal with the poor." The organization resulting from the negotiations, "Rochester Jobs Incorporated," was the pattern for the "National Alliance of Businessmen," created by Henry Ford, II, "a somewhat vaguely constituted body with a goal of finding jobs for 500,000 in 50 cities," as *The Wall Street Journal* put it. Individual member firms were asked to pledge to hire a certain number of hard-core jobless. "The biggest factor in the success of the Rochester plan is a revision of hiring standards by businessmen." Ed Croft, director of Rochester Jobs Incorporated, explained: "Back in 1962, employers hired only high-school graduates. By 1965 they would accept applicants who had completed government training programs. Now, they no longer ask about an applicant's education." Some idea of how the companies in Rochester were trying to hire Negroes is given in a statement from Xerox's vice president for manufacturing, Horace Becker: "I put out an edict stating that in new employment we should shoot for 50 percent black."[6]

The aforementioned Irwin Miller in 1969 summoned his business colleagues to think and act anew and to consider affirmative action policies: "Up to now business has reacted to the impact of race on the communities in which it is located. We know now in business how important it is to act rather than react. Is it unthinkable that we should *plan* the total racial integration of each of our businesses, even to the point of importing members of minority groups?"[7]

A survey of executives of *Fortune's* 750 largest companies revealed that 78 percent of fourth and fifth level executives agreed with "lowering the company's employment qualifications to hire more from disadvantaged groups," though their lower level colleagues disagreed.[8] General Electric (GE), in a study published in 1968, identified the urban minority problem as "the dominant one on the domestic social, political, and economic scene for the next ten years." In January 1970, GE noted that "business leaders must ensure that their decisions and actions are formulated with the broadest possible social and community implications in mind."[9] No mention at all was made of management prerogative in the pamphlet. Instead, it spoke soberly of the need for cooperation between business leaders and government in the face of possible crises.

Just as particular institutions were moving toward affirmative action solutions to widespread questioning of their legitimacy and because of specific threats to their stability, economic conditions also became more amenable to affirmative action—better, perhaps, in the late 1960s than at any time since World War II. In the first place, affirmative action policies became more viable than they had been in the past as contractors became more plentiful and contracts more scarce. Pressure from the government could be brought to bear and contractors could no longer afford to pick and choose contractual arrangement. As such, affirmative action far better suited conditions of recession than other civil rights policies. Paul Moreno suggests that contractors, who had disadvantages in government dealings during the 1930s, held the upper hand with massive defense spending in the late 1940s and 1950s.[10] But at the end of the 1960s contractors faced a bear market. In 1969, despite predictions that the economy would pick up, "fourth-quarter output actually declined by 1.4 percent (annual rate), and the recession that [chairman of the Council of Economic Advisers Paul] McCracken said would not happen, began."[11] Thus, construction and many other blue-collar industries floundered at the time and many of the military and space program contracts dried up in the early 1970s as the Vietnam War effort and the space programs were cut back. A viable affirmative action plan became an asset in the battle to secure a valuable contract.

Because more U.S. workers in the 1970s than at any other time in history depended, directly or indirectly, upon the federal government for their wages, "rulemaking to bind recipients to federal dollars," in Graham's words, became an option.[12] Affirmative action in its new guise would now be brought to bear on a large percentage of the U.S. workforce. As well as an estimated one-third of the U.S. workforce working for government contractors, 15.2 percent of the civilian labor force worked for the government at either the federal, the state, or the local levels.[13] The changing economic structure was tilting toward more government control (rather than less, even during the reigns of Republican presidents who wished to roll back government). When direct control is added to indirect control exercised through contracts, it is hardly surprising that economists at the White House held out great hope for at least the possibility of effective enforcement of affirmative action.

There was also a merging of the public and private spheres occurring in economic terms, as private industry began to rely more heavily on government patronage, having the effect of breaking down barriers to government interference long held within private industry. Economists Walker and Vatter also note that the extent of government involvement in the economy went further than the statistical evidence might have suggested: "[W]e can add to the government's spending growth the element of *pervasive public involvement* in much, if not most, of the economy's activities" [emphasis in original]. They argue that the public/private distinction within the economy had become increasingly meaningless with a "contemporary fusion of the public with the private" spheres extending beyond strictly economic terms "by virtue of the vast extension of government's nonpecuniary interventions in economic affairs."[14]

Part of what Vatter and Walker referred to here is the merging of goals. The federal government took on the economic goals of business in the postwar period when it privileged growth as the technical solution to many—if not all—social problems. Not only did defense spending mean that the government became a mighty consumer of private goods, the growth imperative became an accepted justification for public involvement in private enterprise. Concomitantly, business took up what had been social concerns when it adopted the human relations management theories mentioned above that saw humanistic goals as part and parcel of business affairs.

The involvement of the government in the economy meant that even if large government contractors had not wished the government to take some measures to ensure stability, they might not have had the power to resist a determined administration. By the time Nixon took office, the time when government contractors had dictated the terms was over. Comparing the period 1961–1968 with that of 1969–1983, the annual compound rate of growth of all government purchases of goods and services slowed from an average of 5 percent to 0.6 percent.[15] With the winding down of the Vietnam War and the attempts by the Nixon administration to cut the federal deficit, contractors were left in a weaker position. Competition became fiercer, leaving the government in a far stronger bargaining position. The unions—an important bastion of resistance to affirmative action—were also forced on the defensive by the slowdown.

Enter Richard Nixon

The times called for a president who was not closely associated with the liberal programs and institutions of the 1960s. Only such a leader had the freedom to experiment with different programs. Nixon had the job of slowly extricating the issue of race from the democratic arena altogether. However, Nixon did not at first seriously consider overhauling race relations; his only remit was to "lower our voices," to calm an inflamed situation. Initially, Nixon followed the civil rights efforts of the Johnson administration, hoping to effectively enforce the existing legislation in order to promote order and faith in the law. His initial choice for secretary of Health, Education, and Welfare (HEW), Bob Finch, explained that "We didn't need some new theory in the field of civil rights enforcement . . . the question became 'How are we going to rationalize it?'"[16]

A Political Crisis

Nixon proposed compromises. On CBS radio on June 27, 1968, Nixon departed from the "law and order" theme with which he was attracting panicking white Americans:

> Faced with epidemic disorder, one part of the answer is both to strengthen and to use the forces of law. But this by itself is not enough. If we are to restore domestic peace, we sooner or later must bring those who threaten it back within the system.
>
> What we need is not one leader, but many leaders; not one center of power, but many centers of power.
>
> Every idea has its time. And the time is now for the idea of an expanded democracy, of moving government closer to the people, of breaking massive problems into manageable pieces. This is the way people can participate, they can be involved, their voices can be heard and heeded.
>
> One of the first tasks of the next president should be to set in motion a searching fundamental appraisal of our whole structure of government—not only of our federal departments and agencies, but also of state and local government, and its relation to the federal structure. . . .
>
> I do think that as we make government more responsive, as we rekindle trust and reestablish a sense of community, we can bring many back within the system.[17]

Several aspects of this speech stand out, especially for foreshadowing themes that would later become prevalent. Some sort of measures to include the alienated within the system would be necessary that would accomplish the task of "breaking massive problems into manageable pieces." No longer were the problems referred to (this speech, delivered in the month after the rioting following Martin Luther King, Jr.'s assassination, obviously pertained to rioting when it mentioned "epidemic disorder") to be *resolved*, they were simply to be made more *manageable*. This allowed housing to be approached separately from education and employment to be addressed separately from voting rights. The whole emphasis on decentralization removed the federal government from any national leadership obligations on race.

What was missing from the speech, or any of Nixon's speeches touching on race in the 1968 election? Any reference to the American dilemma. In 1955, Nixon had pledged allegiance to the Myrdalian moral mission in a speech on civil rights: "We must never forget that laws and judicial decisions alone will not accomplish our objective. There must be created in the hearts and minds of people a desire and a will to carry out the letter and the spirit of the law. This can be accomplished only through intensifying our programs of education and persuasion." But, in 1968, these programs lay abandoned by the federal government. In 1956, in another civil rights speech, he said: "Race and religious hatred strike at the roots of that remarkable unity that is the achievement of our nation. For the survival of our highest ideals, we must eradicate them from the face of our society."[18] Yet, there was no talk of eradicating the problem in 1968, only of breaking huge problems into more manageable pieces.

Nixon did not so much give up on black Americans (though, as we shall see, he had no faith in the inherent abilities of African Americans) as give up on whites (though the effect on black Americans has been far worse). By breaking up the racial problem into more manageable pieces, Nixon signaled his intention to change the role of federal government in relation to race problems, a precursor to affirmative action.

There is other evidence that Nixon had some grasp that the nature of the crisis and that fundamental changes were needed. In the White House, Nixon acted to restore public order, and stability had to be regained. In White House speechwriter Ray Price's (rather poor) attempt at a poetic phrase, Nixon wished to "lay a hand on the nation's fevered brow."[19] Outside the administration, the pundits agreed. Political pundits Richard M. Scammon and Ben J. Wattenberg referred to "Nixon's go-slow, antifrenetic style of government."[20] Left-wing editor of *Dissent* Irving Howe told the National Black Economic Development Conference held at the end of April 1969 that: "The main goal of the Nixon Administration is the restoration of social order—social peace— in the United States. How this is to be achieved—by blunt oppression, meliorist legislation, or both—the Nixon people don't yet know."[21]

Nixon carried the battle to the campuses of the nation in 1969. A historical curiosity, given the relatively apolitical nature of U.S. campuses today, is the extent to which Nixon and members of his administration worried about campus unrest. But the question for the Nixon team in 1969 "in its simplest form, was whether rule by mob would supplant rule by the democratic system."[22] Throughout 1969, a constant theme was the specter of disorder and chaos. In a statement on campus disorders issued on March 22, 1969, Nixon warned in stark terms of the danger: "The process is altogether too familiar to those who would survey the wreckage of history: assault and counterassault, one extreme leading the opposite extreme, the voices of reason and calm discredited. As Yeats foresaw: 'Things fall apart; the center cannot hold.' None of us has the right to suppose it cannot happen here."[23]

Even in remarks given at an annual meeting of the U.S. Chamber of Commerce, Nixon's theme was campus disturbances.[24] Perhaps his most prominent attack on campus disorders, however, was at the dedication of a library at General Beadle State College in South Dakota, chosen as a venue because it was isolated from the anti-Nixon sentiment in more prominent campuses. Here he linked the issue of campus disorder with other ills affecting the country:

> We live in a deeply troubled and profoundly unsettling time. Drugs and crime, campus revolt, racial discord, draft resistance—on every hand we find old standards violated, old values discarded, old precepts ignored. . . . As a result of all this, our institutions in America today are undergoing what may be the severest challenge of our history. But the challenge I speak of today is deeper—the challenge to our values and to the moral base of authority that sustains those values.[25]

Nixon administration officials panicked abut the moratorium, held on October 15, 1969. The "New Mobe"—the Mobilization to End the War in Vietnam—threatened a massive march in Washington on November 15, 1969. It would be made up largely of students around the country who would descend upon the city. Within the Haldeman and Ehrlichman White House records, many intelligence reports were filed, indicating that, despite Nixon's apparent disinterest (he let it be know that he would be watching a football game at the time the march was due to be held), the administration was actually deeply worried about the event.[26]

In a record of a meeting with the President in 1969 (the exact date is unclear but the document is contained in a file marked 1969), Ehrlichman noted the priorities of the administration as "1. Vietnam, 2. Inflation, 3. Youth disaffection, 4. Politics" (which included "a. Attack on military [including ABM fight] b. School issue, c. Other)," indicating the importance the President put on "youth disaffection."[27] Continuing investigations begun by his predecessor, Nixon also ordered investigations into whether student leaders were trained and financed by communists.

Especially in the area of civil rights, the Nixon administration continued many of the policies begun under the Johnson administration, despite Nixon's apparent promises to Southerners that school desegregation would be slowed. There is evidence in the files of a fair amount of confusion over civil rights strategies of the new administration. Leon Panetta, chief of Health, Education and Welfare (HEW)'s Office of Civil Rights until Nixon fired him in 1970, spelled out his objections: "The trouble was that no one really understood what Nixon had said or promised during the campaign, and his statements were shrouded in ambiguity and controversy."[28]

Upon taking office, HEW secretary Robert Finch was left with some problems by his predecessor, Wilbur Cohen. Cohen had ruled that five school districts—including two in Strom Thurmond's South Carolina—had to lose federal school funds for failure to submit desegregation plans meeting HEW's guidelines. On January 24, Finch told undersecretary (and liberal California Republican) John Veneman that he had "lost" on the fund cut-off. Finch said that the President wanted the fund cut-off stayed for sixty days. The alternative plan was that the five districts would be cut off from their federal funds effective January 29, but if they came up with acceptable plans within sixty days, they could recover all the funds (and two districts did so). Finch wrote to Chief Judge John R. Brown on August 19 asking for a stay until December 1. On October 29, despite a contrary ruling by the circuit court, the Supreme Court decided that "the obligations of every school district is to terminate dual school systems at once and to operate now and hereafter only unitary schools."[29] Nixon, however, distanced himself from the machinations between HEW and Justice. At a press conference on September 26, Nixon made his famous formulation that "there are those who want instant integration and those who want segregation forever. I believe that we need to have a middle course between those two extremes."[30]

To liberals, Nixon appeared to be backing away from civil rights commitments of the previous administration. In April Nixon requested Congress to reduce the enforcement program for fair housing by four million dollars. In June, the Justice Department came out against extending the Voting Rights Act of 1965, offering a substitute that would end the special sanctions against the South. However, the president stayed above the fray. At the ground level, HEW continued insisting that Southern schools desegregate. Many within the Nixon administration, at least at the lower levels, approved of more strident action by the agency to desegregate schools, buoyed in their opinions by court decisions like *Green v. School Board of New Kent County* (1968) which ruled that so-called freedom of choice plans, where schools simply opened their doors to children of any race, were not adequate if they did not result in integrated schools. *The Baltimore Sun*'s headline summed up the difficulties that ensued as Nixon's balancing strategy and his attempt to find a nonexistent middle ground on this issue lead to each side vying for the president's favor with ever-increasing energy and desperation. On July 1, 1969 the paper warned: "INTEGRATION WAR LOOMS INSIDE GOP."[31]

By this time, however, speechwriter William Safire had recorded that Nixon thought he was "in mortal danger of being perceived as a liberal. Worse, he felt this false perception could lead to a weakening of America's national will."[32] Nixon began to distance himself from the liberal camp. However, he still made no hard and fast decisions that might indicate the direction in which he felt his administration should proceed on civil rights. Panetta recorded the disputes that occurred. The extent of revolt in HEW was evident when eighteen hundred employees signed a petition asking Finch to explain the Administration's civil rights policy. Panetta faced calls for his resignation from right-wingers in the Nixon team like Harry Dent (the former Strom Thurmond aide and self-proclaimed architect of the "southern strategy"), congressional liaison Bryce Harlow, and Patrick Buchanan, and he actually submitted his resignation in early October of that year. Panetta, who displayed a crusading and perhaps naïve belief in the Republican commitment to immediate and comprehensive school desegregation efforts, did not have his resignation accepted until February 17, 1970—a testament to the fact that the Nixon administration's position on school desegregation remained fluid in 1969.[33]

Other key figures in the administration about the Nixon civil rights agenda in 1969 agreed that no new strategy was employed in 1969. Moynihan remarked that "The decision not to repudiate the social goals [of previous administrations] was signalled, but never quite articulated. . . . Whatever the case, comparatively clear decisions were made. There was not to be a restoration. There *was* to be continuity."[34] Conservatives within the cabinet agreed. Harry Dent complained to Spiro Agnew that the "southern strategy" was not really being employed at ground level: "I don't need to tell you that I have been extremely concerned about the apparently schizophrenic posture of this Administration, brought about mainly by the vacuous and ultra-liberal utterances from HEW."[35]

A copy of a *Columbia* magazine editorial from August 11, 1969 held in the Nixon files noted the careful attempt of the president to calm the waters on domestic issues: "Listening to President Nixon's 'New Federalism' address on domestic matters, one marvelled at how carefully he steered between the extreme positions of liberalism and conservatism."[36] Virtually the only guidance on policy issues by Nixon left things very vague. Nixon instructed his aides about domestic policy in a meeting in July that "just 'cause it's new doesn't mean it's right—but if it's old, it's wrong." At another meeting Nixon "emphasized p.r. will be important—but don't want to do anything we can't deliver on—present case as exciting way as we can but first must be sure we can produce."[37] Despite Nixon's seeming sympathy toward the plight of the white South, there was little action in this direction. John Mitchell's famous admonition to black leaders, "instead of listening to what we say . . . watch what we do,"[38] accurately described the operations of the administration in 1969. And the record in terms of school desegregation indicates that this strategy bore at least some fruit. Nixon, mirroring his foreign policy strategy of playing opposing forces against each other, leaving maximum room to maneuver, was clearly present here.

Though violence and disruption were key concerns, when creating numerous experimental programs, policy elites worried about alienation and disaggregation long after the noise of riots and disturbances subsided. After 1970 the deeper (though less immediate) nature of the crisis began to be apparent. Though riots and student unrest by no means ended—especially the latter after the invasion of Cambodia became public knowledge—there was no return to the days of consensus, full employment, and great hope for the future. As Finch told the press in 1972 (in a passage underlined by Nixon), there continued to exist at the time a "general syndrome of distrust about all our institutions—the Church, corporate life, labor unions and higher education."[39] Yet these were precisely the institutions celebrated by Gunnar Myrdal that had linked Americans with their government and within which they had realized a common purpose.

Perhaps most worrying to the administration was the fact that the very top layers of American society refused to defend these institutions and expressed deep hostility to the Nixon administration. In a letter to the president, aide and intellectual-in-residence Daniel Patrick Moynihan indicated how he thought the rot had started. He informed the president that the "many businessmen" he had spoken to since leaving the administration all seemed to hate the Nixon administration.

> I have been astonished—that is the word—at their hostility to the administration. . . . As best I can tell, they mostly get this belief from their children who absorb it in the atmosphere of the elite universities. But they believe their children, and in consequence detest the administration. . . . (Y)ou will recall I came down to Washington to work for you deeply concerned about the stability of the nation. I remain concerned. Vast changes have been made for the better. But in an odd way, appearances are worse.[40]

Just as disturbing, perhaps, was the fact that none of the programs or policies initiated by Nixon alleviated any of the ill feeling. Garry Wills emphasized the inexorable nature of the crisis: "What is hard, and essential, to convey is the *interaction* of resentments. The bitterness moved in crossing tides, an acid weave of right and left, old and young."[41] Lowi expressed the same problem in a different way: "It is as though each new program or program expansion were an admission of prior governmental inadequacy or failure without necessarily being a contribution to order and well-being."[42]

The End of a Sense of Mission

The Kennedy administration, whatever its weaknesses, at least had a secure sense of mission. The space race, the incursion into Vietnam, the innovative attack on poverty, the preparation of civil rights legislation—were all undertaken with a sense of purpose and a confident outlook on the future. Kennedy believed in his own leadership and in progress. Johnson believed in Kennedy's mission and, at least at the outset of his own administration, in his own role in creating the future. He believed that, with the political will to succeed, integration between black and white citizens was imminent, the Great Society was achievable, and that both the war on poverty and the war in Vietnam would be won.

The sense of mission within the Nixon administration was by no means as clear. In response to the pervasive criticism of the United States by citizens of all political persuasions, the Republican Party published a bulletin entitled "What's Right With America" in the run up to the 1970 elections. The prognosis of even the keenest Nixon supporters was that the nation was distressed; "What's Right With America" intended to rebut that fear. The contrast with the hopeful progress promised by previous administration was stark. Beside giving some idea of why the Republicans did badly that year, the bulletin indicated that no overall goals replaced those of the eradication of poverty and the destruction of the racial divide.

The pamphlet began somewhat lamely: "First let's look at just a few examples of the progress that this great country has made in the past 50 years." Clearly, it was clutching at straws: "In 1920, the population of this country was 106 million, half of what it is today," it boasted at a time when Malthusian sentiments were once more on the rise (presumably, Republicans were claiming at least some credit for this surge). "And fifty years ago there was no regularly scheduled radio broadcasting in the United States."[43] "What's Right With America" managed to miss the truly great American achievements of the twentieth century that a European schoolboy could reel off without having to think. The slick advertising men that had so impressed Joe McGinnis in the 1968 election campaign presumably had other jobs by 1970.

However, what was really lacking from the pamphlet was, as George Bush, Sr. once put it, the "vision thing"; without a sense of the future, it was difficult to detect the meaning of the past. Ironically, the pamphlet drew attention to the lack of understanding within the administration of where the country should be headed. A half-hearted and fruitless attempt at creating a set of new goals to that end characterized the first couple of years of the new administration.[44]

The problem with giving up on the Great Society was that optimism about its success had cohered not just federal government but "the system as an interlocking set of institutions and organizations, both public and private, formal and informal, by which we run society and make our decisions . . . institutions locked together by mental attitudes and sets of assumptions about the nature of American society, about people and what is good for America."[45]

Nixon had been elected in 1968 calling for peaceable relations between Americans by "lowering our voices." He clearly stepped back from the grand promises made by his predecessors. But any attempt at creating new goals by fiat ran onto stony ground. Though Myrdal, Schlesinger, and others helped to develop the American Creed as a goal, they did not "invent" it in committee rooms; it was in step with (and in some ways, an expression of) the aspirations of most Americans in the postwar period. Racial equality, which was undoubtedly a primary goal of the Johnson administration, was not supported by all but at least followed logically from the "equalizing" tendencies of the Creed that had some resonance in the growth years of the 1950s. In short, it lent itself toward the overall goals of the American Creed and could claim to be the realization of the Great Society. It had a powerful sense of uplift that, clearly, the Nixon administration could not match.

In 1970, Nixon could only attempt to make a virtue of dissent from the Great Society, emphasizing, in common with most Republican politicians in the postwar period, the mysterious wonders of "diversity." Politically, he relied almost completely upon resentments and negative campaigning (to be discussed later). However, Nixon understood at least semi-consciously the limitations of attacking the Great Society without having anything to put in its place. In some ways, because of the ubiquity of the postwar symbols and structures, because of the near complete consensus on various different aspects of postwar liberal values, the problem alluded to by Christopher Lasch—that humanity is in need of a new religion which, by its very nature, cannot be invented—beset the intellectuals and policy makers of the time.[46]

Some have assumed that this problem of lack of belief and lack of ideals is a problem inherent to capitalism. As political economist Joseph Schumpeter noted, the "relentless rationalism" of capitalism brings into question even its most useful institutions. "The capitalist process rationalizes behavior and ideas and by so doing chases from our minds, along with metaphysical belief, mystic and romantic ideas of all sorts." Later, Schumpeter stated: "[T]he *emotional* attachment to the social order—[that is,] the very thing capitalism is constitutionally unable to produce—is necessary in order to overcome the hostile impulse by which we react to them [day-to-day grievances]. If there is no emotional attachment, then that impulse has its way and grows into a permanent constituent of our psychic set-up." This provides a theoretical model, at least, within which to understand some of the events of the late 1960s and early 1970s, especially the resentment that led to the election of Nixon in 1968 and 1972. Nixon's curious use of that hostile impulse or resentment, especially in relation to affirmative action, will be discussed later.[47] In any event, the Nixon administration lacked a convincing reason for being. At the suggestion of his advisor, Daniel Patrick Moynihan, Nixon created the National Goals Research Staff with presidential assistant Leonard Garment in charge. (Garment later likened his appointment to "putting Homer Simpson in charge of the space program.") Before it was quietly abandoned, its one report, fixed with an ameliorative-to-the-point-of-meaninglessness title (*Towards Balanced Growth: Quantity With Quality*), was met with a balanced lack of interest by the press.[48] Throughout his tenure in office, Nixon rued the lack of goals. Even in late 1972 Nixon complained that "What we lack in Admin is basic philosophy." Nixon thought that he and his close aides should "sit down + establish four goals for next 4 yrs," among which should be "destroy old lib estab." All was expendable and open to new ideas. Nixon toyed with creating a new party, leaving the Republican Party behind. These observations were only mirroring past complaints. An undated paper from 1970 frets: "Rightly or wrongly by some we are accused of being inconsistent and without purpose on many domestic issues. These [sic] could be several reasons—the Administration is too open—there are no established priorities—our programs have lacked a plan for follow through."[49]

Toward Experimentation

The effect of all of these crises was to clear away barriers to experimental programs that might before have been unthinkable. After the storms of 1968, the immediate task the newly elected administration faced—beside calming protest—was to put into place mechanisms designed to restore authority. This process had to come from the top down. A new purpose, a new mission had to be created that might allay the crisis of self-belief. Yet, as the ruminations within the Nixon cabinet suggest, it proved elusive. The problem was that without this project, there was no hope in carrying anyone else along, in creating enthusiasm. The crisis of belief extended downward. The bureaucracy, as discussed in the last chapter, had no particular direction after the discrediting of many of the Great Society programs. As political scientist Richard P. Nathan noted, discussions of "delivery problems" and "performance gaps" were in vogue in the late 1960s.[50]

Most of the political mechanisms in place since the New Deal to integrate various different groups within American society, as we have seen, appeared to be failing. Jerris Leonard produced a thoughtful piece on federalism and revenue sharing, later to be a key program within the Nixon domestic agenda. While federalism had long been a programmatic unifier within the Republican Party (opposing the centralism of the New Deal), Leonard related it to the problem of alienation and the relationship between the citizen and government in the United States. Federalism thus became more than simply a political glue for the Republicans—it emerged as a possible solution to the "depression of the national spirit." If a centralized purpose could not be recreated, perhaps local leadership could fill the void. People could determine their own goals and government could, in the modern parlance, "facilitate" them.

Conclusion

The case for affirmative action being a continuum from postwar trends and movements lies less in the calls for quota policies heard from civil rights groups than in the trend to reformulate what had been political problems into management issues. Just as the major political clash between labor and capital became "human relations" problems to be micromanaged on the shop floor, so did the race problems of the 1960s. Nixon, as we have seen, played a role in breaking up what was seen as an insoluble problem into "manageable pieces." Future research might profitably concentrate on the parallels between the incorporation of class-based political problems into those of management theory with the role of affirmative action in reducing a massive political problem to one to be resolved by administrators and human relations practitioners.

However, in the period just before the implementation of the Philadelphia Plan, when Nixon and his new administration were considering it, there was no deep philosophical justification but simply contingency. Only later would complex and nuanced theories justify and give meaning to what would eventually be called affirmative action. Then, though the term existed and was used in relation to the Philadelphia Plan, its meaning lacked the precise and all-encompassing meaning of the term today.

By 1969, the pieces were in place to at least experiment with limited affirmative action programs. The barriers that prevented Kennedy and Johnson from implementing such programs had mostly collapsed. The business objections to affirmative action of maintaining the prerogative to hire, fire, and promote whoever they choose had been superseded by fear of social disintegration. By this time, business was crying out for the government intervention into these areas that had been so jealously guarded in previous eras. Even if those directly involved objected, their voices would be drowned out by those anxious about black insurrection. Of course, Nixon had no stake in the Democratic alliance between labor and the civil rights movement—he had every reason to divide them. Unions had little influence with Nixon.

The ghettos were still seething with resentment and some attempt had to be made to reach out to ghetto residents. As Nixon told television audiences during the 1968 campaign, "[Y]ou have a person who has a stake in our system, he is going to stand up for our system. It's just as simple as that."[51] Compared with handing over local police duties in ghetto areas to organized criminal gangs, or even to some of the aforementioned programs dreamed up by Johnson's Bureau of the Budget, the Philadelphia Plan (discussed in the next chapter) looked eminently sensible and, as is indicated by business support for the idea, fairly conservative.

Very importantly, an affirmative action program dealing with jobs was deemed unlikely to create the sort of virulent white hostility that still disturbed the elite. On Myrdal's rank order of discrimination, listing areas where integration caused most friction, jobs came last. Programs to integrate neighborhoods following the passage of the 1968 Civil Rights Act created strong resistance. So too did the integration issue dominating the headlines in 1969: school desegregation. The power and influence of unions, one of the key objectors to affirmative action programs involving employment in the past, was on the wane. They could no longer mobilize their membership in the way they had in the past. Though George Wallace was undeniably still a threat, Nixon succeeded in appearing as the "sweet and reasonable" middle, as his aide John Ehrlichman put it, on the prominent issue of school desegregation, convincing Southerners that he was on their side by slowing down demands for school integration while, at the same time, insisting that it would take place.[52]

The Philadelphia Plan was, in 1969, cheap, easy, and available. It did not depend, as did the majority of suggestions within the Kerner Commission Report, on channeling huge amounts of fiscal resources into problem areas. It was also becoming a more realistic option in terms of contract compliance. With a more competitive environment, contractors were becoming more willing to agree to conditions that, when contracts were plentiful, they may have resisted.

However, before Nixon became president, the crucial step had not been taken. Ever after, the civil rights crusade of housing and school integration continued, attesting to the power even of the shadow of the Myrdian paradigm. Many still hoped—even if they found it more difficult to believe—that the educative role of the federal government would be maintained and that racial divisions might still be eradicated rather than simply managed. Liberals understood implicitly that employment quotas would set labor against the civil rights movement. To implement a policy that may not work, though it would undoubtedly be destructive, was simply too risky, liberals felt. Consequently, Johnson, having issued the executive order (11246), resisted enforcing it in a direct way, still hoping to cajole, bully, convince, and even beg Americans to voluntarily take action.

Nixon, as will become apparent in subsequent chapters, had a different conception of what affirmative action was meant to do. However, even he had not quite given up on voluntarism and, as far as the records show, never imagined that this experimental program would evolve into the dominant paradigm for race relations policy.

Notes

1. Cited in Lionel Lokos, *The New Racism: Reverse Discrimination in America* (New Rochelle, NY: Arlington House, 1971), 14.

2. Alan Brinkley, *Liberalism and its Discontents* (London: Harvard University Press, 1998), 165.

3. John D. Skrentny, *The Minority Rights Revolution* (Cambridge, MA: The Belknap Press of Harvard University Press, 2002), 86.

4. See Elton Mayo, *The Social Problems of Industrial Civilization* (New York: Arno Press, 1977 [1933]). Andrea Gabor, *The Capitalist Philosophers: The Geniuses of Modern Business—Their Lives, Times, and Ideas* (New York: Three Rivers Press, 2002).

5. Cited in Hugh Davis Graham, *The Civil Rights Era: Origins and Development of National Policy 1960–1972* (New York: Oxford University Press, 1990), 116.

6. "Answer to Riots—The Rochester Plan," *U.S. News & World Report* 67 (August 4, 1969): 58–61, 60; David Brand, "Negroes on the Job: For Business, Motive Can be Enlightenment or Selfishness," *The Wall Street Journal*, March 5, 1968, 18. John D. Skrentny also noted the participation of business in *The Ironies of Affirmative Action: Politics, Culture, and Justice in America* (London: University of Chicago Press, 1996), 89–91.

7. Irwin Miller, "Business Has a War to Win," *Harvard Business Review* 47, no. 2 (March/April 1969): 4–12, 164–68, esp. 6–7.

8. Cited in Irwin Miller, "Business Has a War to Win," 194. See also Herman Belz, *Equality Transformed: A Quarter-Century of Affirmative Action* (London: Transaction Publishers, 1992), 103–4.

9. *A Decade of Tensions and Decisions: The Minority Environment in the Seventies* ("For Circulation Among General Electric Management"), January 1970, copy in 1972 Onwards, box 4, WHCF: Subject Files: HU (Human Rights), [Ex] HU 2, NPMP.

10. Paul E. Moreno, *From Direct Action to Affirmative Action: Fair Employment Law and Policy in America, 1933–1972* (London: Louisiana State University Press, 1997), 70.

11. Allen J. Matusow, *Nixon's Economy: Booms, Busts, Dollars, and Votes* (Lawrence: University Press of Kansas, 1998), 33.

12. Hugh Davis Graham, "Legacies of the 1960s: The American 'Rights Revolution' in an Era of Divided Governance," *Journal of Policy History* 10, no. 3 (1998): 159–72, esp. 164.

13. Graham, *The Civil Rights Era*, 341.

14. Harold G. Vatter and John F. Walker, *The Inevitability of Government Growth* (New York: Columbia University Press, 1991), 212–13. See generally their section on the changes in distribution heralded by government intervention, 212–23.

15. Figures from Vatter and Walker, *Inevitability of Government Growth*, 209.

16. Robert H. Finch, discussant, in *Richard M. Nixon: Politician, President, Administrator*, ed. Leon Friedman and William F. Levantrosser (New York: Greenwood Press, 1991), 173–75, esp. 173.

17. "Toward an Expanded Democracy," an address by Richard M. Nixon: CBS Radio Network, June 27, 1968, 1968 Presidential Campaign: RNC news releases 8/23/68–9/25/68, comment 8/26/68–11/4/68, Nixon speeches 10/67–9/25/68, 1968 Nixon Campaign: Press Releases and Nixon Speeches, box 5, RNC Records.

18. Text of address by Vice President Nixon, Alfred E. Smith Memorial Dinner, New York City, 18 October 1956, "Speeches, 1956," box 17, RNC Papers.

19. Ray Price, *With Nixon* (New York: The Viking Press, 1977), 47.

20. Richard M. Scammon and Ben J. Wattenberg, *The Real Majority* (New York: Coward, McCann & Geoghegan, Inc., 1970), 297.

21. "Nixon's Dream and Black Reality," Irving Howe in the National Black Economic Development Conference, 27–29 April [presumably a preconference position paper], [Minority Business] National Black Economic Development Conference [CFOA 7261], Box 125, WHCF: SMOF: Garment, NPMP.

22. Price, *With Nixon*, 49.

23. Statement on Campus Disorders, March 22, 1969, *PPPUS: Richard Nixon, 1969* (Washington, D.C.: U.S. GPO, 1970), 236.

24. Remarks at the Annual Meeting of the Chamber of Commerce of the United States. April 29, 1969, *PPPUS: Richard Nixon, 1969*, 334.

25. Address at the dedication of the Karl E. Mundt Library at General Beadle State College, Madison, South Dakota, June 3, 1969. *PPPUS: Richard Nixon, 1969*, 236–37.

26. An entire file in Ehrlichman's files was dedicated to the event. See "MOBE," box 20, WHSF: SMOF: John D. Ehrlichman, NPMP. See also Memoranda for the President's File (November 1969), box 138, WHSF: SMOF: H. R. Haldeman: Haldeman Notes, NPMP.

27. Handwritten note on White House stationery, presumably by Ehrlichman, no date (found with other material from 1969), 105 Closed [desegregation] [1 of 2], WHSF: SMOF: John D. Ehrlichman, NPMP.

28. Cited in Roland Evans, Jr. and Robert D. Novak, *Nixon in the White House: The Frustration of Power* (New York: Random House, 1971), 155.

29. See Evans and Novak, *Nixon in the White House*, 142–59.

30. The President's News Conference of September 26, 1969, *PPPUS: Richard Nixon, 1969* (Washington, D.C.: U.S. GPO, 1970), 755. See also Evans and Novak, *Nixon in the White House*, 156.

31. Leon E. Panetta and Peter Gall, *Bring Us Together: The Nixon Team and Civil Rights* (New York: J. B. Lippincott Company, 1971), 213.

32. William Safire, *Before the Fall: An Inside View of the Pre-Watergate White House* (New York: Doubleday and Co., 1975), 135.

33. Dean Kotlowski presents Panetta's removal as evidence of Nixon's determination to stamp out liberals: "Nixon had even less patience with liberals. In early 1970 he removed Panetta as chief of HEW's Office of Civil Rights. Dean Kotlowski, *Nixon's Civil Rights: Politics, Principle, and Policy* (London: Harvard University Press, 2001), 34. The fact that Nixon kept Panetta's resignation on his desk for some months while Buchanan and others bayed for his blood indicates that Nixon was anything but sure of his direction in 1969.

34. Daniel P. Moynihan, *The Politics of a Guaranteed Income: The Nixon Administration and the Family Assistance Plan* (New York: Random House, 1973) 69.

35. Memo for Harry Dent from the vice president, May 29, 1969, 105 Closed [desegregation] [1 of 2], box 30, WHSF: SMOF: Ehrlichman, NPMP.

36. Copy of editorial of *Columbia Magazine* (August 11, 1969), Ehrlichman Memos 1969–1970, box 1, WHSF: SMOF: Harry S. Dent.

37. Handwritten notes by Haldeman of a cabinet meeting held January 22, HRH Cabinet Notes January 69—Memos/Ron Ziegler (March 1969), box 49, WHSF: SMOF: Haldeman: Alpha Subject Files, NPMP.

38. Cited in Safire, *Before the Fall*, 265.

39. March 27–31, 1972, box 40, President's Office Files (POF): ANS, NPMP.

40. Moynihan letter to the president, March 8, 1971, "Moynihan Letter Flap," box 86, WHSF: SMOF: Charles M. Colson, NPMP.

41. Garry Wills, *Nixon Agonistes: The Crisis of the Self-Made Man* (Boston: Houghton Mifflin Company, 1970), 38.

42. Theodore Lowi, *The End of Liberalism: Ideology, Policy, and the Crisis of Public Authority* (New York: W. W. Norton and Co., 1969), 69.

43. "What's Right with America" campaign—1970 [CFOA 5016], box 54, WHCF: SMOF: Leonard Garment, NPMP.

44. Contained in folder marked "Campaign—1970 [CFOA 5016], box 54, White House Central Files: Staff Member and Office Files: Leonard Garment: NPMP. See Joe McGinnis, *The Selling of the President 1968* (New York: Trident Press, 1969), in which the author presents Nixon's image in the 1968 election as a creation of clever advertising men.

45. Excerpts from a statement by Roger W. Wilkins, Director, Community Relations Service, U.S. Department of Justice, before the National Advisory Commission on Civil Disorders on September 21, 1967, National Advisory Commission on Civil Disorders—Records, November–December 1967, box 465, Brooke Papers, LOC.

46. Lasch echoes one of the chief problems faced by conservatives over the past two centuries. "Maybe religion is the answer after all," he shrugs. Christopher Lasch, *The Revolt of the Elites and the Betrayal of Democracy* (London: W. W. Norton & Company 1995), 72.

47. Joseph A. Schumpeter, *Capitalism, Socialism and Democracy* (London: George Allen & Unwin Ltd., 1961), 127, 145. See also Daniel Bell, *The Cultural Contradictions of Capitalism* (London: Heinemann, 1976).

48. See Leonard Garment, *Crazy Rhythm: My Journey from Brooklyn, Jazz, and Wall Street to Nixon's White House, Watergate, and Beyond* . . . (New York: Times Books, 1997), 175–77.

49. Handwritten notes of a meeting held on 12/10, H Notes October–November–December 1972 [11-17-72 to 12-21-72] part II, box 46, folder 2 [of 25], documents from boxes 46–48, Contested Documents: WHSF: SMOF: H. R. Haldeman, "Talking Paper—Image of the President to Date, Image of the President—Near Future, Domestic Program Progress Report, Vietnam Problem Progress Report," Alphabetical Subject File: Ehrlichman "Scrapbook" Items [Memoranda from the President] [2 of 2], Box 19, WHSF: SMOF: John D. Ehrlichman, NPMP.

50. Richard P. Nathan, *The Plot That Failed: Nixon and the Administrative Presidency* (London: John Wiley and Sons, Inc., 1975), 15.

51. Transcript of Eastern Regional Live TV, October 25, 1968, RNC 1968 Campaign: Press Releases and Nixon Speeches, box 5, 1968 Press Releases and Nixon Speeches, Records of the RNC.

52. John Ehrlichman, *Witness to Power: The Nixon Years* (New York: Simon and Schuster, 1982), 228–29.

II
RICHARD NIXON: LIBERAL ANTI-HERO

6

The Genius of Deflation

In a very real sense, he is the manifestation of the death of a national god.[1]

IF JOHN F. KENNEDY, with his optimistic activism, his immense confidence, and his high hopes for the future of the country, personified the bright side of American liberalism, Nixon was surely its dark, cynical side. Kennedy, though hesitant about racial issues, appeared to rise to the occasion when confronted by them during the election campaign of 1960, whereas Nixon, racially liberal in the past, shrank from the task. As Garry Wills observed in 1969, "(t)here is a genius of deflation that follows Nixon about."[2] In 1954, before the onset of riots, before the civil rights movement came to prominence, Nixon shrugged: "I sometimes almost give up hope that we will ever be able to make much progress among the so-called minority groups, but we must of course continue to try."[3] Kennedy created a mystique and maintained his image as the brave, even heroic figure for whom anti-communism meant bearing any burden, paying any price. Nixon used anti-communism to smear rival politicians. Yet both men were integral to liberalism and the differences between them were not as great as they first appear. The end of ideology that Daniel Bell pointed to may have afforded Kennedy the chance to use his office to accomplish great things but it also bred the venal, "aprincipled" political chicanery for which Nixon is rightly condemned.[4] They were simply two sides of the same coin.

But who was more effective? Kennedy led a charge into the future but, as Daniel Bell noted: "The paradox of the Kennedy administration was that its very élan and activism—the need to seem and to be effective—both in the foreign field and at home, stimulated and unleashed the forces of turbulence which racked the United States in the 1960s."[5] Nixon was forced to beat an orderly retreat from the Kennedy and Johnson promises that could no longer be kept. And he did so extremely effectively, considering Johnson's ambitious attempt to muscle through radical domestic reform at the same time that winning the war in Vietnam failed so publicly. Nixon's historical role as reorganizer or rationalizer of a system in real danger of bankruptcy, his actions to create a new basis for the authority of the status quo, have not yet been appreciated. Affirmative action was part of this retreat and was effective enough to appear as a victory today.

It is difficult to imagine Nixon in Kennedy's role. He was no natural reformer. Recoiling at the prospect of having to sign the constitutional amendment giving eighteen- to twenty-year-olds the right to vote, he posed a number of alternative solutions to the crisis affecting youth. He gave a rather tall order to his speechwriter Pat Buchanan who was put in charge of creating "a new conservative youth movement." Nixon commanded Buchanan (Pat Buchanan!) to "Make it 'out' to wear long hair, smoke pot and go on the needle. Make it 'in' to indulge in the lesser vices, smoking (cigars, preferably—non-Castro!) and alcohol in reasonable quantities on the right occasions."[6] The analysis of Buchanan's success in leading the youth of America away from its vices is not indicated in the files. However, this was by no means the most toe-curlingly embarrassing project. After observing the popularity of Woodstock and other rock music festivals, plans were afoot to organize a concert that would no doubt have attracted, well, dozens of young people. The White House "salute to youth" planned to have as its main attractions the "Mike Curb Congregation" and the Partridge Family![7] Relinquishing these strategies, attractive as they were, the presidential Nixon decided—sensibly—to sign the constitutional amendment.

Richard Nixon would have liked to have had the opportunities that John F. Kennedy did. "There must be some 'malevolent law,'" commented Nixon appointee Paul McCracken, "that places Republicans in power when it is hard to be a hero."[8] He stood on a significantly lower platform than Kennedy. In foreign policy, Nixon knew that the United States had to become more modest in its commitments. As he put it in a meeting recorded by the ever-assiduous Charles Colson, the up-and-coming White House aide who became famous after the Watergate revelations: "Balance of Power Politics—keep balancing power centers acc. to self interest and [their?] self interest—Pragmatic, cold, calculating—only way now with rising power of Japan economically, China militarily—only way now to maintain peace—before it was possible with policy of containment—no longer a practical possibility."[9]

The same "pragmatic, cold, and calculating" self-interest directed Nixon in domestic policy, though it would be a mistake to see it, as some historians do, purely in electoral terms. When one of Ehrlichman's underlings wrote to him complaining that "at least as far as domestic legislation is concerned, I believe that an image has been created that the President doesn't really believe in some of the things he has proposed," Ehrlichman noted, presumably only to himself, that "Problem here is—he doesn't."[10] Even regarding school desegregation, where it appears obvious that Nixon played to the hostility of his Southern white constituents, contradictory impulses were in evidence. In a meeting with Ehrlichman regarding school desegregation, Nixon worried that "(i)t may not work. [George] Wallace and others may stir it up—Don't tell me there may be good politics in this." His responsibility, he said, was "not to let the country come apart—it won't on this Goddamn issue or this silly decision." He added, "Don't be the aggressor with the South in an agonizing experience—the racist dogs will be in full cry & will effect the decent people."[11]

There are few areas within the Nixon administration more contradictory and confusing than civil rights. The Nixon administration boosted nonmilitary racial and ethnic minorities among federal workers to 19.5 percent; it more than doubled aid to black colleges and increased minority business aid by 152 percent. The percentage of black children in all black schools decreased from 40 percent in 1969 to 12 percent in 1972, effectively desegregating more children than had all previous administrations since the 1954 *Brown* decision combined.[12] Topping Clinton's attempt to gather a cabinet that "looked like America," Nixon offered Housing and Urban Development (HUD) to the head of the Urban League, Whitney Young, and the U.S. ambassadorship to the United Nations to black Republican senator Edward Brooke of Massachusetts. While Young and Brooke declined the offers, James Farmer, one-time executive director of the Congress on Racial Equality (CORE) accepted a job as undersecretary of Health, Education, and Welfare (HEW) in 1969. Nixon also appointed Walter Washington as the first black Mayor of Washington.[13] He enthusiastically backed the creation of a "Negro history week."[14]

Yet, when asked to establish a holiday in honor of Martin Luther King, Jr. he wrote "No, Never."[15] He referred to "these little Negro bastards on the welfare rolls at $2,400 a family," hardly the language of a sympathizer.[16] He also maintained that blacks were genetically inferior to whites, could never hope to achieve parity, and that there had never been an adequate black nation.[17] He depended on segregationists like Strom Thurmond for support, used the coded language of "law and order" to play on racial fears, attacked busing to achieve racial balance in schools, and even voiced opposition to "quotas" in the run up to 1972.

In the context of the times, especially in relation to civil rights issues, Nixon was definitely in the conservative camp. His assessment by contemporary observers within the civil rights movement was overwhelmingly negative. For them, as for many modern historians, Nixon was a politician of the right, and all analysis of his actions stemmed from that basic fact. "For the first time since Woodrow Wilson," said the chairman of the board of the NAACP in 1970, "we have a national administration that can be rightly characterized as anti-black."[18] Roy Wilkins, the executive director of the NAACP, said that Nixon wished to "turn the clock back on everything" and had sided with the "enemies of little black children."[19] Affirmative action was, tellingly, ignored by these contemporary observers.

Historians are apt to be more circumspect in their judgment, often speaking of the essential duality of Nixon. Many see a relatively liberal "Jekyll" Nixon in 1969 being taken over by a darkly conservative "Hyde" later in his first term. William Chafe, a trenchant critic of the Nixon administration and writer of one of the most popular books on the post-1945 era, noted the "dual personality of Nixon."[20] Civil rights lawyer Eleanor Holmes Norton saw "two civil rights Nixons, neither of them particularly principled," though the more liberal one on civil rights apparently died in 1970.[21] Michael Genovese saw a shift rightward on civil rights in late 1970, one that married Mitchell's "southern strategy" with Nixon aide Daniel Patrick Moynihan's "benign neglect" strategy: "If there were two Nixons on civil rights early in 1969, by late 1970, it was the anti-civil rights side of the Nixon personality that would come to dominate the policy and political agenda."[22]

Another important theme appearing in many biographies and histories that links assessments of Nixon's civil rights perspectives sees Nixon as lacking any permanent principles. Those hostile to Nixon usually refer to Watergate as the most important (but not the only) indicator of his lack of any real principles. Nixon defender Joan Hoff also speaks of Nixon's "aprincipled" behavior.[23] Connected to this theme of Nixon forsaking civil rights once it appeared politically expensive not to do so is the idea that Nixon lost interest in domestic policies and left others to create domestic policies. Hugh Davis Graham is perhaps the best known exponent of this view. Graham states in an article entitled "The Incoherence of the Civil Rights Policy in the Nixon Administration," that "no coherent theory of civil rights to govern the new Republican administration's policy choices" arose. Graham pointed to a policy vacuum that was filled with "aggressive men . . . pursuing their own agendas. The result was a confusing and indeed quite contradictory array of civil rights initiatives and policies."[24] In many ways, this perspective, in relation to Nixon's personal beliefs regarding race, is that he had none and did whatever was expedient in terms of votes. Vernon Jordan of the Urban League said of Nixon: "He didn't care about the basic issue."[25] James Farmer said of his former boss: "He had no strong feelings on any social issues. He was capable of doing either good or bad with equal facility."[26]

The "aprincipled" (that is, lacking principles rather than being willing to abandon them for the sake of expediency, as "unprincipled" might imply) theme is perhaps the most important consensus about the Nixon character, one that links his many actions as president. According to this version of events, the lack of principles meant that no moral barriers would get in the way of political goals. Hence, Watergate. Hence, the southern strategy. Hence the leftward and rightward "zigs" and "zags" and the criticism from Patrick Buchanan as well as from numerous liberal pundits. And hence, the inability of scholars and insiders in the Nixon White House to find coherent themes with which to characterize the Nixon presidency. Nixon thus becomes the archetypal modern political villain, one for whom power is no longer, as it was for Johnson, simply a means to achieve goals, be they noble or ignoble, progressive or simply deluded. Nixon was, as the *New Yorker* put it, the "man to whom nothing mattered except power."[27]

The problem with all of these perspectives is that they are locked in a left and right framework. Once it is admitted that Nixon's actions mean that he cannot be easily placed in either the liberal or the conservative camps, problems ensue. Nixon was thus "schizophrenic" because his actions, in left and right terms, contradicted each other. He was "aprincipled" because he showed no consistent preference for either side; if his actions cannot be easily bracketed, then he must have no principles whatever. This view assumes that all real principles emanate from some point on the liberal/conservative nexus.

Such analyses of Nixon blur the profound differences between our own time and Nixon's, ironically preserving the postwar ideological categories at a time when their usefulness in understanding contemporary developments lessens almost by the day. Fighting these increasingly irrelevant battles on the pages of histories and biographies risks missing the real connections between Nixon's time and our own, the underlying developments that determined the present and will likely influence the future, and, hence, Nixon's importance as a president. This is not to argue for some banal "third way" (which also situates itself somewhere in relation to the other two) but simply to insist that looking at the development of some social phenomena requires different analytical tools. The implication here is that we need to back away from apparent arguments and look at what lies beneath the surface.

One of the fascinating aspects of Nixon is that he characterizes so well the dominant ideology of the postwar period. As Garry Wills commented, Nixon was a "postwar man. Politically, he does not preexist the year 1946."[28] Likewise, Nixon's final publications, warning of the potential rise of the Soviet Union, indicate that he remained trapped in the Cold War even after the Soviet flag was lowered at the Kremlin. Thus, if many of his biographers remain trapped within this historical framework, Nixon remained even

more the prisoner of these parameters. His bemusement at the "new politics," the counterculture, and the rejection of the older postwar morality reflected that of many of his peers.

Yet Nixon also had an occasionally preternatural acuity. From the evidence
contained in the Nixon Presidential Materials, Nixon was at his most perceptive when discussing ideas with intelligent men and women. Suddenly, he
would rise above the day-to-day presidential grind to deliver philosophical insights from a great height. In February 1972, Nixon told his then-speechwriter
William Safire that health would be the most important issue of the future.
"My intuition tells me that's coming on big."[29] In discussion with Elliot
Richardson in 1971, Nixon casually noted that therapy was taking over what
had formerly been the function of ministers and priests in American society
and that this might have an important effect on American society in the future.[30] Many of his insights on foreign affairs came after long discussions with
Henry Kissinger. Many insights on domestic affairs came after conversations
with or in response to memoradums from Daniel Moynihan, for a time the
president's domestic policy muse.

Of course, what was liberal in 1965 may appear conservative today. What is
considered the most progressive radical perspective on racial issues today—
insisting on the primacy of black identity—would have been unpardonably
conservative at a time when integration was still the aim. John D. Skrentny
noted that "progressive thinkers in 1967 shared a view with civil rights conservatives of the 1970s, 1980s, and 1990s: that the Civil Rights Act proscribed
only intentional discrimination, outlawed only hiring practices which inten-
tionally used an individual's race against him or her."[31]

In relation to affirmative action, the pragmatic Nixon was not entirely
bereft of principle. Historians have pointed to liberals within the Nixon
staff—especially Ehrlichman, Moynihan, and Garment—as largely responsible for what are often seen as progressive moves on civil rights, including
affirmative action.[32] This is at least partially true, as is the contention that
political gain could be made from dividing the Democrats between civil
rights and labor supporters on the issue of minority hiring "goals and
timetables" in the construction industry. But there was also a more personal
basis to Nixon's commitment to affirmative action that must be discussed—
the right to earn.

The Nixon Philosophy and Affirmative Action

During his tenure as vice president, Richard Nixon had overseen the administration's efforts in the civil rights field; he had been favored by civil rights lead-

ers over John F. Kennedy in the 1960 election as the candidate of choice for black Americans before Kennedy's highly publicized intervention after the arrest of Dr. Martin Luther King, Jr. Throughout his presidency, he saw himself as a man prepared to "do what's right" for African Americans. As biographer Stephen Ambrose indicated in his even-handed assessment of Nixon, he never appealed directly to the white backlash and privately as well as publicly told GOP candidates that they could never win by outsegregating the Democrats.[33]

Nixon's occasional but seemingly genuine sympathy for the plight of black Americans no doubt came from what Leonard Garment called an "instinctive sympathy for the underdog."[34] Sudden, deeply felt moments of passion occasionally emerge in the Nixon records, apparently triggered by some event or issue. In response to a news item about a plane crash involving the Wichita, Kansas, football team, where insurance companies said they that may not pay claims because the pilot was improperly certified, Nixon wrote, no doubt harking back to his days playing with a small-town, local football team: "Flanigan—Get on this—Don't let these bastards get out of paying this claim."[35]

On more than one occasion, Nixon told a story that especially affected him about a son, graduating from an Ivy League college, who was ashamed because his father was not university-educated and appeared crude. Nixon told his aides that "nothing bothered him more than this because the young man's education was obtained only because of the hard work of the father." He added at one meeting where he told the story, "[T]he worst thing you can do to a man is snub him; it's worse than exploiting or enslaving him."[36] Here, the president of the United States reveals an earlier version of himself—the young man who attended university when his father could not. It also revealed the continuing sensitivity about the rejection he felt he had experienced from Eastern elite circles. The insecurity borne of rejection both by the best New York law firms and by the FBI after Nixon graduated from Duke, the alienation he felt from his Eastern Establishment "friends" who led the movement to get Eisenhower to drop him from the Republican ticket in 1952—all remained with him throughout his life and might have had some bearing on his attitudes toward race.

A second, related characteristic was Nixon's resentment of privilege. Parmet suggests that Nixon's attachment to the Republican Party may have been related to this hatred of the elite, rather than antipathetic to it: "More than conventional Republican conservatives, however, Nixon kept seeing conflict in terms of a class struggle."[37] Many accounts analyze the Nixon character in terms of class hatred and resentment against more privileged classes. Virtually all observers see this as a flaw, as one of many of the undesirable aspects of the man, such as his virulent hatred of the press.[38] It is also possible to see this quality in a positive light, both in energizing Nixon's campaigns and projects and in that it may have lent sympathy to the plight of others. This "negative" characteristic might have had a positive effect on Nixon's attitudes toward race.

The Private Nixon and Race

The everyday conversations in the records of the most recorded president in history give an interesting insight into the assumptions underlying Nixon's civil rights actions. However, care must be taken. Political figures tend to avoid speaking "off the cuff" about issues like race, especially in periods where the possibility of race riots appears real. Additionally, it is difficult to know whether use of the word "nigger," for instance, is a careless use of a term that was accepted when the subject using it grew up or an attempt to denigrate African Americans. In today's climate there is a hypersensitivity to words, which makes condemnations of historical figures based on the language they used tempting. However, even Nixon existed in a very different historical context where language was assigned less importance. Moreover, what evidence there is can often be contradictory. With these caveats in mind, it is possible to view Nixon's attitudes as fairly typical of his time.

Both Nixon himself and friendly biographer Herbert Parmet contend that Nixon inherited a moral position regarding civil rights from his Quaker upbringing: "His Quaker background was notably free of such [racial] bias, and nothing in the record contradicts that history for either the man's public or personal life." J. Larry Hood saw Nixon's experience at Duke University, where he experienced a Jim Crow society first-hand, as important in making him a committed racial liberal.[39] Nixon himself cited reasons for his self-professed racial liberalism as his "background—background of my college education, Quaker school, and the like."[40] As early as 1946, before the Hiss affair, the Douglas campaign, and Truman's overwhelming interest in either subject began, Nixon stated that "We must be vigilant against the doctrines of the Bilbos and the Talmadges and the Gerald L. K. Smiths, who are just as dangerous to the preservation of the American way of life on the one hand as are the Communists on the other."[41] If we are to accept Myrdal's rank order of discrimination, Nixon could have counted himself as among the most liberal of parents in the 1950s. When in Washington, Nixon sent his daughters to Horace Mann, a public integrated school, and later to Sidwell Friends School, an enlightened Quaker institution that had no racial or religious barriers.[42] It is likely that he was more predisposed toward liberal attitudes on civil rights than many of his compatriots. But he was more than ready to jettison any Quaker principles, as his participation in World War II demonstrates.

Yet Nixon's real faith was in anti-communism and this fired his early interest in civil rights. He touched on this theme in nearly every speech he made about race and civil rights. In a transcript of a radio/television speech made in 1953, the then-vice president thundered: "Every act of racial discrimination or prejudice in the United States hurts America as much as an espionage agent who turns over a weapon to a foreign enemy."[43] At a rally in Harlem in 1956, Nixon stated: "During the next four years there is no single issue which will be more important than civil rights. . . . This is not a matter of charity or of politics—it must be done because of what it means to our economic strength here at home: *what it means to our standing throughout the world*" [emphasis added].[44] Again, in 1957, he emphasized that discrimination was a liability because "(e)very time there is an instance of discrimination in the United States, it gives the Communists a weapon which they can use against us."[45]

Anti-communism was, after all, the force that had enabled him to achieve national political prominence and retained a personal meaning for him throughout his life.[46] It took on a near-religious importance, as he stated decades later: "Anti-communism is not a policy. It is a faith—faith in freedom."[47] This belief in his country—expressed as anti-communism—fueled an early racial liberalism. And, as long as Soviet propaganda effectively attacked the United States's record on race, Nixon remained, at least rhetorically, racially liberal.

Nixon the Racist?

An oft-repeated accusation regarding race was first aired by his aide John Ehrlichman in his memoirs of the Nixon years. Ehrlichman remembered:

> Twice, in explaining all this to me, Nixon said he believed America's blacks could only marginally benefit from Federal programs because blacks were *genetically inferior* to whites. . . . Blacks could never achieve parity . . . but, he said, we should still do what we could for them, within reasonable limits, because it was the "right" thing to do.[48]

Questions over the accuracy of Ehrlichman's memory have created something of a controversy among historians. No one has yet found any mention in the documents released by the Nixon Presidential Materials Project (NPMP) to back up Ehrlichman's memory of the phrase "genetically inferior." It is possible, of course, that Nixon explicitly told Ehrlichman to keep these comments off the record or that any recording of them has been deemed to be personal or private and has thus been withdrawn from the Nixon Presidential

Materials Project, the guardian of the Nixon papers and arbiter of what is public and what is private among the Nixon papers.

Nevertheless, there is enough evidence now to suggest that Nixon did express the sentiments repeated by Ehrlichman. Nixon's other right-hand man, H. R. Haldeman, published his daily diaries of life in the Nixon White House. The entry for Monday, April 28, 1969 seems to back up Ehrlichman's recollections. In it Nixon claims that the "whole problem" of welfare was "really the blacks." Nixon ruminated that "there has never in history been an adequate black nation, and they are the only race of which this is true." "Africa is hopeless," he claimed, "the worst there is Liberia, which we built."[49] Nixon also showed an interest in racial theories. He asked his chief advisor on racial problems, Pat Moynihan, for thoughts on an article in *The Atlantic Magazine* by Richard Herrnstein entitled "I.Q." (Herrnstein would later become infamous for coauthoring with Charles Murray, *The Bell Curve*). Moynihan's response, released in October 1996 after originally being withdrawn, shows that Nixon brought up the subject of black inferiority at a cabinet meeting when discussing the infamous article by Arthur Jensen published in the *Harvard Education Review*. Jensen claimed that the differences between black and white I.Q. test scores were more likely to be genetic rather than environmental.[50]

The advice that Moynihan gave him in this letter was perhaps more important than what either of them thought of the articles, and Nixon took it. Moynihan treated race as an issue that had to be managed, not resolved "Frankly, I don't see how a society such as ours can live with this knowledge. . . . I need not go on: the "danger" of this knowledge is self-evident."[51] Moynihan outlined to Nixon that "a primary problem is how to deal with the widespread legal and social expectation of equality of outcomes with respect to socially defined groups, primarily racial, ethnic, and religious groups."[52] Underlying this advice was fear rather than optimism about racial issues. The major decision, one that Nixon, in asking for the comments, must have been considering, was how much effort should be put into programs based on the assumption of racial equality and how much should be going into those that simply attempt to "contain" racial issues. In an earlier memo, Moynihan gave advice about crime. He expressed his opinion about the difficulty of the issue. The advice, which Nixon underlined and marked beside it, "Correct," would have been apposite for race relations: "What you can't control, you had better not draw attention to."[53]

Beside the implication that Nixon and his administration implemented affirmative action though they knew it would never produce equal results, the most important implication of the Moynihan memo—if it is accepted that its sentiments broadly reflected Nixon's on the issue—is that Nixon held no particular views on race apart from the fact that it was a troublesome problem in the United States. Nixon maintained an open mind on the scientific and moral question of black inequality. The evidence shows at the very least an equivocal approach by Nixon to questions of black and white equality. At times, it seems, Nixon thought that blacks and whites would eventually integrate. When discussing who might fill Supreme Court vacancies, he had originally favored Jewish Republican Rita Hauser, a longtime Nixon supporter. But then he saw an article (yet another rehearsal of issues still emerging today) that quoted her as seeing no Constitutional impediment to same-sex marriages. Nixon said: "There goes a Supreme Court Justice! I can't go *that* far; that's the year 2000! Negroes [and whites], okay. But *that's* too far!"[54] The comment is very interesting considering that today some states have sanctioned same-sex marriages whereas the rate of intermarriage between Americans of European origin and those of African American origin remains incredibly low (5 percent for black men and 2 percent for black women).[55]

Though Nixon was somewhat back and forth on racial issues—often depending on his mood, a certain pessimism pervaded later memos. Commenting on a piece by Charles F. Palmer, president of the National Student Association, in which he promised that, unless the problems of the "repression of black, brown, and red people," poverty, the Vietnam War, the environment, and women's and workers' rights were resolved, students would continue to protest. Nixon underlined a sentence—"until these things have changed" and wrote: "1. They are being changed, 2. Except for V. Nam, *none* will ever be solved."[56]

To sum up his perspectives on race, the issue was, to Nixon as well as to most postwar liberals, outside his most important concerns—except in its ability to destabilize the country. This was the most important motivation behind his implementation of affirmative action, rather than any sudden burst of enthusiasm for civil rights. The actual scientific issue of whether or not black Americans could ever be equal may have influenced his prognosis on issues like busing and other issues connected with education, however. Thus, a policy connection with these private thoughts cannot be entirely disregarded, even if we admit that his first consideration was his "obligation not to have the Goddamn country blow up" as he succinctly put it in one meeting.[57]

The Right to Earn and Affirmative Action

It is possible to see, after considering Nixon's ambivalence toward the issue of race, a nonracial motive for Nixon's espousal of affirmative action. Many observers miss the most important principle governing the decisions of the "aprincipled" Nixon, especially in regard to affirmative action—the right to earn. As Garry Wills observed, "Nixon believes in civil rights, only he believes a man's first right is the right to earn."[58]

The right to earn was a postwar value, the extension of the American dream to the permanent workforce. Here was a direct connection to a key aspect of the American Creed—that through participating fully in the American institution of hard work (the Protestant work ethic), all Americans may be rewarded with full participation in American life. The positive side of the anticommunism to which Nixon subscribed so fervently was the belief that American capitalism remained the best, fairest system in the world. He passionately believed that, as he put it in his famous "Bridges to Human Dignity" radio address in 1968, "there is no greater bridge to human dignity than the pride that comes with well-earned success in the free enterprise system."[59] "A good job is as basic and important a civil right as a good education," Nixon told readers in his autobiography *RN*.[60] In the last of his autobiographies, *In the Arena*, published in 1990, Nixon repeated his idea that "(t)he mainspring of capitalism is the rewarding of work and efficiency."[61] The subject of this belief in the rewarding of work and efficiency was the mirror image of Nixon himself—of humble roots but, through hard work, an achiever who "paid his dues" and *earned* success.

Though an intelligent man, Nixon never subjected this idea to any real scrutiny and it becomes clear that this belief was a simple faith borne of his own experience rather than an intellectual understanding of the relationship of dissident Protestant sects to capitalist ideology. He proudly recounted being told that he had what it took to learn the law—"an iron butt."[62] His book, *Six Crises*, published after his defeat by Kennedy in the election of 1960, told of the struggles during his political career.[63] "Nothing of any value, in business, in culture, in politics, in sports, or in any other field, was created without struggle," he lectured more recently. "Struggle is what makes us human instead of animals," meaning, presumably, the struggle to improve rather than the struggle to survive.[64] Equally, Nixon believed that nothing could come from nothing. Wills described the strength of this feeling within Americans—none more so than Nixon—in the 1960s: "A total disorientation comes over the American, a vertiginous fear that the law of moral gravity has been rescinded, when he thinks that someone might actually be getting something for nothing."[65]

This right to earn, or work ethic, was, of course, not exclusive to Nixon—it found a resonance among many at the time. It can be seen as a defensive response to the pervasive questioning of American capitalist values occurring at the time, championing the American Dream. Gunnar Myrdal wrote in 1961 that work was "the basis for self-respect and a dignified life."[66] Nixon was consistent in wishing to extend the right to earn to black Americans. Indeed, he saw lack of the right to earn as the major problem affecting black Americans.

In 1956, Nixon told a rally in Harlem: "But in order to *have* human rights, people need property rights—and never has this been more true than in the case of the Negro today."[67] In the 1968 campaign, Nixon referred to "(t)he forgotten Americans, the hard-working, the tax-paying Americans, [who] are black as well as white."[68] His election pitch to black Americans was often cited:

> Black extremists are guaranteed headlines when they shout "burn" or "get a gun." But much of the black militant talk these days is actually in terms far closer to the doctrines of free enterprise than those of the welfarist [1930s]—terms of "pride," "ownership," "private enterprise," "capital," "self-assurance," "self-respect"—the same qualities, the same characteristics, the same ideals, the same methods, [that] for two centuries have been at the heart of American success. . . . What most militants are asking for is not separation, but to be included in—not as supplicants, but as owners, as entrepreneurs—to have a share of the wealth and a piece of the action.[69]

As Ambrose notes, Nixon's black capitalism idea "implied a willingness to put aside the goal of an integrated society to concentrate on improving conditions in the ghettoes."[70] But it also testified to Nixon's faith, redolent of Milton Friedman's aforementioned confidence, that capitalism was the solution to the race problem. Cynics might object that, yet again, this was simply the political Nixon attempting to divide what had been solidly Democratic constituencies. It is certainly true that, if this was the aim, it patently failed, although it did unite black radicals with conservatives.[71] However, as indicated above, Nixon's commitment to keeping the programs built on this principle going outlasted the furor about black capitalism. That Nixon was a "true believer" in the right to earn is demonstrated by his willingness to countenance such a radical program as the Family Assistance Plan (FAP). The FAP would have scrapped the welfare system and replaced it with an income floor. Though he had effectively given up on it as too costly by July 1970 (see chapter 8), his hatred of what he felt were the debilitating effects of welfare on individuals outweighed worries he had about the effect on the American economy. He resisted considerable opposition to his plan from conservatives (and liberals) both inside and outside of the administration to jettison the plan earlier.[72]

More importantly for this discussion, the right to earn served as Nixon's overarching justification for all of the affirmative action programs. His statement to Congress defending the Philadelphia Plan in 1969 made it abundantly clear that it was this right to which he referred. Affirmative action first became important to Nixon as it afforded the opportunity to earn to black Americans:

> The civil rights to which this administration is committed is one of demonstrable deeds—focused where they count. One of the things that counts most is

earning power. Nothing is more unfair than that the same Americans who pay taxes should by any pattern of discriminatory practices be deprived of an equal opportunity to work on federal construction contracts.[73]

He told William Safire, "That's why we have to hit this minority enterprise thing so hard—sure they laugh at it—but better jobs, better housing, that's the only way Negroes are going to be able to move to Scarsdale."[74] Nixon, it might be added, had a 100 percent record—both in 1969 and 1972—of defending affirmative action programs when they faced real challenges. His famous attack on quotas implied for many that Nixon was rescinding his support of affirmative action. Phillip Hoffman, president of the American Jewish Committee, wrote to both candidates in the run up to the 1972 election asking what they thought of quotas. The president wrote back on August 11, 1972 declaring:

> With respect to these affirmative action programs, I agree that numerical goals, although an important and useful tool to measure progress which remedies the effect of past discrimination, must not be allowed to be applied in such a fashion as to, in fact, result in the imposition of quotas, nor should they be predicated upon or directed towards a concept of proportional representation.
> I have asked the appropriate departmental heads to review their policies to ensure conformance with these views.[75]

There was no necessary contradiction at that stage between this perspective and his espousal of various affirmative action programs. He was simply asserting the "right to earn" he thought affirmative action afforded to black Americans for whites, too. It was not until some years later that the two appeared inextricably opposed, an anomaly dealt with in the last section of this book.

Conclusion

If Nixon embodied the dark side of liberalism, its crisis of meaning, he also personified its flexibility, its willingness to experiment, and its transition to new values. Though Garry Wills was undoubtedly correct to characterize him as a postwar man, he also set up key aspects of (what could be very awkwardly phrased as) the post-postwar era.

In historical texts, Nixon's duality is central to assessments of this complex character. The light and dark tableaux, the obscured division between shadow and shadowmaker so eloquently recounted in David Greenberg's *Nixon's Shadow: The History of an Image*, the caring and fatherly figure and the venal demographer, the statesmanlike figure magnanimously stepping aside for Kennedy in the interests of his country and the villainous Watergate plotter—all reflect the complex reality of the man.[76] Perhaps the hatred with which he is still regarded comes because Nixon represents something deep down within some American liberals that frightens them. They are purged of their guilt about many of the darker recesses of liberalism—McCarthyism, nagging doubts about Kennedy's character, the debacles of the Vietnam War, the failure of the Great Society—by attacking "Tricky Dick."

Placing his pronouncements and reflections within the historically specific context of the times, however, gives us a much less emotive assessment. He mirrored the ambivalence of the postwar liberal commitment to progress. Andrew Hacker somewhat cynically observed that within the American mind—and, no doubt, within Nixon's—two inclinations were at war: the hope that blacks were equal and the suspicion that they were not. Hope energized the civil rights actions of the Johnson era; suspicion led Nixon to sponsor programs more designed to stabilize race relations than to move toward racial equality.

In that he was a resolute defender of capitalism at a time when opposition to "the system" was rife, Nixon was undoubtedly conservative. He pushed affirmative action strategies, radical departures as they were, because he had to make capitalism appear fair at a time when most doubted it was. The ever-prescient Garry Wills observed:

> The remedy was obvious, for those still trying to make individualism work: one must contrive the systematization of luck. The advocate of competition, the one who is truly concerned with maintaining the contest, will be most interested in giving all runners a chance . . . To protect the game, the government would give everyone a *new deal*, making sure it was a *fair deal*. . . . There might be debate on questions of fact—that is, how much "activism" a referee must engage in to keep the game fair—but there was no disagreement on the principle: the game must go on. And no final disagreement on the referee's job: to provide an equitable basis for the game. Roosevelt, in his second inaugural address, stated the principle this way: "If the average citizen is guaranteed equal opportunity in the polling place, he must have equal opportunity in the market place."[77]

The core belief of this "apricipled" president was in the American Dream. Reflecting his own personal experiences, Nixon believed fervently that the market rewarded those who worked hard but that a fair system must give everyone that chance. He passionately believed that the game must go on—affirmative action reflected an attempt to restore faith in the American Dream, in the idea that capitalism was an inherently just system among the large numbers of Americans who, by this time, dissented from this national religion. However, his espousal of affirmative action also reflected his cynicism about the abilities of African Americans and about the willingness of the nation to include its most troublesome minority.

Notes

1. Charles P. Henderson, *The Nixon Theology* (New York: Harper and Row, 1972), 210.

2. Garry Wills, *Nixon Agonistes: The Crisis of the Self-Made Man* (Boston: Houghton Mifflin Company, 1970), 6.

3. Cited in Dean Kotlowski, *Nixon's Civil Rights: Politics, Principle, and Policy* (London: Harvard University Press, 2001), 17.

4. "Thus modern, mature democracies representing the end of ideologies have, in effect, separated ethics from politics; and ideology, insofar as it continues to exist in modern society, is nothing more than a cynical propaganda cover for the specific self-interest of competing groups." Stephen Rousseas and James Farganis, "Retreat of the Idealists," *The Nation* 196, issue 17 (March 23, 1963): 18–22.

5. Daniel Bell, *The Cultural Contradictions of Capitalism* (London: Heinemann, 1976), 178.

6. Memo for Pat Buchanan from the president April 21, 1970, Memos—April 1970, box 2, folder 1 of 6 [Documents from boxes 1–9], Contested Files: WHSF: SMOF: President's Personal Files, NPMP.

7. Memo to Dwight Chapin and Alex Butterfield from Constance Stuart, September 2, 1971, H. R. Haldeman June–December 1971 [1 of 3], box 3, WHSF: SMOF: Colson, NPMP.

8. Cited in Allen J. Matusow, *Nixon's Economy: Booms, Busts, Dollars, and Votes* (Lawrence: Kansas University Press, 1998), 15.

9. Colson written notes, June 16, Presidential Meetings and Conversations [6 of 6], box 18, WHSF: SMOF: Colson, NPMP.

10. Memo for Ehrlichman from Ken Cole, August 3, 1971, JDE notes of meeting with the president—1-5-71 to 4-21-71 box 5 [6 of 6], Ehrlichman "Scrapbook" Items [memoranda from the president] [1 of 2], folder 2 of 5 [boxes 16–22], Contested Files: WHSF: SMOF: Ehrlichman, NPMP.

11. Handwritten notes of a meeting held on 4/21/71, JDE notes of meeting with the president—1-5-71 to 4-21-71 box 5 [6 of 6] Contested Files, box 1 [documents from boxes 3–14]: WHSF: SMOF: Ehrlichman, NPMP.

12. Hugh Davis Graham, *The Civil Rights Era: Origins and Development of National Policy, 1960–1972* (New York: Oxford University Press, 1990), 446–47.

13. Stephen E. Ambrose, *Nixon, Volume II: The Triumph of a Politician 1962-1972* (London: Simon and Schuster, 1989), 236; Melvin Small, *The Presidency of Richard Nixon* (Lawrence: Kansas University Press, 1999), 36.

14. Memo from David N. Parker to Haldeman, February 8, 1971, box 3, WHCF; Subject Files HU [Ex] HU, NPMP.

15. News Summaries—January 11, 1970, WHCF: POF: ANS, NPMP.

16. Cited in "All the Philosopher King's Men," from a May 13, 1971 taped conversation between Nixon, Haldeman, and Ehrlichman transcribed by James Warren, *Harper's Magazine* 300, no. 1797 (February 2000): 22–24, esp. 22.

17. John D. Ehrlichman, *Witness to Power: The Nixon Years* (New York: Simon and Schuster, 1982), 222–23; H. R. Haldeman, *The Haldeman Diaries* (Sony CD-ROM, 1994), April 28, 1969, H Notes January–June 1969 [January–April 1, 1969] part 1, Haldeman Notes: box 40, WHSF: SMOF: H. R. Haldeman: Haldeman notes, NPMP.

18. Cited in William Chafe, *The Unfinished Journey: America Since World War II* (New York: Oxford University Press, 1995), 253.

19. Cited in Herbert S. Parmet, *Richard Nixon and His America* (London: Little, Brown and Company, 1990), 597.

20. Chafe, *The Unfinished Journey*, 427.

21. Eleanor Holmes Norton, "Civil Rights: Working Backwards" in Alan Gartner et al., *What Nixon is Doing to Us* (New York: Harper and Row, 1973), 201–15, esp. 204. Much material that emerged concerning Nixon's psychological make-up also pursues this theme.

22. Michael Genovese, *The Nixon Presidency: Power and Politics in Turbulent Times* (London: Greenwood Press, 1990), 83.

23. See Joan Hoff, *Nixon Reconsidered* (New York: Basic Books, 1994), 3.

24. Hugh Davis Graham, "The Incoherence of the Civil Rights Policy in the Nixon Administration" in *Richard M. Nixon: Politician, President, Administrator*, ed. Leon Friedman and William F. Levantrosser (New York: Greenwood Press, 1991), 159–72, esp. 165–66.

25. Nicholas Lemann, *The Promised Land: The Great Black Migration and How It Changed America* (London: Macmillan, 1991), 203.

26. Lemann, *The Promised Land*, 203.

27. Cited on the cover of Ambrose, *Nixon: Volume II: The Triumph of a Politician*.

28. Cited in Herbert S. Parmet, *Richard Nixon and His America* (London: Little, Brown and Company, 1990), 19.

29. Cited in William Safire, *Before the Fall: An Inside View of the Pre-Watergate White House* (New York: Doubleday and Co., 1975), 554.

30. Handwritten notes of a meeting held on 5/27/71, JDE notes of meeting with the president—1-5-71 to 4-21-71 box 5 [6 of 6], Nixon Presidential Materials Staff: Presidential Materials Review Board: Review on Contested Documents (hereafter "Contested Files"): White House Special Files (WHSF): Staff Member and Office Files (SMOF): John D. Ehrlichman, NPMP.

31. John D. Skrentny, *The Ironies of Affirmative Action: Politics, Culture, and Justice in America* (London: University of Chicago Press, 1996), 95.

32. Hoff, *Nixon Reconsidered*, 56).

33. Ambrose, *The Triumph of a Politician*, 89.

34. From an interview with Leonard Garment conducted by the author on May 15, 1997.

35. News Summaries (no date), News Summaries—October 1970, box 31, WHSF: SMOF: POF, Contested Files, NPMP.

36. Memorandum for the president's file, July 26 1971—Subject: Meeting with Nixon, Ehrlichman, Connally, Shultz, and Colson, White House/Strategy Memos, box 14, WHSF: SMOF: Colson, NPMP.

37. Parmet, *Richard Nixon and His America*, 189.

38. See Dr. Eli S. Chesen's *President Nixon's Psychiatric Profile: A Psychodynamic-Genetic Interpretation*, (New York, P. H. Wyden, 1973); Dr. David Abrahamsen's *Nixon vs. Nixon* (New York: Farrar, Strauss and Giroux, 1977); Bruce Mazlish, *In Search of Nixon: A Psychohistorical Inquiry* (London: Basic Books, Inc., 1972); Fawn M. Brodie, *Richard Nixon: The Shaping of His Character* (London: W.W. Norton & Company, 1981). All mention this feature of Nixon's personality as a flaw.

39. J. Larry Hood, "The Nixon Administration and the Revised Philadelphia Plan for Affirmative Action: A Study in Expanding Presidential Power and Divided Government," *Presidential Studies Quarterly* 23 (1993): 145–67.

40. *Congressional Quarterly: The Public Records of Richard M. Nixon and Henry Cabot Lodge*, article contained in file marked "Congressional Quarterly," box 17, RNC records.

41. Speech given at East Whittier Friends Church, October 8, 1946, *Statements Made by the Vice President Concerning Civil Rights in the Early Part of His Public Career*, Speeches, 1957, box 17, RNC records.

42. Parmet, *Richard Nixon and His America*, 268.

43. *Transcript of a Radio-TV Speech to the American Public*, December 23, 1953, Speeches 1953, box 17, RNC records.

44. *Excerpts from Address of Vice President Richard M. Nixon to a Rally in Harlem*, New York, October 31, 1956, Speeches 1956, box 17, RNC records.

45. *Statements Made by the Vice President Concerning Civil Rights in the Early Part of His Public Career*, Speeches 1957, box 17, RNC Records.

46. In 1990, after the Berlin Wall had fallen, Nixon still insisted that communism was a threat in his memoir, *In the Arena: A Memory of Victory, Defeat, and Renewal* (New York: Pocket Books, 1990). Even in a 1992 publication, *Seize the Moment: The Challenge for America in a One-Superpower World* (New York: Simon and Schuster, 1992), he continued to warn of the dangers of socialism.

47. Nixon, *In the Arena*, 364.

48. John Ehrlichman, *Witness to Power: the Nixon Years* (New York: Simon and Schuster, 1982), 222–23.

49. Haldeman, *The Haldeman Diaries* (Sony CD-ROM, 1994), April 28, 1969, H Notes January–June 1969 [January–April 1, 1969] Part 1, Haldeman Notes, box 40, WHSF: SMOF: Haldeman: Haldeman Notes, NPMP.

50. Letter to Jensen from Moynihan, April 2, 1969, [Ex] HU2 Equality—Beginning 4/2/69, WHCF; Subject Files HU [Ex] HU, NPMP.

51. Memorandum for the president from Daniel P. Moynihan, September 20, 1971, president's handwriting, December 1–15, 1971, box 2 (folder 2), WHSF: SMOF: POF, Contested Files, NPMP.

52. Memo for the president from Moynihan, September 20, 1971.

53. Memorandum for the president from Daniel P. Moynihan, November 13, 1970, president's handwriting, November 1970, box 1 [folder 1] (boxes 1–13), WHSF, SMOF: POF, Contested Files, NPMP.

54. Cited in Ehrlichman, *Witness to Power: The Nixon Years*, 239.

55. John D. Skrentny, *The Minority Rights Revolution* (Cambridge, MA: The Belknap Press of Harvard University Press, 2002), 345.

56. Annoted memorandum for the president from Moynihan, 8/4/1970, president's handwriting, August 1–15, 1970, box 7, WHSF: SMOF: POF: president's handwriting, NPMP.

57. Handwritten notes 6-19-70, JDE notes of meeting with the president—1/1/70–6/30/70 [5 of 5] box 1 [documents from boxes 3–14], WHSF: SMOF: Ehrlichman, Contested Files, NPMP. Nixon repeated the "do what's right" phrase with regards to civil rights on many occasions throughout his presidency.

58. Wills, *Nixon Agonistes*, 582.

59. Cited in "Remarks of the Honorable Robert H. Finch before the Conference of Regional Education Laboratories," July 17, 1969, file marked "Admin Civil Rights," box 422, Brooke Papers, LOC.

60. Nixon, *RN*, 437.

61. Nixon, *In the Arena*, 353.

62. Cited in Small, *The Presidency of Richard Nixon*, 5.

63. See Richard Nixon, *Six Crises* (Garden City, NY: Doubleday, 1962).

64. Nixon, *In the Arena*, 119.

65. Wills, *Nixon Agonistes*, 244.

66. Cited in Gareth Davies, *From Opportunity to Entitlement: The Transformation and Decline of Great Society Liberalism* (Lawrence: University Press of Kansas, 1996), 50.

67. Excerpts from an address of Vice President Richard M. Nixon to a rally in Harlem, New York, October 31, 1956, Speeches 1956, box 17, RNC records.

68. Statement of Richard M. Nixon, CBS Radio Network, October 30, 1968, RNC 1968 Campaign: Press Releases and Nixon Speeches, box 5, 1968 Press Releases and Nixon Speeches, RNC Records.

69. Bridges to Human Dignity, an address by Richard M. Nixon on the NBC Radio Network, April 25, 1968, box 5, 1968 Nixon Campaign: Press Releases and Nixon Speeches, RNC Records.

70. Ambrose, *The Triumph of a Politician*, 124.

71. Nixon didn't lack for critics of the black capitalism idea. Congressional liaison Bryce Harlow told Ehrlichman in the summer of 1969 that "not one nongovernmental witness, from Roy Innis, chairman of CORE, to the American Bankers Association commended the Administration" regarding black capitalism (memo from Harlowe to Ehrlichman, August 9, 1969, files of John Ehrlichman re: EEOC #379 [CFOA 7730], box 86, WHCF: SMOF: Garment, NPMP.) See also Frederick E. Case, *Black Capitalism: Problems in Development* (New York: Praeger, 1972) and Theodore L. Cross, *Black Capitalism* (New York: Atheneum, 1969).

72. See Alex Waddan, "A Liberal in Wolf's Clothing: Nixon's Family Assistance Plan in the Light of 1990s Welfare Reform," *Journal of American Studies* 32 (1998): 203–18.

73. Cited by Gerald Ford in *CR*, 91st Congress, vol. 115, 40906. See also Robert P. Schuwerk, "The Philadelphia Plan: A Study in the Dynamics of Executive Power," *University of Chicago Law Review* 39 (1971–1972): 723–60, esp. 749.

74. Safire, *Before the Fall*, 237.

75. Letter contained (loose) in box 4, [Ex] HU 2 1972 onward, WHCF: Subject Files: HU (Human Rights), NPMP.

76. David Greenberg, *Nixon's Shadow: The History of an Image* (New York: W.W. Norton and Co., 2003).

77. Wills, *Nixon Agonistes*, 226.

7

The Philadelphia Plan

I F PROOF WAS NEEDED of Nixon's role in the creation of affirmative action, it can be found in the story of the 1969 Philadelphia Plan, which required all contractors working on large federally funded projects to adopt "numerical goals and timetables" to assure the desegregation of their workforces. Nixon was determined to make the plan, devised under Johnson but shelved after challenges to its legality, workable.

The Philadelphia Plan represented both a clear break from and a continuation of past policy. The break, of course, was that the federal government officially contradicted its educative role, relinquished its color-blind approach, and acknowledged the existence of racial divisions which previous administrations had been so determined to deny. As discussed previously, the Philadelphia Plan implicitly condemned the institutions that Myrdal had privileged and undermined all other previous hiring, firing, and promotion systems.

However, it also represented continuity. Not only was the Philadelphia construction industry the target of a long-running campaign by civil rights activists but the city was one of a number of cities threatened with rioting and disorder. With a population of some two million blacks, there was an element of immediacy and contingency to the efforts of the Johnson and then the Nixon administrations.[1] Nixon's Philadelphia Plan—despite its enforcing the hiring of minorities—can be viewed within the context of the voluntaristic civil rights efforts of the Johnson and Kennedy administrations. In many ways—especially in its lax enforcement—it sought to pressurize rather than to force. Furthermore, it continued the focus upon the ghetto rather than on strengthening the black middle class.

Most texts dealing with affirmative action assume the Philadelphia Plan was the most important model for affirmative action programs still in place today. Jill Quadagno, author of *The Color of Welfare*, argued that "the Philadelphia Plan worked" in creating black employment and in instituting successfully affirmative programs.[2] Hugh Davis Graham, whose texts on the history of civil rights policy appear in the footnotes of every text dealing with the issue since *The Civil Rights Era* was published in 1990, notes that, after Nixon's effective defense of the Philadelphia Plan in December 1969, "(t)he tide of affirmative action thereby turned sharply towards minority preferences." However, Graham cites the obscure bureaucratic Order No. 4, the order issued by the Labor Department on January 23, 1970 that extended the requirements of the Philadelphia Plan to nearly *all* government contractors (and soon included women in the list of beneficiaries), as being that which universalized affirmative action in the United States.[3]

Although Graham is right to mark Order No. 4 as an important historical precedent, it is possible that the Philadelphia Plan and Order No. 4 acquired much of their importance in hindsight. This chapter will argue that the significance of the Philadelphia Plan and Order No. 4 has been misunderstood. First, neither the Philadelphia Plan nor the "hometown solutions," voluntary plans modeled on the Philadelphia Plan agreed upon in other urban areas, can be regarded as successes. Progress, when it existed, was painfully slow. Most of the original "hometown plans" were torn up and rewritten within a year of being implemented. Progress for blacks employed in the construction industry took place in tens rather than in thousands of jobs. The impact of the Philadelphia and hometown plans upon black employment in the inner cities at a time when the construction industry suffered under the recession of the early 1970s was, not surprisingly, negligible. There is no evidence that Order No. 4, despite its near universal coverage, was implemented as anything more than an attempt to placate the construction industry by extending its strictures to other industries. As far as the records show, Nixon never mentioned Order No. 4 and seldom mentioned the Philadelphia Plan after the battle in Congress in December 1969 to have it rescinded. Up until September 1971 (at least) not one contract had been canceled nor had any contractor been debarred under the Philadelphia Plan or Order No. 4 despite many calls from such organizations as the Congressional Black Caucus for stricter implementation.[4] The Civil Rights Commission observed that "violation of the Philadelphia Plan has been widespread."[5]

Second, the Philadelphia Plan, designed to combat black unemployment in the ghettos, was effectively shelved by the Nixon administration almost as soon as it was implemented, though not for the reasons imagined by some historians. Nixon's rethink of civil rights strategies in 1970, to be discussed later, shifted policies away from the ghettos and toward those that could "help themselves"—the black middle class.

Nixon only mentioned the Philadelphia Plan when his administration's civil rights record was being attacked. Few others thought that the Philadelphia Plan was significant at the time. It was less contentious than open housing and certainly less contentious than busing to achieve racial balance—the issue of the day during Nixon's first term. The plan was insignificant to the Democratic Party at the time, so much so that they were willing to outlaw preferential hiring and, therefore, scrap the Philadelphia Plan, in return for cease and desist powers for the Equal Employment Opportunities Commission (EEOC) in 1972. Had they succeeded in their attempt, a much different history would now be being written. (This anomaly between the arrival of such a significant piece of legislation and the deafening silence from those who would later praise or decry affirmative action will be explored in later chapters). Nor, as we have seen, was the theoretical premise behind the plan new or unfamiliar as a concept.[6]

This chapter also highlights the importance of the congressional battle over the future of the Philadelphia Plan. Here, it is possible to see that the majority of the political and business elite had now been won over to the need for a new race relations strategy. The conservative reasons for opposing affirmative action that had helped prevent its adoption in previous years had now been surpassed by concerns about racial conflagration.

Background to the Philadelphia Plan

Originating in 1967, though following a long history of civil rights activism over the issue of black participation in the construction workforce in the city, the Philadelphia Plan hoped to break the grip of lily-white unions on the construction trades in Philadelphia, including sheet-metal workers, plumbers, roofers, structural ironworkers, steamfitters, and elevator constructors with a combined membership of between 8,500 and 9,000. These few offending locals remained defiantly lily-white, highly paid, and highly visible.[7] The goal was to force integration on six offending locals in Philadelphia by concentrating irresistible economic leverage on the region's builders. The method was to set no firm target numbers (this would suggest illegal quotas[8]) but to hold up contracts until bidders submitted detailed manning tables that listed specific numbers of minority members they promised to hire. Contractors who submitted the lowest bid after all contractors received the same pre-bid specifications were termed "apparent low bidders" while their manning tables were examined, after which the contract could be signed.[9]

The issue of union discrimination, while not new, had previously been avoided in the interests of Democratic Party unity. However, protests organized to highlight the lack of black faces on construction sites, often in black neighborhoods, proved increasingly hard to ignore, especially after the Watts riot in August 1965 pointed toward the cities as the epicenter of race relations problems.[10]

Part of the problem was that, as per arrangements formalized during the New Deal, craft unions had exclusive jurisdiction over particular skills within a given territory. Employers were not free to hire from outside the union hiring hall, having signed exclusive contracts with the union(s) involved. New employees were, in general, referred by existing employees to the hiring hall where they would begin an apprenticeship program administered within a particular area by a Joint Apprenticeship Program, subject to the Bureau of Apprenticeships and Training within the Department of Labor and made up of union and employer representatives. Apprenticeships for skilled trades generally took between three and five years. Furthermore, the parties ostensibly governed by Title VII of the 1964 Civil Rights Act were numerous. Construction contracts were generally given to a general contractor who subcontracted out most of the work to several specialized contractors. Thus the activities of various unions, several levels of contractor, the Joint Apprenticeship Programs and whatever federal, state, or local agencies were involved needed to be policed.[11]

Government action against recalcitrant contracting companies proved successful in the case of the Newport News Shipbuilding and Drydock Company in 1966, though a case could certainly be made that it was only because of very visible black pickets that the company agreed.[12] Though the Office of Federal Contract Compliance (OFCC) established a *pre-award* program for the construction industry only in May of 1966, it was not until the Philadelphia Plan was implemented that a true test of this new method of enforcement took place. Abortive plans were attempted in St. Louis, San Francisco, and Cleveland.[13]

In Philadelphia, an obscure interagency board—the Federal Executive Board—had the purpose of coordinating the disjointed programs of federal agencies in Philadelphia (similar boards existed in other U.S. cities). In the plan, the contract compliance committee would set no firm targets, as this would suggest illegal quotas. Instead there were ranges of 4 to 8 percent set for 1970, 9 to 15 percent for 1971, 14 to 20 percent for 1972, and 19 to 26 percent for 1973.[14] Contracts would be held up until bidders submitted detailed manning tables that listed by trade the specific numbers of minority workers they pledged to hire. The plan was attractive to the federal government because it was locally organized.[15]

There is little evidence that the plan was originally adopted as anything other than an emergency measure to reduce tension within some urban areas. Johnson's secretary of labor, Willard Wirtz, speaking to the AFL-CIO's Building and Construction Trades Department, promised them that Philadelphia was an exceptional case. John Macy, chairman of the Civil Service Commission, assured anxious members of Congress in January 1968 that "There are no intentions to implement such a plan on a nationwide scale."[16]

Legal scholar Peter Nash claims that 1,400 minority workers were brought into the Philadelphia area construction industry as a result of the first Philadelphia Plan.[17] However, when opposition to the plan grew, the federal government abandoned it. Johnson was diverted by an agreement between unions and federal agencies that occurred in early 1968. Construction unions, happy at the prospects of a building boom, agreed to train underqualified slum dwellers in new, government-funded "trainee" categories. The Philadelphia Plan was rescinded with the result that, according to Nash, "many of the 1,400 beneficiaries did not remain on Philadelphia area construction sites."[18]

Beside union resistance, the Johnson administration faced the opposition of Elmer Staats, the comptroller general of the United States, who ruled that post-award contractual stipulations were illegal and stated in November 1968 that all pre-award contractual requirements not specified would be disallowed. The Department of Labor failed to challenge the ruling.[19]

Nixon to the Rescue

Only the incoming Nixon administration saved the plan. To the surprise of civil rights activists, the new administration, elected eleven days before Staats handed down his ruling, made some efforts to resuscitate the plan. Secretary of labor-designate George P. Shultz announced to the Industrial Relations Research Association on December 30, 1968 that the nation's most important problem was black unemployment—above productivity, inflation, and industrial unrest. He spoke of the need for special measures and claimed that, in the new, straitened circumstances employers "cannot conduct business as usual."[20]

The new administration set to work to iron out the problems of the Philadelphia Plan. Black Republican entrepreneur Arthur Fletcher, assistant secretary of labor, was placed in charge. Labor Department hearings in Philadelphia occurred on August 26 and 27, 1969, after Fletcher had announced the new order on June 27. Confidently, Shultz announced on September 23 that other plans called "hometown solutions" would operate similarly to the Philadelphia Plan but would be tailored to the specific needs of cities. Opposition in Congress grew, however, particularly from the guardian subcommittee on Separation of Powers, headed by North Carolina Democrat Sam Ervin. Ervin and some cronies hatched a way of defeating the Philadelphia Plan by attaching a rider to a minor Senate appropriations bill that stated that no congressional appropriation would be available to finance, either directly or indirectly through any federal aid or grant, any contract or agreement which the comptroller general did not approve.

"Demonstrable Deeds" and the Battle in Congress

To today's reader, the most curious aspect of the debates on the Philadelphia Plan in both houses of Congress in December 1969 was the lack of discussion of affirmative action itself. Opponents focused on the implied appropriation of congressional powers. In his opening statement in the hearings, Ervin assured members that "During the next two days, our purpose will not be to debate the wisdom of the Philadelphia Plan."[21] Proponents of the Philadelphia Plan avoided discussions of the potential implications of the plan, preferring to discuss broad civil rights imperatives.

Nixon, while perhaps not paying attention to the minute details of the plan, was at least aware of it and certainly approved its implementation. On November 21, in his usual day-to-day meetings with his closest staff, Nixon mentioned the Philadelphia Plan as part of an effort to expand employment of the "hard core unemployed."[22] However, on December 18 the conservative forces launched a successful surprise attack in the Senate on the Philadelphia Plan.

The sides of the battle were confusing—the issue split both parties. Those supporting the rider (and thus opposing the Philadelphia Plan) included Southern Democrats, those with close ties to labor, Southern Republicans like Strom Thurmond of South Carolina and John Tower of Texas, as well as a string of non-Southern Republican conservatives like Barry Goldwater and Paul Fannin of Arizona who were concerned about the usurpation of congressional power by the White House. In opposition to the rider were Republican moderates like Bob Dole of Kansas, who would later defend affirmative action when standing as Republican candidate for president, Gerald Ford of Michigan, whose recent defense of affirmative action figured in the 2003 *Gratz v. Bollinger* Supreme Court decision, as well as progressives, Northern Democrats, and liberals.

Most liberals defended the Philadelphia Plan on the basis that the rider attacked all civil rights efforts by the federal government. As Republican senator

Jacob Javits of New York stated it, the question was "Why this 155 millimetre howitzer is used to knock off a small target, the Philadelphia Plan." Those liberals supporting the rider often did so because they supported or were sponsored by organized labor. Conservatives, while sometimes raising the stipulations in Title VII of the 1964 Civil Rights Act, usually decried the usurpation of congressional power by the executive branch of government. As Nebraska Republican Roman Hruska said, "[I]t is not only the Philadelphia Plan that is involved." Despite a concerted defense, those opposing the Philadelphia Plan triumphed in this first vote. By a vote of fifty-two to thirty-seven, the Senate voted that the rider was germane to the bill concerning Hurricane Camille.[23]

After these losses the Nixon forces were immediately galvanized into action. There is much evidence that Nixon became personally involved in the considerable effort dedicated to saving the Philadelphia Plan. Immediately after the Senate vote, he drew up plans to galvanize the civil rights movement in support of the Philadelphia Plan in an extracongressional campaign.[24] He also issued powerful statements opposing the rider. Unlike some of his allies in the Senate, Nixon made the Philadelphia Plan the focus of his defense and made no attempt to bargain with the conservatives, as he had earlier the same year over school desegregation. He opened his first statement to Congress on the subject with the contention that "the House of Representatives now faces an historic and critical civil rights vote." In the second of Nixon's statements to Congress, read out by Jerry Ford in the House, he defended the idea of the Philadelphia Plan in the name of taxpayers, white and black.[25]

By December 22, when the House debated the bill in its entirety, the pro-rider forces were on the defensive. It is worth noting that much of the civil rights support for the Philadelphia Plan was lukewarm, complaining that it was one of the more conservative measures that might be taken to strengthen civil rights. However, the pro-Nixon forces were successful in convincing most Democrats that the rider might have prevented *any* civil rights plan that used financial leverage to pressure public and private institutions into redressing civil rights concerns. Augustus Hawkins, a black Democratic Representative from California, opposing the rider, complained that the Nixon administration, rather than voting for Hawkins's bill to strengthen the powers of EEOC, "prefers to confuse the issue with a new and different approach unsupported by a single civil rights authority or organization." He continued, saying that "it must be understood that this plan is only one, and not necessarily the best of tools for opening opportunities."[26] Continuing but also confusing the metaphor, Bob Eckhardt of Texas expressed the frustrations of Democrats supporting a Republican initiative. "I grasp this small forceps even though it has been in the hands of the other party and there have been much larger tools and more effective ones that they have eschewed."[27]

At the end of the debate, those opposing the rider had 208 votes, those in favor 156. Republicans supported Nixon 124 to 41.[28] Though the bill was returned to the Senate the same day, the pro-rider forces had been soundly defeated. A roll-call vote to drop the rider succeeded.[29]

Order No. 4

Clearly, Shultz and the rest of the administration had initially expected little opposition to the Philadelphia Plan and saw the potential to make a distinctive contribution to civil rights based on the growing strength of the federal government in relation to contractors. In a Department of Labor press announcement released on September 23, 1969, Shultz confidently announced that "we expect the Plan developed for use in Philadelphia to provide useful general guidelines." "The Nixon Administration now has a civil rights vehicle" announced Fletcher.[30]

The enforcement process detailed in the order showed a continuum with more voluntary measures of the Johnson administration. The administration was determined to use sanctions only as a last option and that it expected compliance to be fairly automatic. First, there was "conference, conciliation, mediation and persuasion." Next, if that failed, employers would be issued a "show cause" order, asking them to show why action leading to debarment and contract termination should not be taken. Third, the employer would be issued with a notice of intent. Last, if all else failed, came contract termination and debarment from any more government contracts until "the contractor has established . . . personnel and employment policies in compliance with the provisions of" the executive order. Much of this process had been in place for over a decade.

According to Peter Nash, the OFCC simply seized upon an old compliance procedure included in the procurement procedure that had been included in the procurement regulations at the request of the vice president in 1956 whereby contracting officers are obliged to evaluate a prospective contractor's ability to comply with the equal opportunity clause. It had never been used because "there existed no standards against which to make such a determination." Order No. 4 remedied this problem. However, it is important to keep in mind that, as with the Philadelphia Plan, an employer needed only to show that a "good faith effort" had been made to achieve the goals that had been agreed upon.[31]

Shultz issued Order No. 4 on February 3, 1970. Published in the *Federal Register*, the new order required contractors to file an affirmative action program within 120 days of signing a contract. Employers' plans would identify the "underutilization" of blacks, Spanish-surnamed Americans, American Indians, and Asians. Such underutilization would be determined from, among other things, the "minimum population of the labor area surrounding the facility" and the "percentage of the minority work force as compared to the total work force." The contractor must indicate "specific goals and timetables" based on these criteria. The order included the Philadelphia Plan's insistence that contractors must only show that a "good faith effort" was made to achieve the goals.[32]

It is possible that this move was less an attempt to generalize the stipulations of the Philadelphia Plan than a defense against the charge of inconsistency from builders who were taking Shultz to court. Certainly, *The Wall Street Journal* cited a "knowledgeable source" who explained that this was the real reason behind the order. Whatever the case, no action was taken to ensure compliance with these stipulations outside of the construction industry until years after its implementation.[33]

Opposition to the Philadelphia Plan was so quiet that it was usually discussed openly as a "quota plan" even by its defenders. The *New York Times* reported blandly that "Allen [Dr. James E., U.S. Commissioner of Education] Bids School Aides Around Country Back Job Quotas for Minorities." Similarly, legal scholar James E. Jones, defending affirmative action programs in 1970, simply referred to "employment quotas." The term "quotas" was the common descriptor of affirmative action programs taken on by the government. Outside of congressional and union leadership circles, neither the term nor the policy excited any controversy whatsoever until late 1971.[34]

The Hometown Plans

An indication that the Nixon administration meant to pressurize rather than force contractors with the Philadelphia Plan is the emphasis it put on so-called "hometown plans" after the Plan was implemented. On January 25, 1970, the *New York Times* reported that a "hometown solution" had been created. Chicago had been, in late 1969, subject to black picketing of construction sites and thus had need of some sort of a solution. Interested parties, including the main contractors, city and state officials, and local civil rights activists had drafted a plan in response. The result, agreed upon by Shultz and Mayor Richard Daley, promised to provide four thousand new jobs a year for five years for minorities in private and public construction. Daley hailed it as "an example to the entire nation."[35]

The courts began imposing judgments specifying numbers of minorities to be hired in 1969, following the federal logic of the Philadelphia Plan. They also backed up these federal initiatives when they were challenged. However, they defended them as individual solutions to ameliorate tensions within the inner cities rather than as part of a definitive model of race relations. When a court instructed sheet metal workers unions to take a percentage of minority applicants for apprenticeships, it felt compelled to say that "we impose no quotas, we grant no preferences."[36] Judge Charles R. Weiner held that the Philadelphia Plan "does not require the contractors to hire a definite percentage of a minority group" and emphasized the call for a good faith effort defensible in court.[37] As Moreno notes, the court's defense against the charge that the Philadelphia Plan violated congressional intent centered on the fact of the construction industry's specificity. No new general model of affirmative action emerged with the Philadelphia Plan. It is instructive that the court made these arguments in 1971, long after order No. 4 was in effect. Rather than judicial activism, this was closing down escape routes for unions that defied what was still prodding—albeit a rather muscular and forceful prodding—by the federal government.[38]

On February 9, Shultz designated nineteen cities as targets for adoption of more hometown solutions, warning that they would have Philadelphia-type plans imposed upon them if they failed to come up with an acceptable hometown solution. On March 18, the *New York Times* reported hopefully that hometown plans had been implemented in Chicago, Pittsburgh, and Boston. "The more success such attempts achieve, the less need there will be for Philadelphia Plans and other forms of government compulsion."[39]

The hometown plans—or hometown solutions, as they were sometimes called—resembled previous business initiatives like those detailed in chapter 5 rather than government programs. Targets and goals were agreed upon by local parties before gaining the federal government's seal of approval and thus varied greatly from city to city. There were no sanctions imposed against those contractors not honoring the agreement. They *were* voluntary, proof that the Nixon administration still hoped to accomplish, just as Nixon had in the 1950s, the voluntary desegregation of American workplaces.

Nixon's Motives

As indicated on the first page of this book, Nixon's ruminations about the future of race relations in the United States began just days after his Philadelphia Plan victory in Congress. He was unsure of what he had accomplished with the Philadelphia Plan. It had been greeted as too little by civil rights advocates and as special punishment for unions by George Meany. Historians have pointed out the political motives Nixon had for backing the Philadelphia Plan. Presidential aide John D. Ehrlichman remembered that Nixon thought Shultz had shown "great style" in devising a plan that divided two stalwarts of the Democratic Party: blacks and labor. On this issue, as Ehrlichman observed, the AFL-CIO and the NAACP would be locked in combat, leaving the Nixon administration in the "sweet and reasonable middle."[40]

But the Philadelphia Plan also threatened to split the "southern strategy's" core coalition of Republicans and Southern Democrats. Though it undoubtedly set core Democratic constituencies against each other, neither did it unite the Republican Party. As Nixon ruefully commented to a news summary shortly after the administration's victory in Congress, "(w)hile our 'Libs' won't agree this hurts us with our constituency—we gained little on the play."[41]

Nixon also employed what John D. Skrentny has called "the politics of preemption."[42] John Finney of the *New York Times*, in a piece published in February 1970, used the word preemption when characterizing the first year of the administration. It had, he said, shrewdly succeeded in "taking away or neutralizing every issue that might be exploited by the Democrats."[43] In attempting to neutralize attacks from liberal and radical quarters, Nixon did not forget the right wing of his constituency. But attorney general John Mitchell's widely reported maxim—"watch what we do, not what we say"—applied not just to the administration's dealings with the South.[44] And, as speechwriter William Safire once said of Mitchell, Nixon "saw the need to lean right when you were moving left, taking as many conservative friends with you as possible when you had to go in a progressive position."[45]

By concentrating too much on Nixon's political motives it is possible to miss other more immediately compelling reasons to at least augment the doubtful political gains of the plan. The racial violence that flared up in cities like Philadelphia, though nowhere near the level seen in previous summers, took place near construction sites.[46] Mayor Joseph Barr had ordered all construction work shut down for two weeks only to face counterdemonstrations by disgruntled construction workers.[47]

In 1967, the Kerner Commission Report had recommended stronger enforcement of Executive Order 11246 and for revisions to it "particularly as regards labor unions."[48] There were also economic reasons. Construction workers saw 14 percent wage increases in 1969 and, in September of that year, Nixon called for an increase in manpower training and vocational education "in order to achieve a major increase in needed skilled labor for the construction industry. A shortage of skilled manpower is at the root of many problems faced by this industry." Later the same month he responded to a question at a press conference about the proposed Philadelphia Plan by saying "it is essential that black Americans, all Americans, have an equal opportunity to get into the construction unions. There is a shortage in construction workers." The Philadelphia Plan might have been seen as a useful tool to lower the cost of construction labor.[49]

The apparent insignificance of the plan within the wider context of the time renders moot, to some extent, the issue of Nixon's immediate motives in sponsoring it. In 1969-1970, few within or outside the Nixon administration found anything interesting about the issue of preferential treatment in employment.[50] The contentious issue of 1969–1970, reflecting the fact that hopes were still invested in education as a tool for the creation of black equality, was school desegregation. After the *Green* and *Alexander* Supreme Court decisions, Nixon's foot-dragging on forcing southern school districts to desegregate dominated the headlines in 1969 and early 1970, especially after the departure of Leon Panetta, then a liberal Republican lawyer in the Office of Civil Rights within Health, Education, and Welfare. Few had even heard of the Philadelphia Plan.[51]

A response from the Nixon administration to criticism from the Congressional Black Caucus in early 1971 failed to mention the Plan.[52] Occasionally, either Nixon or one of his aides would complain that no one had heard of the Philadelphia Plan. In March 1970 Nixon scrawled in the margins of a memo concerning efforts to publicize civil rights efforts of the administration: "I believe the record is impressive on things done (Phil plan etc.) + things (Family Assistance)." Reflecting the perception that the Philadelphia Plan was buried within other news, Leonard Garment also suggested later in the year a plan to publicize the administration's civil rights efforts with the "Philadelphia Plan Revisited." He mentions "hometown solutions," a "major Department of Labor effort" now functioning in 102 cities.[53]

Generally speaking, discussion of the issues of preferences, quotas, and affirmative action was nearly nonexistent at the time. The issues made little impact in the *New York Times*. In 1970 the Philadelphia Plan received mention in the paper (mostly in relation to the hometown plan in New York) each month until October. In 1971, the plan received mention only five times. In 1970 or 1971 the terms "affirmative action" or "quotas" did not attract enough attention to merit an index category.[54]

The Democrats Attack Affirmative Action

Proving how different the context in which the issue was raised in 1972, the *New York Times* reported in September 1971 that the Democrats were willing to outlaw preferential hiring altogether in exchange for cease and desist powers for EEOC. To win the support of Democratic Representative Edith Green of Oregon, who, according to the *New York Times*, maintained a substantial following among conservative Democrats, Democratic leaders agreed to sponsor three crucial amendments.[55] One of them would have prevented

EEOC from imposing hiring quotas or requiring preferences. Made by Democratic Congressman John H. Dent of Pennsylvania, it stated that "All authority, functions, and responsibilities vested in the Secretary of Labor pursuant to Executive Order 11246 . . . are transferred to the Equal Employment Opportunities Commission. The Commission shall be prohibited from imposing or requiring a quota or preferential treatment with respect to numbers of employees or percentages of employees of any race, color, religion, or national origin."[56] Dent made it clear that this meant goals, too. "If I did nothing else in this law but wipe out the contract compliance feature and put it under the jurisdiction of EEOC . . . then I would have done sufficiently (sic)."[57] As the *New York Times* noted, this "would rule out the so-called Philadelphia Plan."[58]

In an interesting debate indicating the ideological confusion at that time over the issue of affirmative action, Augustus Hawkins, cosponsor of the bill, had accepted Dent's amendment as one of three to his bill, HR1746. He attacked the Philadelphia Plan as he had in the debate over it in 1969: "In the first year of the operation do you know how many blacks got jobs? Less than 100. Do you know how many women have gotten jobs in the history of the Philadelphia Plan? Not one."[59] Edith Green, who had been a civil rights activist during the 1950s and early 1960s, also attacked quotas. Left-leaning black representative Shirley Chisolm tried to calm the waters, justifying her support for HR1746 by saying that the power to issue cease and desist orders will allow EEOC to "make construction workers and other groups do that which they have to do in order to be able to prevent preferential treatment."[60]

Some who might have voted against HR1746 without the amendment were swayed by the efforts of the Democrats. Most conservatives, however, worried more about what an empowered EEOC might do than about affirmative action programs. HR1746 lost the day. When the substitute Republican-sponsored bill came before the Senate, Sam Ervin, the primary force against the Philadelphia Plan in 1969, failed to raise the forces needed to turn back the Equal Employment Opportunities Act. His amendment that would have banned all agents of reverse discrimination (including, rather awkwardly, the judiciary), lost, twenty-two to forty-four, indicating that the forces that had fought against the Philadelphia Plan were, by 1972, considerably weakened.[61]

The Failures of the Philadelphia Plan and the Hometown Solutions

Beside being fairly obscure at the time, the Philadelphia Plan and the "hometown solutions" could be not counted as successes in their own terms. Jill Quadagno indicates that, for the intended beneficiaries of the plans, they had been successes: "Yet the Philadelphia Plan worked. Through the early 1970s the Philadelphia Plan was implemented in cities throughout the country. Minority representation in the skilled craft unions increased significantly during this period." She additionally stated that: "Hiring practices among federal contractors also experienced an enormous shift. In 1966 the workforce of federal contractors was disproportionately white; by 1974 their workforce had become disproportionately black."[62] Similarly, Nixon historian Dean Kotlowski announced that "Under the Philadelphia Plan, the most famous imposed plan, with its threats and incentives, contractors exceeded federal hiring goals." However, he cited the authority of the *Department of Labor News*, hardly an unbiased source. The quote by a Filipino electrician, included by Kotlowski with apparently unintentional irony, gives some indication of the numbers involved: "I think it's working. There are three of us here as a result."[63]

All the evidence, however, seems to contradict Quadagno's and Kotlowski's assertions. Neither the Philadelphia Plan nor the hometown plans worked. Certainly (and as Kotlowski notes), the hometown plans were near catastrophic. The Chicago Plan that Mayor Daley had hailed as "an example to the entire nation," the first of the hometown plans, failed to live up to Daley's (or, more to the point, black Chicagoans') expectations. Within eight months, the Civil Rights Commission complained that there were only seventy-five minority members in any of the training programs set out in the Chicago Plan, the *Washington Post* spoke of the "disarray" of the Chicago Plan and Herbert Hill, one of its architects, flatly called it a "failure."[64] Some months later it collapsed amid a financial scandal in which the plan's director, Alderman Fred Hubbard, disappeared and was later accused of embezzling more than $100,000 in federal funds designated for the program.[65]

Some problems were common to all of the hometown plans. Relations between the various groups effected by the plans, while only occasionally as rancorous as those between blacks and white construction workers in Seattle, were difficult. For example, in Chicago, a new plan launched in July of 1972, which promised to hire more than ten thousand minorities for construction jobs by 1975, had to be scuttled when one of the local black groups, the Coalition for United Community Action, and a Spanish-speaking group, the Spanish Coalition for Jobs, protested that their position within the plan was not equal to that of the Urban League. Two months later, the plan was resuscitated but, after nine months of the plan being in operation, the Urban League pulled out, complaining about the refusal of unions and contractors to uphold the targets set for them. Finally, in January of 1974, an imposed plan was installed.[66]

Beside the imposition of Philadelphia Plan-style plans in five cities, the number of the original 102 cities with "functioning" hometown plans had dwindled to 45 in April 1972. Throughout the early months of 1972 Assistant Secretary of Labor Richard J. Grunewald traveled the country relaunching hometown plans. By July there were fifty federally approved plans with cities such as Peoria, Illinois, promising to reserve 158 construction jobs for minorities over the next five years.[67] In 1973 OFCC conducted what it termed a comprehensive audit of the voluntary plans then in practice. It found that in terms of "placement credits" (OFCC's term for the successful placement of minority workers in construction jobs,) 3,243 had been achieved against total goals and targets of 6,573. Four out of forty plans attained or exceeded their targets but, in two of those, individual participating trades had failed. As the Civil Rights Commission observed, many of the 3,243 "worked only thirty days or slightly longer." The Commission concluded its assessment of the audit reports by saying that "(t)he audit results almost certainly exaggerate the achievements, if any, of the plans."[68]

Imposed Plans

The Congressional Black Caucus, the U.S. Civil Rights Commission, Arthur Fletcher, and other civil rights interests felt that all the plans should be made involuntary.[69] But the imposed plans fared little better than the voluntary ones. Again, problems ensued that had bedeviled the hometown plans. The first was that, because of the way the construction industry worked, results would not pour in quickly if they poured in at all. Apprentices took three to five years to learn a trade before they could become qualified, might drop out before their apprenticeships were complete, and had no guarantee they would become qualified journeymen. An indication of this problem can be seen in Chicago where seventy-five minority members were accepted on training programs. Of the forty-six that were placed in on-the-job training, only five were employed in 1974.[70]

There were only two ways, given limited resources, of measuring success or lack of it. First, contractors could report how many minority "man-hours" had been worked as opposed to all hours worked. There were several problems inherent to this method of monitoring. It relied on the honesty of the contractors in reporting accurately. Because of the specifications on the forms used, the term *minority* was not broken down into its constituent parts.[71] It was favored by Department of Labor press releases probably because results could be made to look favorable even if they were insignificant. For instance, one press release in December 1973 reported that in Philadelphia, out of 3,818 hours worked by plumbers and pipefitters during a ten-month period, 852 of them had been by minorities. This made up 22 percent, within the range of targets and goals of 20 to 24 percent set by the Philadelphia Plan. However, when taking into account the estimated average for the construction industry at that time of 39.1 hours per week, the total minority employment was equivalent to *one* unspecified "minority" person working half of the ten-month period.[72]

The second method of monitoring employed by OFCC was a count, made on-site on a specific day. Difficulties also existed here. First, the visit was arranged. Some contractors, it was reported, employed a method of avoiding an accurate count by "motorcycling"—sending a minority worker from site to site—or by "checkerboarding"—sending all minority employees to federally financed projects (the only ones inspected by OFCC officials). Richard Rowan and Lester Rubin, who conducted a study of the effectiveness of the involuntary Washington, D.C. plan, observed: "Minorities are not being left on the bench when contractors need them for compliance purposes. . . . [R]elatively few minorities are being used to meet man-hour goals and that permit-holders—not new union members—are being used to meet the requirements."[73]

Not surprisingly, few sanctions were imposed, despite ensuing problems in the imposed plans. By September 1970 it had been reported that "violation of the Philadelphia Plan is very wide-spread."[74] But OFCC's movement toward effective sanctions proved tortuous. Debarment actions were initiated against seven companies. Seven notices of intent to impose sanctions were sent in 1970. Yet, by September 1971 an OFCC memorandum revealed that "these sanctions [cancellation of contracts and debarment] have never been used in the construction industry."[75] By July 1975 only six construction contractors had ever been debarred or had agreed to consent decrees. All but one of the debarment orders had been lifted by August 1974. Not that the situation in Philadelphia had changed—it was still included on the list of imposed plans in March 1975.[76] As the *Chicago Tribune,* perhaps indulging in a bit of *schadenfreude* after the debacle of Chicago's hometown plan, remarked in 1972, the Philadelphia Plan "nominally had sanctions that in the event proved unenforceable."[77]

Contraction of Construction

Though it might be argued that black Americans gained symbolically by the appearance of minority laborers on construction sites, few of the badly-needed jobs materialized. Any advance in the interests of unemployed black youth came in the thousands when the problem was properly measured in the millions. Over one year in operation, the Philadelphia Plan gained forty-one jobs for minorities on construction sites while the black unemployment rate remained at 12 percent. The hometown plans, numbering over a hundred and covering whole states in some instances resulted in a little over three thousand job placements by 1973—hardly enough to cheer the millions of unemployed and underemployed African Americans.[78] In terms of participation in the referral units in building trade unions, there was little progress. Between 1970 and 1972 the number of black union members rose by 3 percent. However, the total proportion of blacks within building trade unions did not change.[79]

Far more effective in the construction industry than affirmative action programs was the onset of recession and "stagflation." The great expectations expressed earlier collapsed. In 1969 NAACP national labor director Herbert Hill noted of the construction industry: "It is a huge industry with vast growth potential. . . . The estimate of the U.S. Department of Labor that the construction industry will require one million more workers by 1975 may be most conservative."[80] By May 1971 the *New York Times* reported a "slowdown in housing construction and purchase." The national unemployment rate grew to 4.8 percent—the highest in five years—and among inner-city blacks in Philadelphia the rate was over 12 percent. The open shop share of construction workers doubled from 20 percent in 1968 to 1975. Union membership—and a guarantee of decent wages—was also declining. In 1970 construction workers had been among the highest paid workers. By the end of the decade their weekly earnings declined by more than 12 percent. By 1974 unemployment among all construction workers had skyrocketed to 12.4 percent.[81] Instead of blacks moving up to participate on an equal level with whites in a high-paying industry, the entire industry declined so much that the unemployment level within it matched that of inner-city blacks.[82]

Beginning in 1970 Nixon began to direct civil rights efforts toward the black community outside of the ghettos, the subject of chapter 8. Nixon initiatives like the Philadelphia Plan and the hometown solutions—aimed at ghetto employment as they were—could not be dropped but could be left to languish after their enforcement proved complicated. Though other civil rights initiatives fared reasonably well, the Philadelphia Plan and the other hometown solutions effectively disappeared. In early 1974, Paul Delaney of the *New York Times* commented that "(m)inorities, especially blacks, had seen one of the Administration's main efforts in civil rights—the various plans to put minorities in construction jobs—die for lack of enforcement."[83]

Conclusion

The Philadelphia Plan was an important but transitional phase of affirmative action, a landmark in the journey between voluntaristic affirmative action of the Myrdalian era and subsequent enforced affirmative action. Its importance has not so much been overstated as misunderstood. The debate in Congress stands as a historical record of the final destruction of those institutions that had in the past prevented serious consideration of affirmative action. But its full implications emerged only later.

The Philadelphia Plan was certainly not intended to be the model for new policy. It was, of course, originally a Johnson administration program and, in its assumption of permanent job growth and the hope that it would set an example that would result in voluntary efforts by companies, it shares more with the Great Society than with the affirmative action of today. However, even within these terms it was a conservative measure, a cheap alternative to the more elaborate efforts at creating African-American equality, at best a very small victory in what was then still a considerable drive for civil rights.

The Philadelphia Plan was itself doomed to failure *because* it was a transitional phase. The Philadelphia and hometown plans were still subject to debate. Goals and targets were hammered out in smoky public meeting attended by union officials, civil rights groups who were as often at odds with each other more than the unions, and public officials. Much posturing and little progress took place. Any signs of underrepresentation could be seen on building sites and could result in a picket by civil rights groups. Unions might strike if they felt the burden too onerous. Thus, plans that completely did away with any of the old institutional impediments—including civil rights groups and unions—might be more promising. They, and Nixon's conscious move away from the ghettos in 1970, are the subject of the next chapter.

Notes

1. Thomas J. Sugrue, "Affirmative Action from Below: Civil Rights, the Building Trades, and the Politics of Racial Equality in the Urban North, 1945–1969," *The Journal of American History* 91, no. 1 (June 2004): 145–73.

2. Jill Quadagno, *The Color of Welfare: How Racism Undermined the War on Poverty* (New York: Oxford University Press, 1994), 80.

3. Hugh Davis Graham, *The Civil Rights Era: Origins and Development of National Policy, 1960–1972* (New York: Oxford University Press, 1990), 412.

4. The Black Caucus, in a report issued on April 16 1971, labeled the Philadelphia Plan a "cruel delusion" to black construction workers. See Black Caucus Report and Reviews [6 of 6] [CFOA 463], box 47, WHCF: SMOF: Garment, NPMP.

5. Herbert Hill, "The Construction Industry: Evading the Law," *Civil Rights Digest: Quarterly Publication of the United States Civil Rights Commission* (Washington D.C.: U.S. GPO, April 1975), 78; U.S. Civil Rights Commission (USCRC), *Federal Civil Rights Enforcement* (Washington, D.C., U.S. GPO, September 1970), 209.

6. See Byron E. Shafer, *Quiet Revolution: The Struggle for the Democratic Party and the Shaping of Post-Reform Politics* (New York: Russell Sage Foundation, 1983).

7. James E. Jones, Jr., "The Bugaboo of Employment Quotas," *Wisconsin Law Review* 27 (1970): 341–403, esp. 343.

8. The 1964 Civil Rights Act, Section 703(j), Title VII, expressly outlawed the imposition of employment quotas of minorities or anyone else. See Robert P. Schuwerk, "The Philadelphia Plan: A Study in the Dynamics of Executive Power," *University of Chicago Law Review* 39 (1971–1972): 723–60.

9. Jones, "The Bugaboo of Employment Quotas," 343–45; Schuwerk, "The Philadelphia Plan," 739–40; Graham, *The Civil Rights Era*, 287–90.

10. See Kevin L. Yuill, "The 1966 White House Conference," *Historical Journal* 41, no. 1 (May 1998): 259–82.

11. See chapter 7, "The Construction Industry Problem" in Alfred Blumrosen, *Black Employment and the Law* (New Brunswick, NJ: Rutgers University Press, 1971), 304–27.

12. See chapter 8, "The Newport News Agreement" in Blumrosen, *Black Employment and the Law*, 328–407.

13. USCRC, *Federal Civil Rights Enforcement* (1970), 39–41; Jones, "The Bugaboo of Employment Quotas," 343–46; Graham, *Civil Rights Era*, 278–87.

14. Schuwerk, "The Philadelphia Plan," 742; USCRC, *Federal Civil Rights Enforcement* (1970), 41; Jones, "The Bugaboo of Employment Quotas," 347–48; Graham, *Civil Rights Era*, 278–87.

15. Ibid.

16. Graham, *Civil Rights Era*, 290–91.

17. Nash, "Affirmative Action under Executive Order 11,246," 233–34.

18. Nash, "Affirmative Action under Executive Order 11,246," 234; Graham, *Civil Rights Era*, 294–95.

19. USCRC, *Federal Civil Rights Enforcement* (Washington, D.C.: U.S. GPO, 1969) 143; Graham, *Civil Rights Era*, 290.

20. Graham, *Civil Rights Era*, 323.

21. *Congressional Record (CR)*, 91st Congress, Vol. 115, 40039.

22. Handwritten notes on yellow lined pad, dated 11/21, read "Schultz—collective bargaining—govt. attitude—long range urges expansion of employment of hard core unemployed. Phil. Plan." H-Notes July–December 1969 [October–December, 1969] part II, Haldeman Notes: box 40, WHSF: SMOF: Haldeman: Haldeman Notes.

23. *CR*, 91st Congress, Vol. 115, 39966.

24. John D. Skrentny, *The Ironies of Affirmative Action: Politics, Culture, and Justice in America* (London: University of Chicago Press, 1996), 205.

25. Cited by Gerald Ford in *CR*, 91st Congress, Vol. 115, 40906. See also Schuwerk, "The Philadelphia Plan," 749.

26. *CR*, 91st Congress, Vol. 115, 40917. Later in the debate, a cable from the Civil Rights Commission was inserted into the CR opposing the rider (as was one from Americans for Democratic Action). *CR*, 91st Congress, Vol. 115, 40921.

27. *CR*, 91st Congress, Vol. 115, 40920.

28. *CR*, 91st Congress, Vol. 115, 40921.

29. *CR*, 91st Congress, Vol. 115, 40743.

30. Department of Labor press release, "Statement by Secretary Shultz on Philadelphia Plan Guidelines," September 23, 1969; and "For Backgrounder on the Philadelphia Plan Vote," no date, Philadelphia Plan [2 of 2] [CFOA 1265], box 143, WHCF: SMOF: Garment, NPMP.

31. Nash, "Affirmative Action Under Executive Order 11,246," 250, 253. Herbert Hill criticized this aspect of the Plan in "The Construction Industry: Evading the Law," 22–36.

32. Graham, *Civil Rights Era*, 342.

33. "In Brief," *The Wall Street Journal*, January 30, 1970, 1.

34. "Allen Bids School Aides Around Country Back Job Quotas," *New York Times*, February 15, 1970, 3; Jones, "The Bugaboo of Employment Quotas."

35. USCRC, *The Federal Civil Rights Enforcement Effort* (1970), 205–07.

36. *United States v. Sheet Metal Workers* (1969), cited in Schuwerk, "The Philadelphia Plan," 760.

37. Moreno, *From Direct Action to Affirmative Action*, 263.

38. Moreno cites *Local 53, International Association of Heat and Frost Insulators and Asbestos Workers v. Vogler*, 59 L.C. 9195 (1969) as the first "quota ordered by a federal court under the Civil Rights Act" (259). Again, there is no evidence that this court decision was not intended simply as a single decision pertinent only to this union. It ordered a union to make referrals on a one-to-one, black-white ratio as affirmative action relief, forbidding "preferential treatment." See Moreno, *From Direct Action to Affirmative Action*, 264, 259.

39. Editorial, *New York Times*, March 18, 1970, 46.

40. John D. Ehrlichman, *Witness to Power: The Nixon Years* (New York: Simon and Schuster, 1982), 228–29.

41. January 13, 1970, news summaries—January 1970, box 31, POF: ANS, NPMP. See also Graham, *Civil Rights Era*, 340.

42. Skrentny entitles one of his chapters "The Politics of Preemption." See *The Ironies of Affirmative Action*, 177–219.

43. Cited in "The Administration's First Year—Editorial and Column Reaction," February 13, 1970, PR 16-3 Presidential News Analysis [1969–1970], box 54, WHSF: WHCF: Subject Files: Confidential Files 1969–1974, NPMP. Moynihan also used the term "preempt" in a memo for the president from Moynihan, November 25, 1969, president's handwriting, November 1969, WHSF: POF, NPMP.

44. Cited in William Safire, *Before the Fall: An Inside View of the Pre-Watergate White House* (New York: Doubleday and Co., 1975), 265.

45. Safire, *Before the Fall*, 266.

46. See Sugrue, "Affirmative Action From Below," Graham, *Civil Rights Era*, 335–36. In Pittsburgh in August 1969, a clash took place in which fifty blacks and twelve policemen were injured.

47. "A Rush of Action to Get More Jobs For Negroes," *U.S. News and World Report*, September 15, 1969, 67–68.

48. Memo to the Commission from Ginsburg, November 7, 1967, plus attached "Survey Paper on Short-Term Domestic Program Options," no date, National Advi-

sory Commission on Civil Disorders—Records, November 1967, box 465, Brooke Papers, LOC.

49. Statement on the Construction Industry. September 4, 1969, the president's news conference of September 26, 1969, *PPPUS: Richard Nixon, 1969* (Washington, D.C.: U.S. GPO: 1970).

50. Nixon, according to former Nixon administration staff member Bradley H. Patterson, told the EEOC that there would be "no quotas" while he was president. However, several documents indicate that the term quota was used—apparently unproblematically—to refer to various programs connected to civil rights. See, for example, *The Nixon Administration Civil Rights Report*, which, among its boasts about Nixon's civil rights accomplishments, states that: "The Civil Service has approved a modified quota hiring system for blacks, Spanish-speaking Americans, and American indians (sic) for government jobs." [Ex] HU2 Equality—Beginning 4/2/69, box 3, White House Central Files: Subject Files: HU [Ex] HU, NPMP.

51. Of course, the Department of Health, Education, and Welfare (HEW), for which Panetta worked, did not deal with employment. But Panetta's book makes very clear that school desegregation made headlines while affirmative action did not. See generally Leon E. Panetta and Peter Gall, *Bring Us Together: The Nixon Team and Civil Rights* (New York: J. B. Lippincott Company, 1971).

52. Draft response dictated by Ray Price 5/17/71, Black Caucus Report and Reviews [2 of 6] [CFOA 463], box 47, WHCF: SMOF: Garment, NPMP.

53. Memorandum for the president from Ehrlichman, March 9, 1970, president's handwriting: January 16–31, 1970, box 5, WHSF: POF: President's Handwriting, NPMP. See also memo to the president from Garment, November 23, 1970, [Ex] HU2 Equality—Beginning 4/2/69, box 3, WHCF: Subject Files HU [Ex] HU, NPMP. The downside, Garment explained, would be that George Meany, president of the AFL-CIO, might grumble. Nixon, by that stage busily courting labor with the 1972 election in mind, scotched Garment's idea.

54. See *Index to the New York Times*, 1970 (New York: New York Times Publications, 1971), *Index* 1971 (1972) and *Index* 1972 (1973).

55. "EEOC Bill Compromise," *New York Times*, September 16, 1971, 16.

56. *CR*, 92nd Congress, Vol. 117, part 24, September 15, 1971, 31984.

57. *CR*, 92nd Congress, Vol. 117, 32089.

58. Herman Belz has argued that the choice was between two different ways of administering quotas but the amendment, both in letter and spirit, would have outlawed affirmative action. Herman Belz, *Equality Transformed: A Quarter-Century of Affirmative Action* (London: Transaction Publishers, 1992), 74.

59. *CR*, 92nd Congress, Vol. 117, 32100.

60. *CR*, 92nd Congress, Vol. 117, 39021.

61. Graham, *Civil Rights Era*, 443.

62. Quadagno, *The Color of Welfare*, 80. Her source, Russell K. Schutt, examines black employment in craft unions from 1967–1973 and points to the period before the Philadelphia Plan as the most crucial. See "Craft Unions and Minorities: Determinants of Change in Admission Practices," *Social Problems* 34, no. 4, (October 1987): 388–400.

63. Dean Kotlowski, *Nixon's Civil Rights: Politics, Principle, and Policy* (London: Harvard University Press, 2001), 111.

64. USCRC, *The Federal Civil Rights Enforcement Effort* (1970), 209.

65. "New Jobs Plan: 10,000 Quota Promised For Minorities," *Chicago Tribune,* July 17, 1972, I, 2.

66. "Jobs Plan Scrapped," *Chicago Tribune,* July 18, 1972, I, 2. See also the *Chicago Tribune* editorial July 20, 1972, I, 14. Hill, "The Construction Industry: Evading the Law," 33.

67. "U.S. Approves Chicago Plan," *Chicago Tribune,* January 12, 1972, I, 1, and "Peoria Job Plan Gets Federal OK," *Chicago Tribune,* July 28, 1972, I, 2.

68. USCRC, *The Challenge Ahead: Equal Opportunity in Unions* (Washington, D.C.: U.S. GPO, May 1976), 173, 176, 179. See also Robert W. Glover and Ray Marshall, "The Response of Unions in the Construction Industry to Antidiscrimination Efforts" in Leonard Hausman et al., *Equal Rights and Industrial Relations* (Madison, WI: Industrial Relations Research Association, 1977), 120–40. They argue that the hometown plans were ineffective.

69. Black Caucus Spring 1971 Report and Reviews I [1 of 3] [CFOA 10172], box 48, WHCF: SMOF: Garment, NPMP. See the USCRC report, *The Federal Civil Rights Enforcement Effort: A Reassessment* (Washington, D.C.: U.S. GPO, 1973) and Arthur Fletcher, *The Silent Sell-Out: Government Betrayal of Blacks to the Craft Unions* (New York: The Third Press, 1974).

70. Hill, "The Construction Industry: Evading the Law," 27.

71. USCRC, *The Federal Civil Rights Enforcement Effort: A Reassessment* (Washington, D.C., U.S. GPO, 1973), 74.

72. USCRC, *The Challenge Ahead,* 290. Schuwerk states that the goals were 19 to 26 percent for this year. See Schuwerk, "The Philadelphia Plan," 742.

73. Cited in USCRC, *The Challenge Ahead,* 196. Many of the early assessments of the Plan discuss the problem of motorcycling. See Schuwerk, "The Philadelphia Plan," 751. Nash also mentions the problem and includes a section on the specific problems encountered in Washington, D.C. Nash, "Affirmative Action Under Executive Order 11,246," 241-43.

74. USCRC, *Federal Civil Rights Enforcement* (1970), 209.

75. Cited in Hill, "The Construction Industry: Evading the Law," 28.

76. USCRC, *The Challenge Ahead,* 166, 7. Jonathon Leonard claimed that "enforcement did become more aggressive in 1973" in his oft-quoted article, "The Impact of Affirmative Action on Employment," *Social Forces* 2, no. 4 (October 1984): 388–401, esp. 392. But by the end of 1976 only twelve companies in total had ever been barred from holding federal contracts under the power invested by the OFCC in EO 11246. USCRC, *The State of Civil Rights 1976* (Washington, D.C.: U.S. GPO, February 15, 1977), 17.

77. "Jobs Plan Scrapped," *Chicago Tribune.*

78. Rhode Island and Delaware had plans that covered state rather than metropolitan areas.

79. United States Equal Employment Opportunities Commission (EEOC), *Minorities and Women in Referral Units in Building Trade* (Washington, D.C.: U.S. GPO, 1972), 20.

80. Herbert Hill, "Employment, Manpower Training, and the Black Worker," *Journal of Negro Education* 38, issue 3, American Minority Groups and Contemporary Education (Summer 1969): 204–17, esp. 210.

81. As Schuwerk noted, the Philadelphia Plan was based on estimates of "continued growth in the crafts in question, an assumption that time has found to be unwarranted." Schuwerk, "The Philadelphia Plan," 742–43.

82. "Economic Slowdown Hampers Programs to Aid Poor in Cities," *New York Times*, May 21, 1970, 1; News Report, *New York Times*, March 8, 1970, 2; Edwin L. Dale, Jr., "Rate of Job Growth Remains Sluggish," *New York Times*, January 10, 1970, 15; Quadagno, *Color of Welfare*, 84.

83. Paul Delaney, "US is Spurring Efforts to Fight Job Prejudice," *New York Times*, January 19, 1974, 43.

8

Revenue Sharing and
Other Affirmative Actions

THE FACT THAT NIXON RESCUED the Philadelphia Plan is jarring enough for historians, political scientists, and pundits. That his administration set up the regulatory machinery behind most affirmative action plans of today may prize them from the idea that Nixon's involvement with affirmative action was anomalous, an exception. The Philadelphia Plan was not the only move the Nixon administration made in the direction of affirmative action in its modern sense.

Other experimental programs, easier to implement and less controversial—at least at first—than the Philadelphia Plan, became the model upon which affirmative action operated. These programs were either implemented directly by the Nixon administration or were the result of increases in regulatory pressure by it. They rose in importance when Nixon himself consciously changed the direction of civil rights policy in 1970 from focusing on the ghetto to shoring up the black middle class. Not only was affirmative action not an anomaly, but its rise came, in part, because of the intervention of the thirty-seventh president. This reinterpretation of the purpose of federal civil rights policies cast new light on programs developed during the Great Society and Nixon's first year in office, causing some to grow, like affirmative action in colleges, white-collar work places, and contracts, and others to wither and die. This chapter discusses first, the specific policy mechanisms with which the Nixon administration influenced affirmative action policy, and second, the administration's change of approach to all civil rights policies in 1970.

The Other Affirmative Action Programs

These other policies were not debated in Congress and remained, for the large part, low profile, though they greatly benefited from the apparent legitimacy given them by the successful justification and defense of the Philadelphia Plan. They—not the Philadelphia Plan—set the pattern of modern affirmative action plans in that they were not the result of long, complex, and public negotiations between various local groups of Americans, like the Philadelphia Plan and the hometown plans. They did not emerge from the pressure of pickets by civil rights groups. Instead, they used the enormous and increasing financial muscle of the federal government as leverage. Instead of assisting ghetto residents, they aimed at creating and providing a stable existence for a new black middle class made up of what were then extremely alienated elements.

Reinterpreting EO 11246

One quiet but important initiative by the Nixon administration in 1969 involved a move to reinterpret Executive Order 11246, signed by Johnson on September 23, 1965. EO 11246 required contractors with the federal government to agree not to discriminate in employment on the basis of race, color, religion, sex, or national origin (a 1967 EO superseding 11246 included women alongside minorities). Part III of the order also required recipients of federal financial assistance to require nondiscrimination clauses in construction contracts financed by federal assistance. Though the order had specified any "applicant for federal assistance" for whom "any grant, contract, loan, insurance, or guarantee" might be given, this language appeared in a section dealing with construction contracts and, presumably, referred to areas given grants by the federal government to finance construction. In the four years since the order was issued, it had been applied only to procurement-type contracts and not to grants, loans, guarantees, or other arrangements for federal financial assistance.[1]

Assistant Attorney General Jerris Leonard, then head of the Office of Civil Rights within the Department of Justice, wrote to Attorney General John Mitchell on February 22, 1969 asking him to write to heads of departments that granted financial assistance. Leonard wished to extend the rules on nondiscrimination governing federal contractors to *all* recipients of any sort of federal aid—grant and loan recipients rather than simply contractors. Existing statutory authority could be used to provide "an administrative enforcement mechanism . . . which could be enforced on a day to day basis." The program was originally simply a stop-gap plan, because Leonard felt that court proceedings were normally the best method of enforcement. However, "the sanction of cutting off funds from state and local agencies would also be available, if needed." The proposal provided "a vehicle by which the federal government could enforce the existing constitutional obligation."[2]

On April 14, 1969 Mitchell sent the proposal with his recommendation to Nixon's urban advisor, Daniel Patrick Moynihan, senior counsel to the president Arthur Burns, and congressional liaison Bryce Harlow, among others. Harlow and Burns objected to the proposal on the basis of congressional opposition; Moynihan "wholeheartedly" supported the proposal. Assistant Attorney General (and later, Supreme Court Chief Justice) William H. Rehnquist's office inveighed against the proposal. Rehnquist's assistant, Richard K. Berg, spotted the importance of extending EO 11246 to all recipients of federal government money. Though supportive of the proposal as a whole, Berg argued for a strictly constitutional perspective on 11246 on the basis that the obligation to take affirmative action "has not, to our knowledge, ever received a precise administrative or judicial interpretation, but its inclusion in the passage would certainly appear to denote some broadening of the present legal duties of the affected state and local agencies."[3] Whether Nixon was directly involved in the final decision of whether or not to extend the remit of 11246 (or, as Rehnquist's office had requested, to get rid of affirmative action altogether) is unclear from the correspondence. In any case, Harlow, Rehnquist, and Burns lost the argument.

This subtle reinterpretation of Johnson's executive order by Nixon staff in the spring of 1969 represented a substantial broadening of those affected by affirmative action. A background document noted that "the order has historically been applied only to procurement-type contracts and not to grants, loans, guarantees, or other arrangements for federal assistance" and had "seldom applied" to state and local governments. As the document pointed out, although the order required that construction contractors hired by government and other bodies that received federal assistance not discriminate, the order "does not require that the recipient agency itself not discriminate." Johnson's Attorney General Ramsey Clark, in a letter dated June 20, 1967, had specifically rejected a similar proposal to apply the order in this way.[4]

For the first time since World War II, the concept of contract compliance was broadened and set a pattern for future civil rights enforcement, creating the apparatus to enforce affirmative action "targets" in areas where resistance was likely to be less vociferous than in construction yards. Included for the first time were at least two sites where some of the highest profile affirmative action programs were later implemented. The vast majority of universities and colleges—as recipients of federal aid—now came under the remit of 11246, though few knew it at the time.[5] Local and state governments, employing, at the time, larger and larger numbers of people, had been included in the original order but had, traditionally, not been subject to it. The ease with which the federal government could use economic arm-twisting to pressure higher education authorities and state and local government officials stands in contrast to the difficulty it faced against unions and construction contractors.

EO 11478

A second move by the Nixon administration during the first few months of office pressured the largest single employer in the country, the federal government, to take positive steps to employ minorities. The Kerner Commission Report had recommended that the federal government, "through its Civil Service Commission and other agencies, should undertake programs of recruitment, hiring, and on-the-job training of the disadvantaged and should reevaluate and revalidate its minimum employment and promotion standards."[6] On March 28 Nixon stated: "I want to emphasize my own official and personal endorsement of a strong policy of equal opportunity within the federal government. I am determined that the federal branch of the government lead the way as an equal opportunity employer."[7]

Since 1883, recruitment and promotion within the federal government had operated, by law, within a system of merit. The Ramspeck Act of 1940 prohibited discrimination in federal employment because of race, creed, or color. The fact that merit was formalized within the public sector reflects the fact that there was no automatic discipline of the market to ensure efficiency in federal employment, necessitating law. A search of literature with "merit" in the title shows that, before the 1950s, discussions of merit dealt almost exclusively with the public sector.

Nixon was clearly prepared to transgress this system based on merit and color-blindness in order to include black Americans. In motivating this executive order, Nixon stated that merit was no longer adequate. "Under the merit system of employment we have made progress in recruiting minority group Americans to the federal workforce. . . . Now we need to raise our sights."[8] On August 18, 1969 Nixon issued EO 11478 to ensure that affirmative action took place within government employment. Nixon stressed that more than nondiscrimination would have to occur in federal government employment: "[W]e must, *through positive action*, make it possible for our citizens to compete on a truly equal and fair basis for employment and to qualify for advancement within the Federal service."[9] (Emphasis added.)

Though tentatively enforced at first, departmental heads paid close attention to the fate of the Philadelphia Plan. In November of 1969, the U.S. Civil
Service Commission (CSC) reported on changes that had been implemented
after EO 11478. Full-time Equal Economic Opportunity representatives had
been designated in each CSC regional office to work directly with agencies on
EEO (Equal Employment Opportunity) provision. "Federal agencies have
been directed to develop affirmative action plans in *sufficiently specific detail*
to carry out the new directions in equal employment opportunity. Agencies
have submitted EEO plans; we have reviewed them; and these plans are now
being used to measure agency performance." The CSC had also developed in-
centive programs for "managers, supervisors, and others in achieving EEO"
and "directed agencies to include in the ratings of supervisors and evaluation
of their performance in the area of equal employment opportunity so that a
measure can be made of their commitment to action in this area." Not only
did the phrase "sufficiently specific detail" point to "targets and goals," the
parallels of this enforcement apparatus bears a very close resemblance to the
affirmative action machinery in place within the government and in large corporations today.[10] (Emphasis added.)

EO 11478, perhaps of less-than-heartstopping interest to anyone outside of
bureaucratic circles, became more important, in the end, for the future of affirmative action than the Philadelphia Plan. Dean Kotlowski downplayed the
efforts at affirmative action within federal government employment. The Civil
Service Commission, he said, "preached minimalism, that is, hazy guidelines
and persuasion in lieu of coercion," distinguishing it from the coercive
"model" of the Philadelphia Plan. What EO 11478 did, however, was to give
senior level bureaucrats a new set of operational values, establishing goals that
restored, to some extent, the sense of mission lacking from administrators
since the late 1960s. The system could be made to work for minorities by pro-
ducing specific, realizable goals. This "hazy persuasion" produced far more
jobs for African Americans than the Philadelphia Plan.

"Six Points for Richard Milhous Nixon":
Black Capitalism and Its Aftermath

Another significant contribution of the Nixon administration to creating a
quota-based affirmative action paradigm was the Minority Business Enterprise program and a renewed emphasis on loans to minority businesses
through the Small Business Administration (SBA). As with other programs,
the emphasis behind the SBA changed from the goal of growth (by making
better use of resources) to the goal of equality.

The SBA, created by the Small Business Act of 1953, began a procurement program called 8(a) after the establishment of the OMBE that provided "for the reservation of a certain proportion of government contract business to minority firms."[11] The SBA, the heir of Hoover's Reconstruction Finance Corporation, owed a (perhaps) Progressivist concern about the deleterious effects of absence of competition. Its real remit in the 1950s came from the imperative of growth. Its importance to later affirmative action programs came, as Jonathan Bean indicates, in its enshrining of "disadvantage" of small business. But the SBA justified even this idea of disadvantage within the framework of economic growth. The disadvantage to small business "weakens the competitive free enterprise system and prevents the orderly development of the national economy."[12] The specter of the Soviet Union could be seen looming behind the lawmakers, giving another meaning to the competition to which they referred.

By the time Nixon took office, growth was no longer seen as a panacea to various social problems. But the SBA found new motivation by shifting the emphasis from growth at a national level to the growth of businesses in deprived areas. In his first proposed budget, Nixon designated 40 percent of SBA business loans to minority businesses.[13] Fulfilling his promise made during the 1968 election campaign to give blacks "a piece of the action," Nixon signed Executive Order 11458 on March 5, 1969, creating the Office of Minority Business Enterprise (OMBE). Again, the blueprints for minority business schemes had been drawn but never developed under Johnson, who developed "Project Own" within the Small Business Administration (SBA) in August 1968 to increase loans to black businesses. Johnson had instead emphasized that loans went to help the poor of whatever race in the slums.[14] Nixon publicized the signing of the Executive Order widely. He signaled the direction in which he wished the new agency to progress:

> What we are doing is recognizing that in addition to the basic problems of poverty itself, there is an additional need to stimulate those enterprises that can give members of minority groups confidence that avenues of opportunity are neither closed nor limited; enterprizes that will demonstrate that blacks, Mexican Americans, and others can participate in a growing economy on the basis of equal opportunity at the top of the ladder as well as on its lower rungs.[15]

The new OMBE had no program budget and no authority. The OMBE functioned in a "leadership and catalytic role"; its remit was to coordinate the efforts of future minority entrepreneurs in special impact areas. The Employment Development Agency (EDA) operated in "depressed areas," making business loans where the SBA cut off at $350,000 and providing technical assistance for entrepreneurs.[16]

Few took the idea very seriously when Nixon first touted the idea (including Nixon himself). The Russell Sage Foundation put up money for a conference of scholars on black capitalism. However, as conservative intellectual Irving Kristol indicated to Daniel Patrick Moynihan, many intellectuals had already discarded the idea as hopeless. Kristol said he had "concluded that it [economic regeneration of the ghetto through themes such as black capitalism] has only a little substance, of a not terribly interesting variety, and I therefore lost interest in the conference."[17] Privately, Nixon held out little hope for minority enterprises. Writing notes just five days after signing EO 11458 in the margin of a news report concerning the failure of the Watts Manufacturing Company, Nixon delivered a message to Commerce Secretary Maurice Stans, whom he had asked to manage the new agency:

> To Stans
> This shows the enormous problems in our minority enterprise program
> 1. Any small business has a 75% chance of failing
> 2. Minority small business has a 90% chance of failing good luck![18]

In some ways, OMBE failed to get off the ground in 1969. After it boasted at the start of the program that "hundreds of companies" would make millions of dollars available to minorities, only nine companies, even by the summer of 1970, had kept to their commitment of $150,000 each with two-to-one federal matching money and not all of that nine had granted loans after a year of the program.[19] In June of 1969, Phillip Pruitt, head of the SBA's minority entrepreneurial program, an important creation of the OMBE, resigned with a blast at the administration for failing to give adequate financial support for the high-profile black business program. By the end of the summer Frank Hoy wrote in the *Washington Post* that "[i]t has now become apparent that the practical problems were fundamentally underestimated." A severe critic of "black capitalism" was Andrew Brimmer, the only black member of the Federal Reserve Board and whom Nixon claimed had backed the idea during the campaign. Hoy noted that "(n)ot one non-governmental witness, from Roy Innis, chairman of Congress on Racial Equality (CORE), to the American Bankers Association, commended the administration." Developments during the first year of the OMBE's existence did not augur well for black capitalism, to say the least.[20]

Despite this, the OMBE and 8(a) programs retained a political importance for Nixon. First, the black business initiatives gained the political acceptance across the spectrum, attracting conservatives such as Texas Republican Senator John Tower and California Governor Ronald Reagan. It simultaneously met the liberal demand to "do something" about the ghettos and the conservative proposition that capitalism was the solution to the problems of the ghettos.

Much more importantly, the concept, Nixon hoped, would chip away at the solid wall of African-American opposition to the Nixon administration. Most accounts of the origins of affirmative action fail to emphasize its importance to maintaining support for capitalism inside the ghettos. The vitriol expressed by the Black Panthers against the idea gives some indication that black capitalism undermined the whole concept of "Black Power." In "An Open Letter to Stokely Carmichael" published in the radical magazine *Ramparts* in August 1969, the Black Panther Party's editorial board wrote:

> The Black Panther Party tried to give you a chance to rescue Black Power from the pigs who have seized upon it and turned it into the rationale for Black Capitalism. . . . Even though you were right when you said that LBJ would never stand up and call for Black Power, Nixon has done so and he's bankrolling it with millions of dollars. Now they [the black bourgeoisie] have stolen your football and run away for a touchdown: six points for Richard Milhous Nixon.[21]

As many biographies discussing Nixon's early sports career might note, a Nixon touchdown, metaphoric or otherwise, was somewhat of a rarity. But Nixon was undoubtedly successful not in providing many jobs for African Americans but in splitting civil rights opposition between those who called for an overhaul of the whole system and those who wished to be accommodated within it. Accordingly, the justification for the OMBE and other agencies subtly changed. Instead of dividing resources for the purpose of efficiency, dividing resources became the goal itself. Established for that very purpose, it became a key agency for delivering the symbolic promise of equal opportunity.

Still at the "experimental" stage in 1969, it increased its total worth of minority contracts from $8.9 million in 1968 to only $10.4 million by the middle of 1969. Although Congress appropriated $36 million for SBA loans, Nixon froze the funds, forcing the SBA to rely on bank loans at 12 percent interest. However, during fiscal year 1969, the SBA's loans to minority groups had nearly tripled—from 1,676 contracts worth $29.9 million to 4,120 worth $93.6 million.[22] The OMBE that Nixon had privately mocked grew into a huge and important program. OMBE's operational budget skyrocketed from a pathetic $46,000 in 1969 to $52.5 million in fiscal year 1974.[23] By May 1971, 422 new contracts had been added worth $35.2 million. By the end of that year, there were 811 contracts worth $65.4 million; in fiscal year 1972 a total of 1,714 contracts were worth $149.4 million. Lending to minority enterprises under the program increased from $28 million in 1968 to $217 million in 1971. In 1975 the Small Business Administration gave loans and guarantees to minority enterprises totalling $651 million.[24]

Despite Nixon's early reservations about the OMBE, the agency became an important part of civil rights efforts—not only of his administration but for subsequent administrations up to the present day. In *Fullilove v. Klutznick* (1980), the Supreme Court backed a congressional program that set aside 10 percent of federal construction contracts to firms owned by minorities. The presiding judge noted that Congress, "for the first time in the Nation's history has created a broad legislative classification for entitlement to benefits based solely on racial characteristics."[25] Such was the legacy of this program.

New Federalism and Revenue Sharing

New Federalism became a theme for the Republicans as they looked forward to victory in 1968. This was, of course, the Republican version of "power to the people" and perhaps one of the few common themes tying together the by-then fairly disparate threads of Republicanism. Within the New Federalism theme was an implicit attack on Washington with its largely Democratic federal bureaucracy. Beyond this vague purpose, New Federalism remained very aspecific.

Though Nixon often repeated the importance of New Federalism in public, the subject clearly bored most people. "I . . . think that revenue sharing and government reorganization are probably loosers [sic] insofar as public appeal is concerned."[26] The truth was that a motif for Nixon's domestic program simply eluded them. "We still have the need for deciding a theme for our overall Domestic approach. . . . Obviously we should forget New Federalism."[27]

However, in its broadest possible interpretation, New Federalism did become a theme, and an important one at that. It created a way for Nixon to devolve responsibility for reform away from the federal government to state and local government, allowing them to set the agenda rather than following one to be set nationally. Thus the responsibility to fight poverty, to make the cities more habitable, to train young people for meaningful work, to destroy the ghettos became—to a much larger extent than under Johnson—localized. New Federalism also removed civil rights issues from the public forum by setting them up as nonnegotiable, formalized requirements attached to federal monies. In doing so it effectively froze the movement for civil rights reforms. Percentages would be negotiated away from the public eye and enforced quietly.

One of the problems that prevented the reinterpretation of EO 11246 from being effective was the complex nature of the distribution of federal funding. The profusion of block grants administered by the Johnson administration made it difficult to regulate equal employment within the recipient bodies. The recipient bodies varied in their makeup and many were simply unprepared to report accurately on the makeup of their workforces or the workforce of any contractor. Giving grants to local elected authorities at least eased the difficulties of monitoring and ensured that regulatory procedures could become standardized. Revenue sharing was to become part of Nixon's attempt, following from campaign promises, to make government more effective.

Revenue sharing was one of the most consistent aspects of Nixon's (and the Republican Party's) domestic platform, as part of New Federalism. During the previous two Democratic administrations, and particularly in relation to Great Society policies, categorical grants had been given directly to representatives of recipient groups, bypassing local elected authorities. These grants were designed to meet some need that ostensibly met some national need, such as federal aid to disadvantaged children. By 1969 there were at least five hundred categorical grants programs as more and more areas of concern appeared, administered by various agencies in various departments, some inevitably overlapping. The problem of categorical grants had been in existence for some time but had greatly increased during Johnson's tenure of office. As was the case with so many of Nixon's programs, Johnson had begun to move toward reforms but had not implemented his plans by the end of his presidency.[28]

With revenue sharing, Nixon wished to provide funds in the form of block grants directly to state and local administrations, bolstering their authority among recipients, giving them more power and responsibility. The idea Nixon had in mind when he proposed the General Revenue Sharing Act of 1969 (first touted in April 1969[29]) was to strengthen the links between individual citizens and their governments, to revitalize local and state politics. Nixon held forth on the issue continually throughout 1969: "If there is one thing we know, it is that the Federal Government cannot solve all the nation's problems by itself; yet there has been an overshift of jurisdiction and responsibility to the Federal Government. We must kindle a new partnership between government and people, and among the various levels of government."[30] Nixon's impetus toward revenue sharing and reform of the federal grant program was clearly borne of the recognition that the reforms of the 1960s had created an impersonal, bureaucratic, dehumanized, and centralized form of government and that reforms returning power closer to the people had to be implemented. More specifically it was designed to "alleviate a malaise caused by the breakdown of Great Society expectations without overreacting and shutting off aid entirely."[31] Another problem it was designed to address was the alienation of the average American from local politics; voters barely participated in local elections in the late 1960s. It was estimated in 1968, for example, that less than 30 percent of the voter age population casts a ballot in separately held city elections.[32]

Indicative of the paradoxical nature of Nixon's decentralization programs, Nixon made affirmative action clauses a contingency for continued funding. As Richard P. Nathan and Paul R. Drommel characterized revenue sharing, it was a "decentralization instrument with many centralization features."[33] Nixon initially struggled with an uncooperative Congress in his efforts to enact revenue sharing. He managed to create only two block grants before he resigned despite six years of continuous (if not intense) struggle, and both differed substantially from what the president initially proposed.[34] However, when the Revenue Sharing Act was finally signed into law on October 20, 1972, the newly created Office of Revenue Sharing gained power over all aspects of the program being funded through nondiscrimination provisions in the act. For example, if money was used to buy police cars, nondiscrimination provisions of the Revenue Sharing Act then also extended to employment practices, police protection services, treatment in jails, and other functions of the police department. The act provided for auditing including "possible failure to comply substantially with the civil rights provisions of the law." It was the first federal agency to include civil rights matters as part of regular audit requirement.[35]

In revenue sharing, Nixon demonstrated his ability as a policy entrepreneur. It helped to transform affirmative action from a bottom-up demand on the part of civil rights activists in northern cities to a new top-down moral justification for state activities. As Lauren Edelman pointed out, *pace* Kotlowski, "the ambiguity and complexity of compliance standards" of affirmative action ensured that a self-interested affirmative action industry of experts and interpreters was necessary, who in turn propagated affirmative action.[36]

1970: Retreat from the Ghettos

Whereas it might be said that the Nixon administration, in implementing these lesser-known affirmative action policies, "drifted" into affirmative action with little central direction, a shift in the approach to civil rights issues in the first term came right from the top. Nixon consciously rationalized and reorganized civil rights policy in 1970, effectively dividing a policy like the Philadelphia Plan—directed at providing laboring jobs for inner-city blacks—from those concerned with college entrance and white-collar jobs. This was his attempt to split African Americans into more manageable pieces, separating the black middle-class from those who occupied the ghettos.

Nixon's presidency, at least in civil rights terms, is probably best divided in two. The remarkable aspect of the first year of his presidency is the degree of continuity with the Johnson administration. Author (and Nixon advisor)

Richard Scammon assumed Nixon would be "a successor to Lyndon Johnson and consensus, rather than a departure from them."[37] Yet, in 1970, the policies discussed above accelerated after a year in the doldrums. Funding for all civil rights outlays increased each year, hardly an indication of neglect.

Initially, Nixon made no dramatic policy changes, preferring to see whether he could more effectively manage existing policy. However, problems were created by this holding pattern. Though evidence shows that, as he worried about alienating Southern support and failed to blunt liberal criticism, Nixon began to distance himself from the liberal camp, he still made no hard and fast decisions that might indicate the direction in which he felt his administration should proceed on civil rights.

In 1970 Nixon agonized over decisions about the Vietnam War. Most available archives indicate his preoccupation with it and its repercussions in Congress and throughout the American population. It is possible, in the morass of war-related material, to miss one of the most crucial changes for race relations policy of the twentieth century. Many Nixon scholars pay little attention to civil rights changes around this time.[38] However, some historians would agree with Dan T. Carter when he said that "(t)he year 1970 marked a critical turning point for the Nixon administration."[39] Those that feel Nixon was led largely by political considerations see a rightward shift when his more conservative advisors within the administration appeared to win out on several arguments taking place at the time. Nixon speechwriter William Safire and John D. Skrentny, among others, have suggested that the hardhat march against the peace campaigners in New York in May 1970 turned the Nixon administration against early liberal civil rights "blunders," among which they number the Philadelphia Plan.[40] Most agree Nixon clearly wished to capitalize on the sentiments of the "silent majority" that he assumed the hardhats represented. He also feared George Wallace's ability to capitalize on these sentiments. But questions remain about why Nixon continued to pour money into some civil rights strategies while abandoning others.

The most important of the factors leading to the shift was the fact that the immediate turmoil of the late 1960s appeared to be under control. "For whatever reasons—increased legal, extralegal, and illegal surveillance; the end of the draft; the exhaustion of radical cadres—incidents of New Left and campus violence decreased dramatically after 1970."[41] Events such as the "New Mobe" had passed off peacefully, 1969 had been (relatively) trouble-free in the ghettos, if not entirely on the campuses. Nixon's first stated priority upon taking office had been to "lower our voices," to calm what nearly everyone imagined to be an inflamed situation. After a year in office, Nixon took stock of his civil rights efforts. He had done "well where least expected" and "poorly where [he] should have succeeded," commented journalist Joseph C. Harsch in the *Chris-*

tian Science Monitor at the end of 1969. "Administration spokesmen see as their greatest success a general lowering of political temperatures on the domestic scene. . . . Ghetto streets and college campuses have been less disturbed than in previous years."[42]

Nixon's advisors agreed, even the "libs" in the camp. Moynihan wrote in 1970 that "(s)uddenly the riots ended. Again, no one knows why." Moynihan made an important point regarding funding civil rights programs, one that was marked by Nixon: "[T]he principal argument against any decrease in existing programs is that it will automatically trigger such violence."[43] In another 1970 memo, Moynihan advised his president to take credit for the end of the riots: "As you are blamed when it rains (or, in this case, will be if it starts to rain again), you might as well take credit when the sun shines."[44] The more peaceful American scene gave the president more options in terms of policy. Not all civil rights policy would need to have as its major function prevention of rioting. Freed from this reactive imperative, Nixon could more freely redirect policy.

Second, though black rioting seemed to be easing, implacable opposition to the administration appeared to be on the rise and 1969 had shown that continuation of Great Society programs had not placated racial liberals and civil rights organizations. His administration had supported the 1968 Civil Rights Act by bringing suit, in July 1969, against an association of real estate brokers and thirteen of its suburban Chicago members, charging racial discrimination in the sale of housing. Efforts at desegregating southern schools could be called moderately successful, despite the ensuing controversy, and Nixon might have been encouraged by the results of his softer approach to the issue. The 18.4 percent of black pupils attending majority white schools in eleven southern states in 1968 had risen to 38 percent in 1970.[45] He had very publicly issued Executive Order 11458 establishing the Office of Minority Business Enterprise on March 5, 1969. With the Philadelphia Plan, Nixon had proved that he would put himself on the line for a civil rights measure. Yet none of these actions—referred to by administration members as "zigs" to counter conservative "zags"—seemed to please his liberal critics or to "blunt the vigor of their resentment and political opposition" as Nixon put it.[46] He had, in regard to the Philadelphia Plan, "gained little on the play." A disgusted Nixon exclaimed in the summer of 1970 that "(T)he NAACP would say my rhetoric was poor if I gave the Sermon on the Mount."[47]

Third, the threat from the left, in the form of instability and rebellion, was on the wane, the threat from the right appeared to be waxing. Nixon now worried that to continue the programs of the Johnson administration might weaken his fragile electoral base. In 1970, George Wallace appeared to be more of a threat than any Democratic candidate—Nixon secretly poured $400,000 (from his reelection campaign kitty collected and hoarded before the Campaign Reform Act of 1970) into the campaign to elect Wallace's rival in the gubernatorial race for Alabama, Albert Brewer, in an effort to derail Wallace's 1972 campaign for the presidency.[48] As the year progressed, it became obvious that such efforts were not working. The "sweet and reasonable middle" in which Nixon had located himself in 1969 appeared to be disappearing fast.

Finally, evidence indicated, as Nixon had openly suspected, that many of the policies put in place by the Johnson administration designed to reform the ghettos were ineffective. One of the major problems was the apparent unenforceability of policies aimed at gaining compliance for these efforts. Nixon inherited the Johnson strategy to achieve black equality by ensuring that education facilities were equal, by attempting to integrate the suburbs, to create bases for political participation through the Community Action Programs (CAPs) as well as—through the Equal Employment Opportunities Commission (EEOC)—pushing for black employment gains. By 1970, all programs devoted to achieving these ends languished for want of effective implementation mechanisms. Though there were modest gains in southern school desegregation, it was found in northern school desegregation cases that private sector actions in real estate and home lending led to residential segregation that made school integration impossible.

Busing between school districts became the favored remedy of the courts but—quite apart from Nixon's personal reservations—developed into a very messy and costly solution. Additionally, it ran up against concerted opposition from many white (and some black) parents who, for racial motives or otherwise, objected to busing their children to different areas or having black children bused to local schools. Nixon also thought that efforts to desegregate the suburbs would fail. "It is important to break down barriers," Nixon told a reporter in 1967, "but the fellow who spends all his time talking about open housing is pursuing a will-o'-the-wisp. I know that's the exciting way to do things. Marching feet. Protests."[49] After taking office, Nixon felt vindicated in his earlier position. Between January 1, 1969, the date the 1968 Open Housing Act became effective, and July 1970, the Housing Section of the Justice Department—despite its reputation as an activist agency (Nixon frequently complained that it was "against us"[50]), filed only about fifty cases though it received thousands of complaints. By the middle of 1970, the Department of Housing and Urban Development (HUD) had not yet issued regulations spelling out how the act should be enforced.[51] In April 1971 Nixon ordered aides to create a policy that "waffles" open housing and "gets [the White House] out of it." Between 1971 and 1974, the Justice Department annually filed an average of only thirty-five lawsuits per year against persons or communities practising racial bias in housing.[52]

The efforts at strengthening black communities through CAPs and other experimental projects in the ghettos had also failed. As soon as capable leaders emerged, they would make it their first priority to get out of the ghetto, quite naturally. Of equal (if not more) concern to Nixon was the fact that the most effective ghetto leaders tended to be those most vocal in their opposition to "the system."[53] Neither, as has been discussed in chapter 4, could EEOC be counted as a success. Of course, on one level the Nixon administration simply did not make adequate efforts to ensure that many of these programs would work. But it is undeniable that serious problems faced those who would have implemented these programs. Courts could order large corporations or state and local authorities to change their ways with "pattern or practice" suits but what would be the penalties? Who would pay for the resolution of the matter? Who specifically was responsible? The more ingrained within American life the problem of racial divisions appeared to be, the more difficult it became for the courts or the federal government to enforce useful remedies.

But the pressure for the administration to do something about the problem of civil rights, especially from powerful liberal interests, was, if anything, increasing. Evidence of these programmatic failures poured in during Nixon's first year of office, signifying a crisis of enforcement of civil rights legislation. Yet Nixon had promised to enforce civil rights legislation, stating in his 1968 campaign that no new legislation was needed, only the will to make it work. Nixon made it clear that he would "cut and run" rather than invest more time, effort, and money into making these failing programs work.

Helping the Strong Instead of the Weak

Nixon's answer in the face of these problems—following one of the most important and consistent themes of his presidency—was to further change the meaning of civil rights. Splitting of African Americans into middle-class and ghetto residents for policy purposes represented a way of "breaking the problem into more manageable pieces." Instead of policies that aimed at what he felt were impossible goals, policy would be concentrated on making successes of more limited actions. Democratic programs that attempted to create equal opportunities by promising universal benefits, such as model cities, housing funds, emergency public-service jobs for the unemployed and community action programs, would be de-emphasized in favor of programs that were tailored to the black middle class.

The crisis that seemed to immediately provoke Nixon's rethink on civil rights occurred in January 1970. Then, in the memo cited at the beginning of this book, Nixon condemned the administration's civil rights efforts as "a hopeless holding action at best" and signaled his determination to do as little as the administration could get away with in civil rights. This preceded Daniel Moynihan's infamous memo calling for "benign neglect" of the race issue (later leaked to the New York Times), which must have added fuel to the fire. In a lesser-read section of the memo, Moynihan declared: "As you have candidly acknowledged, the relation of the administration to the black population is a problem. . . . I dare say, as much or more time and attention goes into this effort in this administration than any in history. But little has come of it."[54]

However, the immediate trigger for a pervasive rethink seems to be the ongoing debates regarding school desegregation involving HEW, Justice, and the White House. On January 30 Patrick Buchanan's news report noted an article in the Sunday Observer on the decline of integration in the northern schools. Nixon wrote at the top of the page: "E[hrlichman]—I would be interested in reactions by [Secretary of HEW Robert H.] Finch—Moynihan, [Attorney General John] Mitchell to that piece." On February 4, 1970, Nixon decided to "take on the integration problem directly."[55] He then asked for HEW Office for Civil Rights Director Leon Panetta's resignation.

Throughout February Nixon ruminated over the problems of race relations. On February 12 Buchanan declared that the "ship of integration is going down" in a memo that Nixon obviously took very seriously.[56] He spent most of the afternoon of February 18 talking to Harriet Elan, "[White House aide Dwight] Chapin's Negro secretary," in order to gain the opinions of a "responsible, intelligent Negro." Haldeman recorded in his diary that "Obviously, P deeply concerned. Later kept saying to me there's no adequate solution and nothing we can do in the short haul to settle this, it will have to take one hundred years, but people don't want to wait." [57] Nixon attended a meeting with an informal "black group" composed mainly of those concerned with civil rights issues and black administration employees that Moynihan organized on February 28. Notes taken by Haldeman (declassified in 1996) indicate the conclusions Nixon was coming to:

> Shift of policy of helping and backing the strong—instead of putting all effort into raising the weak
> Recognize there is no "black community" . . .
>
> how to give the black middle class cultural legitimacy
> blacks—as things get better—feel small slights more . . .
>
> we should discourage the people who live on agitation
> esp. those on Federal payroll
> create a disincentive for agitation
> build incentives for the strong + positive
> give the fellowships to them instead

don't really know how to help the weak
+ and even if we did—the proportionate cost is so great . . .

devise programs to make sure that for those who have made progress, that progress is permanent . . .
don't aim manpower programs at unemployed black male teenager . . .
directed to street-corner society won't work. . . .[58]

Nixon had consistently opposed "forced integration" in the form of busing but, up until 1970, had kept the programs of the Great Society aimed at alleviating conditions in the black ghettos of American cities. Nixon outlined here a subtle yet significant switch in emphasis for the administration toward racial programs, well before the hardhats marched. The clear message coming from this meeting was: Efforts within the inner city are likely to fail and the focus should now be on creating a stable and strong black middle class.

Coming so soon after Moynihan's "benign neglect" memo, many historians as well as contemporary observers concluded that Nixon's shift in 1970 simply followed Moynihan's advice to the letter.[59] Leaked to the *New York Times* by James Farmer on March 1, 1970, the memo caused Moynihan to offer to resign, given the furor attending its publication (his offer was refused by Nixon). The most cited part of the memo stated:

The time may come when the issue of race could benefit from a period of "benign neglect." The subject has been too much talked about. The forum has been to much taken over to hysterics, paranoids, and boodlers on all sides. . . . The administration can help bring this about by paying close attention to . . . progress . . . while seeking to avoid situations in which extremists of either race are given opportunities for martyrdom, heroics, histrionics or whatever.[60]

Nixon agreed. The meaning of the memo, which was widely interpreted as a prescription to ignore civil rights problems, must be reassessed. The memo insisted that the *issue* of race must be separated from African Americans. The message here, rather than neglect per se, was that racial rhetoric should be toned down, and (perhaps giving it a perhaps undeservedly positive gloss) African Americans should not simply be seen in racial terms. However, it is wrong even to assume that Nixon uncritically accepted Moynihan's message, as many did at the time and historians continue to do. Not withstanding the "I agree" comment, Nixon's notes in the margins of other parts of the memo indicate that he used Moynihan's observations as catalysts for his own thinking rather than direct sources of his ideas. In another section, Moynihan declared:

There is a silent black majority [Nixon circled "majority" and wrote "minority" beside it]. . . . It is mostly working class, as against lower middle class. It is politically moderate (on issues other than racial equality) and shares most of the concerns of its white counterpart. . . . The more recognition we can give to it, the better off we shall be.

Taken altogether, Nixon's thinking on race appears to have been stimulated by this memo but not exactly along the lines set out by Moynihan. Nixon wrote in the margins beside Moynihan's point, "H—follow up (Graham's groups and Browns [?]—Negro business men—bankers—Elks, etc. Let's poll this + go after the probably 30% who are potentially on our side—Garment et al.—are directing our appeal to the wrong group (both in case of Negroes and whites)." In other words, Nixon ignored Moynihan's "working class" category. He did not decide to neglect blacks. Instead, he wished to stop the issue of race from being used as a sledgehammer against his administration. By dividing up black Americans and concentrating on middle-class blacks ("recognize there is no black community"), he could accomplish this goal by achieving some progress for at least some black Americans.[61]

With regard to civil rights, the theme outlined in his statements to the "black group" came up again and again. In a meeting in June consisting of Haldeman, Ehrlichman, and rising star Charles Colson (with other nameless individuals possibly present), Nixon instructed them to pay attention to the black middle class: "There are 35 percent of blacks we can do good with," Nixon told Haldeman. Nixon instructed him to "find $100 mill[ion] for black colleges" which were "vitally imp[or]t[ant] to have . . . so blacks dev[elop] capacity to run something . . . whenever integrated—whites will dominate." From this statement, it becomes evident that this switch in policy direction happened for more than just political reasons. Had Nixon wished only to attract votes, he certainly would not have requested $100 million for black colleges. As Moynihan had pointed out in his January 16 memo (and as Nixon agreed), young educated blacks detested white America and this group could hardly be mined for Republican votes.[62] The administration must, Nixon continued, "encourage the good blacks, find some honest Mexicans—have to develop some 'leadership.'"[63] He worried that the 1964 Civil Rights Act clearly called for efforts to be taken to achieve racial equality but "we recognize clearly that the methods chosen to carry out the law have all failed."[64]

Many of the programs launched with the purpose of aiding black Americans languished. The Philadelphia Plan received little mention within the administration after Nixon's success in ensuring congressional attempts to disallow it failed, as discussed previously. Nixon had set forth the Family Assistance Plan (FAP) on August 8, 1969. However, the plan, with its attention to alleviating ghetto problems (Nixon told Haldeman in the same month that "you have to face the fact that the *whole* problem [of welfare] is really the blacks")[65] and grand universalist designs, was effectively abandoned in 1970. Even after the House of Representatives approved the plan by almost two-to-one on April 16, 1970, Nixon instructed Haldeman to make sure the effort failed.[66]

The Civil Rights Act of 1968 that outlawed discrimination in housing also appears to have been put on hold. A row broke out between the departments of Housing and Urban Development (HUD), with Secretary George Romney at the helm, and Justice over the *Blackjack* case. To exclude a low- and middle-income integrated housing project being constructed within its borders, Blackjack, Missouri, changed its zoning laws. In response, Romney then asked the Justice Department to file suit, a move supported by the Federal Court of Appeals, which ruled that HUD had an affirmative action responsibility to consider what impact site selection would have on integration. In September 1970, Mitchell called Romney to the White House and told him to back off. "The White House decided to study discrimination in housing, putting all policy decisions on hold until the study was completed. For nearly a year, the civil rights laws regarding housing were suspended, though hundreds of grants were approved in the interim."[67]

However, not all black Americans were neglected, lending weight to the theory that Nixon's ultra-political concern with most issues did not extend to civil rights decisions. Despite continued and even increased hostility from civil rights groups, the Nixon administration steadily ratcheted up funding for civil rights programs and civil rights enforcement. In fiscal year 1968, $64 million was earmarked for civil rights programs. In 1969, funding went up to $75 million; in 1970, $94 million; in 1971, $114 million; and in 1972 the figure rose to $141 million. Outlays for Title VI compliance, a problem over which the civil rights movement had attacked Johnson, increased between 1969 and 1972 from $7.5 million to more than $18.6 million.[68]

The beneficiary of this shift in course in 1970 was the black middle class. And, unlike the Philadelphia and hometown solutions, the administration could more convincingly claim some credit. They boasted in 1973 that the total income of blacks rose from $38.7 billion in 1969 to $51.1 billion in 1972. State and local government employment has increased steadily—from 6.3 million employees in 1960 to 12 million in 1975.[69] They could have also pointed to an increase in black and minority employment in full-time state and local government, which, between 1973 and 1974 (after the passage of the Revenue Sharing Act of 1972), increased by 12 percent against a total gain in state and local government employment of nearly 5 percent.[70] Minority enrollment for master's and doctoral degrees increased from 7.7 percent in 1970 to 9.1 percent in 1972. The authors of a study critical of voluntaristic efforts to implement affirmative action programs, had to admit the success of the Nixon administration's pressuring tactics upon minority college enrollment: "(I)t is clear that between 1968 and 1978 these voluntary affirmative action programs did bring thousands of black, Chicano, Native American, and Asian students into universities who otherwise would not have been there."[71] The strategies to build up the black middle classes had worked in a way that attempts to alleviate ghetto conditions had not.

Conclusion

What often remains hidden—and what this chapter has demonstrated—is the consequential nature of the Nixon administration's contributions to affirmative action *after* the revised Philadelphia Plan was devised. The subjective factors outlined in this (and the previous) chapter form just as essential a part of the story as the objective factors outlined in the first section of this book. The desire of Nixon to "lower our voices" about civil rights (when there was and still is much to shout about) helped affirmative action become a management prerogative rather than, as it had been, a demand by protestors.

These hidden policies resemble affirmative action programs of today far more than the Philadelphia Plan, which, with its noisy, participatory, and very public deliberations, appears a child of the 1960s. These were quiet, top-down plans implemented without any of the direct pressure of demonstrations, one more step removed from democratic, participatory politics. The conservative descent of affirmative action today thus becomes apparent. Those who see affirmative action as part of the teleological progression of African Americans in American history must at least reckon with its administrative origins during the Nixon presidency.

If one moment of history can be pinpointed as end of the road for the dream on racial integration in the United States, 1970 is it. That year proved to be a crucial one for the Nixon administration's retreat from civil rights. Contrary to the received wisdom, Nixon himself—not liberal advisors or civil rights activists—steered the administration toward expanding affirmative action policies, if indirectly. First, he consciously gave up on programs aimed at reform in order to achieve stability; these measures were clearly intended to strengthen the "system" by injecting it with a new cultural imperative rather than to eradicate the racial divide. In carving out a new relationship to the black middle classes, Nixon ensured that affirmative action would be defined not on the basis of need but solely on the basis of race.

Notes

1. One Republican document boasted that the Republican Party "put teeth into Executive Order 11246—which sat for four years without significant action after it was issued in 1965." *GOP Nationalities News,* box 125, RNC Records.

2. Memorandum to the Attorney General from Jerris Leonard, February 22, 1969, Files of John Ehrlichman re: EEOC # 168 [CFOA 7730], Alpha-Subject Files, WHCF: SMOF: Garment, NPMP; memorandum to John Ehrlichman from the Attorney General, April 14, 1969, [CF] HU2-2 Employment [1969–1970], box 35, WHSF: WHCF: Subject Files: Confidential Files, NPMP.

3. Memorandum from Richard K. Berg, Office of Legal Counsel, to William H. Rehnquist, assistant attorney general, March 19, 1969, [CF] HU 2-2 Employment [1969–1970], box 35, WHSF: WHCF: Subject Files, Confidential Files, NPMP.

4. Ibid.

5. See Richard P. McCormick, *The Black Student Protest Movement at Rutgers* (London: Rutgers University Press, 1990).

6. *Report of the National Advisory Commission on Civil Rights* (New York: New York Times Publications, 1968), 419.

7. Letter from Bryce N. Harlow, assistant to the president, to Honorable William Clay, House of Representatives, April 11, 1969, boxes 17 and 18 [Gen], WHCF: Subject Files: HU (Human Rights), [Ex] HU2-2 Employment, NPMP.

8. Statement by the president regarding Executive Order 11478, August 11, 1969 vol. 5, no. 32, *PPPUS: Richard Nixon,* 1969 (Washington, D.C.: U.S.GPO, 1970).

9. Memorandum on Equal Employment Opportunity in the Federal Government, August 8, 1969, *PPPUS: Richard Nixon,* 1969, 635.

10. United States Civil Service Commission (USCRC), *Preliminary Report of Minority Group Employment in the Federal Government,* 1969 (Washington, D.C.: U.S. GPO, 1969), 8. See Dean Kotlowski, *Nixon's Civil Rights: Politics, Principle, and Policy* (London: Harvard University Press, 2001), 98.

11. Memo from Shultz to the president (a review of the administration's civil rights programs, received May 18, 1971), Black Caucus I [1 of 2] [CFOA 463], box 46, WHCF: SMOF: Garment, NPMP.

12. Jonathan J. Bean, *Big Government and Affirmative Action: The Scandalous History of the Small Business Administration* (Lexington: The University Press of Kentucky, 2001), 77. The Small Business Act of 1953, Section 9, in Addison W. Parris, *The Small Business Administration* (London: Frederick A. Praeger, 1968), appendix II, 244–76, esp. 268.

13. Bean, *Big Government and Affirmative Action,* 77.

14. Both the Kennedy and Johnson administrations had investigated set-aside programs. See folder entitled [Civil Rights] Background Material for the Reluctant Guardians: A Survey of the Enforcement of Federal Civil Rights Laws by Barney Sellers [CFOA 908], ox 61, WHCF: SMOF: Garment, NPMP.

15. Statement by the president on minority enterprise, March 5, 1969 and attachments, files of John Ehrlichman re: EEOC # 379 [CFOA 7730], box 86, WHCF: SMOF: Garment, NPMP.

16. Draft of Delivery and Coordination Mechanism for Assistance Grants in Support of Minority Business Enterprise by the Interagency Task Force on Assistance Grants for Minority Businessmen, no date, Civil Rights Accomplishments [1 of 2] [CFOA 907], box 57, WHCF: SMOF: Garment, NPMP.

17. Letter from Irving Kristol to Moynihan, March 25, 1969, [Gen] HU2 Equality 1/31/69, box 5, WHCF: Subject Files: HU (Human Rights), NPMP.

18. Staff and department briefs, March 10, 1969, News Summaries—March 1969, box 30: January 1969–September 1969, POF: ANS, NPMP.

19. See "Nixon and Blacks: Substance and Symbol," edit., *The New Republic* (July 18, 1970), 7–8.

20. "Bleak Facts Slow Black Capitalism," Frank Hoy, *The Washington Post*, Sunday, August 31, 1969, in files of John Ehrlichman re: EEOC # 379 [CFOA 7730], box 86 WHCF: SMOF: Garment, NPMP.

21. Cited in Philip S. Foner, ed., *The Black Panthers Speak* (New York: J. B. Lippincott Company, 1970), 105.

22. Anonymous memo to Terrence M. Scanlon, Office of Minority Business, dated December 15, 1969, Equal Employment Opportunities Commission (EEOC)—1970 [2 of 2] [CFOA 7730], Garment: Alpha Subject Files, box 35, WHSF: SMOF: Garment, NPMP.

23. Edward W. Brooke, "Black Business, Problems and Prospects," *The Black Scholar* (April 1975). Copy contained in Subject File: Blacks—miscellaneous 1967–1976, box 415, Brooke Papers, LOC.

24. Shultz to the president, May 18, 1971. Letter to the president from Thomas A. Kleppe 6/6/73, box 5, WHCF: Subject Files: HU (Human Rights), NPMP. Highlights of Administration Initiatives in Civil Rights and Related Programs, Stanley S. Scott, February 1974, box 5, WHCF: Subject Files: HU (Human Rights), NPMP.

25. Hugh Davis Graham, "Civil Rights Policy in the Carter Presidency," in Gary M. Fink and Hugh Davis Graham, *The Carter Presidency: Policy Choices in the Post-New Deal Era* (Lawrence: University Press of Kansas, 1998), 202–23, esp. 208.

26. Memo for Haldeman from the president, March 8, 1971, Haldeman Memos from the President 1971, Box 140, WHSF: SMOF: H. R. Haldeman: Alpha Subject Files, NPMP.

27. Talking Paper re PR. February 16, 1971, Talking Papers 1971, box 153, WHSF: SMOF: H. R. Haldeman—Talking Papers, NPMP.

28. See Timothy J. Conlan, "The Politics of Federal Block Grants: From Nixon to Reagan," *Political Science Quarterly* 99, no. 2. (Summer 1984), 247–70.

29. Special Message to the Congress on Forthcoming Legislative Proposals Concerning Domestic Programs, April 14, 1969, *Public Papers of the Presidents: Richard Nixon*, 1969, 284.

30. Ibid., 287.

31. William Safire, *Before the Fall: An Inside View of the Pre-Watergate White House* (New York: Doubleday and Co., 1975), 229.

32. "New Directions For Urban America," draft 3/19/68, Human Needs, 1968 Republican National Convention, box 60, RNC Records.

33. Richard P. Nathan and Paul R. Dommel, "Federal–Local Relations Under Block Grants," *Political Science Quarterly* 93, issue 3 (Autumn 1978), 421–42, esp. 422.

34. Conlan, "The Politics of Federal Block Grants," 252.

35. USCRC, *Making Civil Rights Sense out of Revenue Sharing Dollars* (Washington, D.C.: USCRC Clearinghouse Publication 50, February 1975), 39.

36. Cited in Frank Dobbin and Frank R. Sutton, "The Strength of a Weak State: The Rights Revolution and the Rise of Human Resources Management Divisions," *American Journal of Sociology* 104, issue 2 (September 1998), 441–76.

37. Cited in Herbert S. Parmet, *Richard Nixon and His America* (London: Little, Brown and Company, 1990), 562.

38. See, for example, Stephen E. Ambrose, *Nixon, Volume II: The Triumph of a Politician 1962–1972* (London: Simon and Schuster, 1989); Dean Kotlowski, *Nixon's Civil Rights: Politics, Principle, and Policy* (London: Harvard University Press, 2001).

39. Dan T. Carter, *From George Wallace to Newt Gingrich: Race in the Conservative Counterrevolution, 1963–1994* (London: Lousiana State University Press, 1996), 39. Ronald Randall identified the shift as occurring in 1971. See "Presidential Power versus Bureaucratic Intransigence: The Influence of the Nixon Administration on Welfare Policy," *The America Political Science Review* 73, no. 3 (1979).

40. News Summaries—January 1970, Box 31, POF: ANS, NPMP. Safire claimed that "most of the zip went out of the integration effort (the "courageous, if short-lived" Philadelphia Plan) after the hardhats marched in support of Nixon on the war." William Safire, *Before the Fall: An Inside View of the Pre-Watergate White House* (New York: Doubleday and Co., 1975), 585. See also John D. Skrentny, *The Ironies of Affirmative Action: Politics, Culture, and Justice in America* (London: University of Chicago Press, 1996), 211–15. Dan T. Carter's *The Politics of Rage; George Wallace, the Origins of the New Conservatism, and the Transformation of American Politics* (London: Simon and Schuster, 1995) argues persuasively that Wallace scared the Nixon team more than any Democrat; see chapter 12, "The Wars of Richard Nixon," 371–414.

41. Melvin Small, *The Presidency of Richard Nixon* (Lawrence: Kansas University Press, 1999), 158.

42. Copy of *Christian Science Monitor* article by Joseph C. Harsch "The Balance Sheet," 12/30/69, president's handwriting: January 16–31, 1970, box 5, WHSF: POF: President's Handwriting, NPMP.

43. Memorandum for the president from Moynihan, November 30, 1970, president's handwriting, December 1970, box 8, WHSF: POF: President's Handwriting, NPMP.

44. Memorandum from Moynihan to the president, November 13, 1970, president's handwriting, November 1970, box 1 (folder 1) (boxes 1–13), WHSF: SMOF: POF: Contested Files, NPMP.

45. The Nixon Administration Civil Rights Report, no date [but other material in the same folder indicates that it was from May 1970], box 2, [Ex] HU2 Equality—beginning 4/2/69, WHCF: Subject Files HU [Ex] HU, NPMP.

46. Memo to John Brown from Bryce Harlow, June 2, 1970, box 2, WHCF: Subject Files HU [Ex] HU, NPMP. See also handwritten notes on yellow lined pad, 7/24,

H-Notes July–December 1969 [July–September 1969], part I, WHSF: SMOF: Haldeman Notes, NPMP.

47. Nixon, *RN*, 436, Graham, *Civil Rights Era*, 345.

48. Carter, *The Politics of Rage*, 387.

49. Ambrose, *The Triumph of a Politician*, 124.

50. Small, *The Presidency of Richard Nixon*, 42.

51. Editorial, "Nixon and Blacks: Substance and Symbol," *The New Republic* (July 18, 1970), 7–8, esp. 7.

52. Cited in Kotlowski, *Nixon's Civil Rights*, 62.

53. See draft reply to Black Caucus recommendation 2, 3, and 4, Economic Security and Economic Development, Federal Assistance to State and Local Government—no date (May 1971 or later). For an extensive discussion on the problems, see Memo from Moynihan to the President, May 17, 1969, box 2, WHSF: POF: President's Handwriting, NPMP. See also Daniel P. Moynihan, *Maximum Feasible Misunderstanding: Community Action in the War on Poverty* (New York: The Free Press, 1969).

54. Memorandum for the president from Daniel Patrick Moynihan, January 16, 1970, president's handwriting: January 16–31, 1970, box 5, WHSF: POF: President's Handwriting.

55. Memorandum for the president from Buchanan, January 30, 1970, president's handwriting: January 16–31, 1970, box 5, WHSF:POF: President's Handwriting; H. R. Haldeman, *The Haldeman Diaries* (New York, G. P. Putnam's Sons, 1994), 126.

56. Memorandum for the President from Buchanan, February 12, 1970, Numerical Subject File 314 [Committee on Educational Quality] [1 of 3] folder 2 of 5 [boxes 16–22], box 1 [documents from boxes 3–14], Contested Files.

57. H. R. Haldeman, *The Haldeman Diaries* (Sony CD-ROM, 1994), February 28, 1970.

58. Handwritten notes 2/28, folder 1 of 25, documents from boxes 1–45, H Notes January–March 1970 [February 21–March 31, 1970], part II, box 41, WHSF: SMOF: H. R. Haldeman, Contested Files.

59. See, for instance, Small, who cites the memo as a "demonstrat[ion] that it [the administration] would not actively pursue civil rights issues." (*The Presidency of Richard Nixon*, 165). Michael Genovese saw a shift rightward on civil rights in late 1970 that married Mitchell's "southern strategy" with "benign neglect." Michael Genovese, *The Nixon Presidency: Power and Politics in Turbulent Times* (London: Greenwood Press, 1990), 82.

60. Memorandum for the president from Moynihan, January 16, 1970, President's Handwriting.

61. Ibid.

62. Ibid.

63. Handwritten notes of a meeting held on 6/26, H Notes April–June 1970 [May 6–June 30, 1970], part II, box 42, WHSF: SMOF: H. R. Haldeman, Contested Files, NPMP.

64. Memo to Jim Keogh from Ehrlichman, June 26, 1969, 105 Closed [desegregation] [1 of 2], box 30, WHSF: SMOF: Ehrlichman, NPMP.

65. Entry for Monday, April 28, 1969, *The Haldeman Diaries*.

66. *Haldeman Diaries*, Monday, July 13, 1970.

67. Jill Quadagno, *The Color of Welfare* (New York: Oxford University Press, 1994), 109. See generally chapter 2 (44–70) of Kotlowski, *Nixon's Civil Rights* for a discussion of Nixon's dealings with open housing and Romney.

68. Draft reply to Black Caucus, Black Caucus I [1 of 2] [CFOA 463], box 46, WHCF: SMOF: Garment, NPMP.

69. Memorandum for Pat Buchanan from Stanley S. Scott, August 31 1973. [FG1-FG 6-11-1/Scott, Stanley S.], box 5, WHCF: Subject Files: HU (Human Rights), NPMP.

70. Nijole V. Benokraitis and Joe R. Feagin, *Affirmative Action and Equal Opportunity: Action, Inaction, Reaction* (Boulder, CO: Westview Press, 1978), 40.

71. Benokraitis and Feagin, *Affirmative Action and Equal Opportunity*, 119–20, 156–57. Benokraitis and Feagin are careful to note that a fair amount of the increases in minority graduate enrollment was made up of Asian enrollments.

III

AFFIRMATIVE ACTION
AND THE NEW LIBERALISM

9

Affirmative Action in an Age of Limits

THE HUGE ECONOMIC GROWTH of the postwar period and, even more, the prospect of continuous growth, helped to rekindle Americans' faith in the future after the dark days of war and depression. There was a connection between growth and democracy established in the aftermath of World War II. As Seymour Martin Lipset noted: "The more well-to-do a nation, the greater the chances that it will sustain democracy." Lipset noted that wealth permitted "those in the lower strata to develop longer time perspectives and more complex and gradualist views of politics." Not only that, but wealth was seen as an inherent equalizer, a guard against the politics of *ressentiment*. Lipset observed, "the more well-to-do and better educated a man is, the more likely he is to belong to voluntary organizations . . . the propensity to form such groups seems to be a function of level of income and opportunities for leisure." In other words, growth underwrote the whole raft of postwar institutions. To the postwar generation of the elite, wealth took on a psychological importance far outweighing its material significance.[1]

Specifically, growth underwrote the belief that America was a land of equal opportunity, the idea that anyone, with some effort and a little bit of luck, could make it. As Louis Hartz noted, Horatio Alger survived the crash of 1929.[2] Even with some Willy Lomans, the system was generally accepted as a fair and equitable distributor of resources. The American Dream was still alive, even in this huge and complex economy. Postwar liberals, though nervous of the fragility of the Alger ideal, nevertheless found it an important component of Cold War ideology. The superiority of the American system lay in the way that the "little guy" could make it big, in its unbounded opportunity.

In the liberal belief system, continuous economic growth—"the pot of gold and the rainbow," as Walter Heller expressed it—created the possibility of progress, both economic and social. Should any minor adjustments be needed, constant economic growth provided very adequate funds for it. The future seemed, at least from a domestic perspective, assured.

What, then, happened when the ideal of sustained and unlimited growth disappeared? If Habermas's *Legitimation Crisis* sketches some of the general dynamics of what was occurring, the story of the onset of the age of diminished expectations indicates the way the crisis played itself out in its historically-specific American setting.

The next two chapters deal with the creation of various elements of a new liberalism shaped around the idea of specific limits to any sort of progress. Chapter 9 deals with affirmative action's part in creating a new subjectivity, a new path of connection between the individual through institutions to the state. It looks at affirmative action's role in providing a new moral legitimacy for certain institutions. It is particularly concerned with the replacement of the goal of growth and national efficiency with the goal of equality of treatment within liberal ideology.

This is the story of the implications of the switch between a land where anyone *could* make it to a land where everyone *should* make it, a redefinition of equality of opportunity. With the arrival of an era characterized by recognition of limits, affirmative action emerged as the way through which a national goal of fair equality could be made concrete. Institutions—business, in particular—could declare their allegiance to the new national goal of equity through affirmative action. While the first part of this chapter discusses the advent of limits and their implications, the second shows that even within John Rawls' abstract reconstruction of liberalism some sort of program similar to affirmative action would have to play a key part.

The End of National Efficiency

Although normally associated with the Ford and Carter presidencies, with the oil crisis and the convergence of inflation and recession that came to be known as "stagflation," the age of limits began in the minds of sections of the intelligentsia well before economic developments seemed to confirm is gloomy predictions. As more and more domestic social problems occurred, national efficiency—which had become important for generating funds for competition with the Soviet Union in arms and the space race, creating a general sense of superiority—became burdened with these domestic problems also.

Early attacks on inequalities were justified in terms of economic efficiency, even if they contradicted the actions of the market. In calling for government assistance to the "disadvantaged," the Small Business Administration (SBA) launched in 1953, as Jonathan Bean has observed, might be said to be the ancestor of governmental affirmative action. A number of contracts were "set aside" exclusively for small businesses, who, it was felt, were disadvantaged by the lack of research and development funds determined as necessary to compete successfully. It was admitted that some adjustments may be necessary to make the market system fair and that it may be necessary to redistribute some resources to the least advantaged. But all of this was done in the name of making the whole system more efficient, a Keynesian oiling of the wheels as much as augmenting moral deficiencies of capitalism.[3] Many of the early justifications of civil rights efforts involved the need for efficiency and intelligent use of available resources.[4] When the social problems loomed large in the mid-1960s, as we have observed in prior chapters, the call was for redoubling efforts at efficiency and wealth creation in order to fund ever-larger programs aimed at resolving them.

Later, however, affirmative action policies became not just possible but necessary. In an age characterized by limits, methods of allocating jobs, awarding contracts, and even deciding who entered college all needed new legitimacy. Whatever system of distribution that replaced the market would have to bear some sort of relationship to a recognizable national goal in order to give it some sort of legitimacy.

This was a process of augmentation rather than replacement. Businesses, of course, continued (and still continue) to operate on principles of efficiency; educational institutions—even more beholden to national imperatives— must still accept students on the basis of ability. Economic growth has occurred within the United States and has been welcomed. But the justification of "national efficiency" is missing from modern rationalizations of business and government decisions, replaced by commitment to affirmative action in the ubiquitous "mission statements" of today.

The End of Growth Liberalism

The Kerner Commission Report remains a remarkable historical document. It indicates that the commitment to the Myrdalian paradigm on race collapsed before the liberal attachment to constant economic growth. Even as it implicates "white institutions" and white people for racism, it regards "the great productivity of the American economy, and a Federal Revenue system which is highly responsive to economic growth" as the cornerstone of efforts against the racial divide in the country. In its goals and objectives, it lists first among nine: "Continued emphasis on national economic growth and job creation so that there will be jobs available to those who are newly trained, without displacing those already employed."[5]

However, the almost messianic regard for economic growth that characterized the pre-Nixon postwar period changed dramatically over the next few years. As Daniel Bell noted in 1976, in a passage that summed up the problems faced by the intelligentsia in the 1970s:

> Growth is held responsible for the spoliation of the environment, the voracious use of natural resources, the crowding in recreational areas, the density of the cities, and the like. . . . Just as the new politics rejected the traditional problem-solving pragmatism of American politics, it now rejects the newer, liberal policy of economic growth as a positive goal for society. But, without a commitment to economic growth, what is the *raison d'être* of capitalism?[6]

What, indeed?

To assume scarcity in the 1950s would have been, as we have seen, almost unAmerican. Yet, by the end of the 1960s, Americans' faith in the sustainability of economic growth and in its ability to resolve social problems was on the wane. Moreover, constant economic growth that had underwritten the civil rights efforts was no longer even seen as desirable. As historian Robert M. Collins has observed, "[t]he economic stagnation, stubborn inflation, and widespread pessimism that marked the 1970s contrasted sharply with the prosperity and confidence of the earlier post-war years. The loss of optimism was manifested in a growing distrust of established institutions and a widespread loss of faith in the curative powers of economic growth."[7] Though gradual, uneven and, in many areas, only partial, the retreat from growth manifested itself both popularly and within the intelligentsia. The new environmental groups celebrating the first Earth Day in 1970 called for "a thorough reassessment and reversal [sic] of unlimited economic growth as an economic goal."[8]

It began long before then. Important presaging ideas appeared, expressed in Rachel Carson's *Silent Spring* and Ralph Nader's *Unsafe at Any Speed* as well as in the Students for a Democratic Society's Port Huron declaration in 1962. In Britain, economists such as E. J. Mishan published critiques of growth that went far beyond J. K. Galbraith's 1958 *The Affluent Society*, which urged more social spending. (In fact, Galbraith did not attack growth; indeed, much of his theory depended on private economic growth to fund public projects).[9] These criticisms acquired a critical mass by the end of the 1960s.[10] By then, few economists expressed unbridled optimism about the curative powers of unbridled growth. Well before the Great Crash of 1929, Gary Gerstle has written, liberals lost faith in capitalism.[11] The same could be said of the 1960s; it was a seedtime for pessimistic ideas about the possibility or desirability of progress.

One of the reasons that affirmative action was not seriously considered during the Kennedy/Johnson era was, as has been noted previously, because affirmative action focused on racial progress as a distributive problem while the direction of policy then was on avoiding issues of distribution by concentrating on increasing production. Those standing on the lower rungs of the ladder of opportunity would at least be able to move upward. As President Johnson told an aide in 1964, anything was possible: "I'm sick of all the people who talk about the things we can't do. Hell, we're the richest country in the world, the most powerful. We can do it all. . . . We can do it if we believe it."[12]

By the time Nixon took office, with troops mired in the mud of Vietnam and riots tearing up the cities, few Americans believed it any more. The assurance of continual material progress appeared not only unrealistic but, to many, even undesirable. "The age of abundance has ended," wrote historian David Donald, summing up the perspective of the 1970s in the *New York Times.* He saw his duty as a historian to "disenthrall" students "from the spell of history, to help them see the irrelevance of the past, . . . [to] remind them to what a limited extent humans control their own destiny."[13] A new era characterized by diminished expectations was emerging.

Several other books appearing at the time captured the mood of the times. The themes running through these books—all published during Nixon's tenure—are remarkably similar. First, they point to a crisis, either imminent or already happening, the result, they say, of an overreliance on technological and economic solutions to problems. The result is, in an overused metaphor, that technology has become a runaway train, threatening to crash and kill its occupants. All point to a new era whereby economic growth is limited or tightly controlled. Most point to the need for a new, more human-centered value system to replace those "econocentric" values of the past. Each book argues that the new focus of American society must now be placed on the sphere of distribution rather than that of production.

One of the most famous expressions of these new perceptions was *The Limits to Growth* but many other "no-growth society" discussions, either inspired by or responding to this book, came forth around the same time, questioning the viability or even the desirability of continuous economic growth.[14] A group of some thirty individuals—scientists, educators, industrialists, civil servants—from ten countries met for the first time in April 1968. In early 1972 The Club of Rome, as they became known, published a report by a subsidiary Massachusetts Institute of Technology (MIT) project team. *The Limits To Growth* presented a glum picture forecasting population growth, resource depletion, food supply, capital investment, and pollution in the future. They forecasted that "(t)he most probable result [of present trends] will be a rather sudden and uncontrollable decline in both population and industrial capacity" unless the world sought equilibrium and a "stationary state" where economic growth was curtailed.[15]

The critic H. L. Mencken noted the eruption of Thorstein Veblen on the American intellectual scene: "Of a sudden, Siss! Boom! Ah! Then, overnight, the upspringing of the intellectual soviets, the headlong assault upon all the old axioms of pedalogical speculation, the nihilistic dethronement of Prof. Dewey—and rah, rah, rah for Prof. Dr. Veblen. . . . His books and pamphlets began to pour from the presses, and newspapers reported his every wink and whisper, and everybody who was anybody began to gabbing about him."[16] Such might have characterized the reception given to The Limits to Growth, if not to its authors. The report reverberated in the newspapers and magazines when it was published, causing a plethora of alarmist articles.

Most leading journals were critical of the report. The New York Times called it "an empty, misleading work." The Times of London called it "pseudo-science at its worst."[17] Yet, after criticizing the specifics of the book, the general point that there were limits to growth found agreement in nearly all reviews. As Rufus E. Miles, Jr., wrote, "The book's sensational doomsday warning seemed to strike a responsive chord—almost untouched by any previous work—in the strong intuitive feelings of many thoughtful citizens that the end of the era of dependable economic growth and high-energy affluence might be nearer than supposed by economic analysts and forecasters."[18] S. Fred Singer, an economist writing in Nation, was among the most critical but agreed that "a kind of self-regulation that uses the laws of economics" was necessary. "I don't feel as optimistic about population growth," he said.[19] Another more substantial review, published the next year, attacked the book savagely, yet agreed that its impact was positive: "As a result of reading The Limits To Growth many people are now thinking anew about long-term problems and discussing them much more seriously. In particular, they are discussing once again whether or not the world is likely to run up against physical limits. This is a very important achievement."[20]

As the critics pointed out, this perception of the limits to growth rested on three assumptions, all of them superficially correct. First, the spectacular growth in the Gross National Product occurring after World War II did not correlate to quality of life (more succinctly, money can't buy happiness); second, the resources of the earth—in some ways the basis of all prosperity—are finite; and third, environmental pollution was getting worse. These observations, however, might have been made at nearly any time. Nor were their prescriptions for a "condition of ecological and economic stability that is sustainable" any guarantee that resources would not be used up. They failed to deal with the important objection that economic growth also can be used to positive effect to clear up pollution, a fact that has been demonstrated by the relative success of Western countries in the battle against pollution. Whatever the criticisms, though, the ideas rapidly became an underlying assumption with which economists had either to agree or explain their disagreements.

The Limits to Growth became a template for works dealing with other topics, indicating that the concept of *limits* went far beyond economic limits. Fred Hirsch transferred the concept of limits in nature to that of American society, urging, in common with so many other social commentators of the 1970s, restraint: "To the extent that the mismatch between current expectations and resources is qualitative rather than quantitative, the restraint necessary would not be patience but stoicism, acceptance, and social cooperation—qualities that are out of key with our culture of individual advance."[21] In a book published in 1988, Nathan Glazer recalled the moment in the late 1960s when an insight came to him that was to dominate his response to social policy from that time onward: that there were definite limits to social policy, that they could not solve all of America's problems.[22]

The implications of many of the books appearing at the time was that some sort of moral correction was needed to augment or perhaps police a wayward technocratic regime. First was the reasoning that human need and technological goals had become unhinged and expressed different interests that must be reconciled. Second, in a zero-sum situation, some system of redistribution based on nonmarket reasoning was needed. Cited in the book, economist Dr. Herman Daly expressed the task for a new government in 1969 as he saw it:

> For several reasons the important issue of the stationary state will be distribution, not production. The problem of relative shares can no longer be avoided by appeals to growth. The argument that everyone should be happy as long as his absolute share of wealth increases, regardless of his relative share, will no longer be available. . . . The stationary state would make fewer demands on our environmental resources, but much greater demands on our moral resources.[23]

In other words, the problem of relative shares would become important, demanding some "moral" (i.e., noneconomic) system to divide resources. Thus, affirmative action appeared to be a potentially useful tool for the prophets of limits, though none came out and said it.

When Alvin Toffler, a then-obscure journalist, published *Future Shock* in 1970, it became an overnight bestseller. Toffler defined future shock as "the shattering stress and disorientation that we induce in individuals by subjecting them to too much change in too short a time." Though often labeled a "futurologist," Toffler explicated deep anxieties about the future, painting an image of technology as a speeding train, still accelerating, with no driver: "The horrifying truth is that, so far as technology is concerned, no one is in charge." *Future Shock* shared with *The Limits to Growth* both this sense of limits to possibilities of the future and an animus toward what Toffler called "econocentric" solutions. Though Toffler may have appeared hopeful in comparison, the message was similar: we must stop economic growth. "Technocrats suffer from econo-think. Except during war and dire emergency, they start from the premise that even non-economic problems can be solved with economic remedies."[24]

After rejecting "econo-think," Toffler—again, in a striking parallel to *The Limits to Growth*—calls for a new, morally-based ethos to replace it. "In its historical time and place, industrial society's single-minded pursuit of material progress served the human race well. As we hurtle toward super-industrialism, however, a new ethos emerges in which other goals begin to gain parity with, and even supplant those of economic welfare."[25] Toffler continued:

> At the same time, in societies arrowing towards super-industrialism, economic variables—wages, balance of payments, productivity—grow increasingly sensitive to changes in the non-economic environment. Economic problems are plentiful, but a whole range of issues that are only secondary economic break into prominence. Racism, the battle between the generations, crime, cultural autonomy, violence—all these have economic dimensions; yet none can be effectively treated by econocentric measures alone.[26]

Expressed here is the sense that economic solutions to social problems have failed, and that cultural problems have impacted upon economic variables. Thus, even for economic problems, extraeconomic solutions will be needed.

British-based author E. F. Schumacher's *Small is Beautiful* echoed and developed many of these themes in 1973, selling over 700,000 copies in multiple languages. Schumacher challenged the doctrine of economic, technological, and scientific specialization and proposed a system for intermediate technology, based on smaller working units, cooperative ownership, and regional workplaces using local labor and resources. Again, Schumacher emphasized the inherent thresholds in the scale of human activity that, when surpassed, produce effects that subtract from or even destroy the quality of all life. He used the examples of cities: "I think it is fairly safe to say that the upper limit of what is desirable for the size of a city is probably something of the order of half a million inhabitants. It is quite clear that above such a size nothing is added to the virtue of city."[27] Schumacher hoped to resolve the problem of the 1970s that he neatly expressed in an article published in *The Nation*:

> From 9 to 5, the businessman struggles for growth, expansion, rationalization, labor saving, job elimination, even automation; all meant, and expected, to lead

to ever increasing prosperity, ease, and happiness. After hours, however, he finds himself bombarded by urgent appeals to limit growth and by prophecies of doom, breakdown of civilization, ecological disaster, and exhaustion of resources. During the day, he studies every conceivable way to speed things up; whereas after hours, he cannot avoid encountering every conceivable argument in books like *The Limits to Growth* and *Blueprint for Survival*, calling for stabilization, for slowing down rather than speeding up.[28]

Again, this was a search for an extraeconomic intervention into the means of production and distribution, an attempt to capture the runaway economic train that no longer seemed to be headed for humanistic goals.

The implications for the United States in particular were large. Collins noted that "[g]rowth has often been America's 'out'—the way, many believed, that the nation could somehow square the circle and reconcile its love of liberty with its egalitarian pretensions."[29] The new focus on the realm of distribution of the stationary state pointed to the problem of just how resources were to be divided. This situation was new. As economist Gian Singh Sahota noted, "the mid-1970s have witnessed a surge of interest in distribution theories."[30] Prior concentration on increased production, as well as the pervasive hostility to all things perceived to be socialist, had rendered discussion of distribution moot.

In a society subsumed by the goal of increasing productivity, the allocation of, for instance, jobs was simply not an issue. If anything, distribution was subsumed within the problem of production. Kermit Gordon noted the postwar understanding of distribution: "the differentials in income are meant to serve as incentives—rewards and penalties—to promote efficiency in the use of resources and to generate a great, and growing, national output."[31] With the previous attitude toward growth, it could be assumed that, with a constantly expanding economy, the pool of jobs would increase. With the goal of increased production, the allocation of jobs was ruled by considerations of efficiency, functional rationality, and what Daniel Bell referred to as "the organization of production through the ordering of things, including men as things."[32] The allocation of the job was seen as a functional question based on productivity.

Individual merit—a value touted by latter-day critics of affirmative action—was also subsumed by production. Those, like Daniel Bell, calling for a return of merit-based allocation of employment opportunities miss this point. As Norman Daniels has explained, there is no reason to understand merit simply as an individual attribute. Merit has, in the past, been linked with productivity—meritorious employees furthered the aim of the company. But productivity has always been seen on a larger scale than simply individual worth. Consider the following case. Jack and Jill both want jobs A and B, and each prefers

A to B. Jill can do either A or B better than Jack. But the situation in which Jill performs B and Jack A is more productive than that of Jack performing B and Jill performing A. The employer, with an eye on macroproduction, naturally chooses the former situation, despite the fact that Jill, being more efficient, deserves the more desirable job. It has never really been the case that the best person available should get the job; other considerations have intervened. The assignment of specific workers to specific jobs has always been dictated by larger productivity questions, themselves subject to even larger considerations dictated by the market. Individual ability and effort, though more important in the drive for national efficiency and growth, did not mean automatic placement in the most appropriate jobs. Thus, many critics of affirmative action hark back to a golden age that never existed.[33]

A Theory of Justice

John Rawls' philosophical works are an important element within the story of affirmative action's rise despite the fact that he does not mention affirmative action in his major texts. In the development of Rawls' theory up until his *meisterwerk*, *A Theory of Justice*, was published in 1971 and in what have largely been justifications for what was contained in that book since then, a remarkably historically accurate parallel to the travails of liberalism and its need for reconstitution exists. In Rawls' 1958 article, "Justice as Fairness," we see an abstract reconstruction of postwar American society. In its 1967 incarnation, Rawls' theory of justice devoted more attention to the "least advantaged" members of society and, in 1971, Rawls emerged with the finished version of his theory that would, he hoped, serve as the basis for a reconstitution of liberalism.

Thus Rawls's theories serve us well as abstract versions of the empirical themes of this book. The following analysis of Rawls' theory understands Rawls' works as prescriptions—albeit expressed abstractly—for various problems besetting postwar liberalism, something with which Rawls would surely not disagree.

The primary philosophical problem with which Rawls engages lies in an impasse that haunted many thinkers in the second half of the twentieth century, between the "good" and the "right," between moral imperatives and utilitarian rationales. Utilitarianism—the greatest good for the greatest number—ran into the difficulty that, according to the theory, it was right to sacrifice the good of one often for the good of many. Such a theory sat uncomfortably in a liberal individualist polity, especially when seen as a basis for majority-minority dealings. By reducing individuals to simple receptacles of happiness, utilitarianism denied that any moral purpose might unite a society or that individual morality had any real role to play. Intuitionism asserts that each person has a power of moral intuition that is essentially rational. It holds that the right is independent of the good, and makes rightness a fundamental, irreducibly moral conception. Intuitionism, however, is in many ways a mere expression of conviction; if two people have different moral intuitions, intuitionism has no answer.[34]

That Rawls made a real attempt at resolving these problems sets him apart from many other philosophers in the twentieth century, who as Kukathas and Pettit note, were "loath to present themselves as defenders of any particular values."[35] It also moved in the direction of resolving a similar question expressed in political theory—the divide between existing conceptions of what is politically feasible, on the one hand, with what is politically desirable, on the other. Such a bridge might have helped bring together academic disciplines that had long developed progressive demarcations between their respective professional spheres such as economics, political science, and philosophy. H. Gene Blocker and Elizabeth H. Smith observe that "Rawls' work can be seen as a way of relieving a major political schism of our time, one which separates the libertarian right from the egalitarian left." They note that, in law, Rawls' theory helped resolve a dispute between legal positivism and those arguing for a natural rights/natural law conception. "Like Kant, Rawls stands as the man in the middle, a mediator of many longstanding disputes."[36] The immodesty of Rawls' theoretical project (though Rawls himself made less grand claims for his theories than have other writers), with its attempt to resolve so many problematic divisions as well as provide a basis for political action, is perhaps its greatest strength.

A Theory of Justice, published in 1971, became, for a time, enormously influential and the book received favorable reviews in the *New York Review of Books*, the *New York Times Book Review*, the *Economist*, the *Spectator*, *Nation*, the *Washington Post*, *The Times Literary Supplement*, and others. No detached philosopher, Rawls was blunt about his project, which was to recreate a basis upon which liberalism might provide a stable order, to recreate the consensus that had held Americans together in the postwar period.[37]

The book is a complex synthesis of twenty years of philosophical development. Rawls dealt with many topics and left many questions—purposefully, it sometimes appears—open-ended in a way that has created vast amounts of material dedicated simply to clarifying the meaning of many aspects of the theory. Key aspects of the theory evolved at different times, though.

Rawls' solution to the schisms that he felt beset liberalism became the heart of his book, a brilliantly simple, elegant, formal maneuver, "one of the loveliest ideas in the history of social and political theory," as Robert Paul Wolff, a trenchant critic, put it.[38] Rawls constructed a formal model of a society populated with rational, self-interested persons that would choose the way in which their society would organize. Called the "original position" (and self-consciously referring to Rousseau's "initial situation"), Rawls posited that these individuals would, if they were rationally self-interested, unanimously choose a set of principles from which institutions and practices within which the players interact might be evaluated. Once they agreed on those principles, Rawls added to the rules of the game, they would have to abide by those principles. His concern was to derive principles of justice from this formal model that might stand as the basis to a just society.[39]

Though Rawls remained abstract in his reasoning, his attention to particular problems reflected his consideration of problems arising at the time. Specifically, it is possible to see in Rawls the changes to liberal thinking from the 1950s to the 1970s. In his theory's original appearance in his 1958 essay "Justice as Fairness,"[40] Rawls derived two principles of justice from this model that reflected the emphasis on equal opportunity. The first was that "each person participating in a practice, or affected by it, has an equal right to the most extensive liberty compatible with a like liberty for all." The second, which would be changed in later versions, was that "inequalities are arbitrary unless it is reasonable to expect that they will work out for everyone's advantage, and provided the positions and office to which they attach, or from which they may be gained, are open to all."[41] Rawls used the expectations of the "representative man" to judge whether an inequality was legitimate; the representative man must believe that an unequal distribution works to his advantages. In other words, if there were a dispute over the rules within, say, a game of baseball, representatives might be made up of pitcher, infielder, outfielder, and catcher, who represented the various different positions within the game. In order to decide the efficacy of the rules, these four players could fairly represent the views of most players.[42] Rawls claimed that the principles were at the same time an accurate reconstruction of our settled moral convictions *and* the solution to the bargaining game. The American capitalist system received a moral blessing since the inequality it generated worked for the good of everyone. When all felt that the game was to their advantage, the theory worked beautifully. What was good was right and what was right was good.[43]

The next version of the theory appeared in 1967, a date of crucial importance in understanding the influences upon Rawls, as "Distributive Justice."[44] He made two revisions to his theory, both of which expressed a solicitude toward the least-advantaged members of his society. He introduced the "veil of ignorance," whereby "no one knows his position in society, nor even his place in the distribution of natural talents and abilities." The second revision was a change in the second principle of justice. Instead of justifying inequalities by their acceptability to everyone playing the game—or of the representative man—inequalities had now to be justified by their acceptability to the "representative man of those who are least favored by the system of institutional inequalities."[45] This new conception has been referred to at various times and by various people as the "difference principle" and the "maximin" conception of justice. Rawls asks the question of "whether it is possible to arrange the institutions of a constitutional democracy so that the two principles of justice are satisfied, at least approximately."[46]

Reflecting the times, Rawls continued to insist that growth and efficiency remained important goals, though they were now measured by how much it helped the least advantaged (instead of the "less advantaged" mentioned in the 1958 version). "The basic structure is perfectly just when the prospects of the least fortunate are as great as they can be."[47] The test of efficiency, then, was its ability to help the least advantaged.[48]

John H. Schaar observed in 1975 that "Rawls proposed a basic shift in our operative definition of equality."[49] Equality of opportunity, in the past, made real the primary liberal tenet that the individual is the basic unit of society. It justified inequality within capitalism by holding aloft the possibility that all individuals have equal chances to hold offices and positions within society. Schaar pointed out that:

> Up until a few years ago, this understanding of equality as equality of opportunity reigned virtually unchallenged. . . . John Rawls . . . proposes that the liberal principle of equal opportunity must, as a requirement of justice, be replaced by a new understanding of "fair equality of opportunity."[50]

Rawls' revisions also had major implications for the *subject* in the new arrangement, somewhat diminished compared to his earlier version, a theme that will be explored further in the next chapter. The "veil of ignorance" reflected the disappearance of the universal "representative man." The veil covered up the particularities of his players and reflected Rawls' attempts to deal with the disappearance of the liberal consensus. It was meant to force consensus upon all players. Stripped of all status, privilege, and prior knowledge, they became the least advantaged or, in the concrete world, "minorities," at least potentially. The veil of ignorance conveyed the new sense of risk and doubts about the future. The concern for the "least fortunate" reflected a concern to minimize risk from what might have been described in the past as "the masses" or "the mob." In the 1960s, of course, this threat appeared racial.

Whereas the previous model had melded the moral imperatives with what was right by showing that what was good for all was also morally just (by showing that all self-interested "reasonable" parties would agree to the present rules), this second version made it problematic. The greatest happiness for the greatest number was not necessarily what was "right." The imaginary administration in Rawls' original position suffered the same legitimacy crisis discussed by Habermas, requiring Rawls to consciously and artificially recreate the morality of the system, to restore what had previously been automatic.

As Ian Shapiro has noted, Rawls downplayed the difference between his original model and this new conception of his theory of justice.[51] In Rawls' terms, pointing out the problems with the "Pareto-optimal" justification for inequalities in his first version of events would "only show what we knew all along," namely that the efficiency of a system and a high degree of equality of opportunity did not guarantee justice.[52]

In the final version, published in 1971, Rawls stapled onto the old concept of equal opportunity new demands for compensation within a new system that would, he hoped, please all "by combining the principle of fair equality of opportunity with the difference principle."[53] A finished version of the principles derived by those in the original position is contained nearly halfway through *A Theory of Justice*:

First Principle
    Each person is to have an equal right to the most extensive total system of equal basic liberties compatible with a similar system of liberty for all.

Second Principle
    Social and economic inequalities are to be arranged so that they are both:
    a) to the greatest benefit of the least advantaged, . . . and
    b) attached to offices and positions open to all under conditions of fair equality of opportunity.[54]

They are, as in the first model, lexically ordered so that the first precedes the second and (b) precedes (a) within the second. In the book, Rawls asserted that those in the "original position" would unanimously choose this set of rules above any other. This was Rawls' attempt at replacing the older consensus, as we discussed in the first section, with a new consensus that might be the basis of liberal society.

Rawls also added extra stipulations to the "veil of ignorance" in the 1971 version. All parties in the original position know much more about the general situation than they did in previous versions. In particular, they must assume that their society needs a system of justice—"moderate scarcity" is assumed so that the players cannot imagine that, with endless abundance, no system of justice would be necessary. This reference to moderate scarcity showed that the disenchantment with growth liberalism had permeated Rawls' theory from the real world. Rawls also had his parties "understand political affairs and the principles of economic theory; they know the basis of social organization and the laws of human psychology."[55] The parties in the original position would choose the maximin rule first. There are only a few alternatives, as Rawls omits, for example, any form of libertarianism, principles requiring distribution according to need, and desert-based conceptions of justice.[56] Rawls also stipulated that "the person cares very little if anything, for what he might gain above the minimum stipend that he can, in fact, be sure of by following the maximin rule. It is not worthwhile for him to take a chance for the sake of further advantage, especially when it may turn out that he loses much that is important to him. . . . The situation involves grave risks."[57]

This much-modified process, whereby the parties of the original position choose the difference principle, is perhaps the most criticized of Rawls' formulations. As Allan Bloom asked, where did Rawls find this "cramped little risk-fearing man" in the original position?[58] However, Rawls made no claim to have derived the choice made by original position parties from their characteristics. Instead, he had, as he admits, made the stipulations conform as closely as possible with the desired result of the maximin principle: "We want to define the original position so that we get the desired solution."[59]

Responses to Rawls

Scholarship has tended to concentrate on criticizing Rawls from either a left or right perspective (along with those from the less-easily categorized communitarian tradition) but many criticisms are common to both, particularly those that deal with the structure of the theory. One of the key problems, it has been pointed out, is that Rawls ignores any questions of production.[60] Myriad problems with the original position have been pointed out, especially the difficulty that the parties of the original position know little about themselves yet have "life plans" (presumably they don't know what they want but they know how to get it!) and very sophisticated knowledge about human psychology, economic theory, and a developed sense of justice. The "veil of ignorance" is uneven in that some things must be known whereas others must remain hidden.[61] Rawls constructed his theory so it would fit intuitively with the existing liberal democratic conceptions, from the result to the method, as he admitted.

However, much of the criticism directed from political perspectives misses the point. From the left, the complaint is that Rawls is simply bolstering the liberal status quo.[62] This is true to an extent, but misses the important point that his model of justice fundamentally changes the existing legitimation for the liberal status quo, providing something qualitatively new. This is what makes Rawls so important. Conservatives and "neo-cons" picked up on this point at the time and accused Rawls of undermining traditional (liberal) universal conceptions of rights, notions of equality of opportunity, and merit. They ignore the bankruptcy of these particular values—the need to overhaul traditional bases of legitimacy—emanating from the failure of the liberal polity to make them truly universal, real for all Americans. In any case, libertarian thinking, by the time that Rawls finished his book, had become counterintuitive in the eyes of most Americans. Like a philosophical version of Franklin Roosevelt or perhaps Nixon (though, of course, in a very different way), Rawls can be seen as doing conservatives a favor despite their antagonism to him.[63]

In many ways, Rawls begins with an impossible problem. For a utilitarian purpose—the survival of democratic liberalism—he wishes to locate or develop a Kantian moral imperative. Rawls' answers to other problems are similarly ironic and even Nixonian. If the question of equality cannot be dealt with politically, remove it from the political/public sphere, which, as Hannah Arendt has shown, is the font of all equality.[64] For the sake of preserving democracy, we must place it beyond the reach of the people. Thus, in a stark parallel to Nixon's actions in the real world, Rawls moved the problem from the unsettled political sphere into the realm of the purely administrative. As Daniel Bell observed: "But in the larger context, the wholesale adoption of the principle of fairness in all areas of life shifts the entire society from a principle of equal liability and universalism to one of unequal burden *and administrative determination*."[65] By showing that all "reasonable" people would agree with his proposition, Rawls short circuits democracy, just as Nixon did by removing race from political discussion.

This is a problem cogently discussed by none other than Jürgen Habermas. The most damaging aspect of the shift in liberalism is its destruction of the public sphere (with, as Habermas notes, concomitant damages to the private sphere).[66] Discussed in Rawlsian terms, Habermas shows that Rawls sets down the rules of the game a priori, making the public good of rights meaningless because they cannot be exercised by the parties themselves. "For the higher the veil of ignorance is raised and the more Rawls' citizens themselves take on flesh and blood, the more deeply they find themselves subject to principles and norms that have been anticipated in theory and have already become institutionalized way beyond their control. . . . Because the citizens cannot conceive of the constitution as a *project*, the public use of reason does not actually have the significance of a present exercise of political autonomy but merely promotes the nonviolent *preservation of political stability*."[67] With a now-familiar irony, we see that Rawls curtails political liberty in order to preserve the system founded upon it and embarks upon dismantling the public sphere because it cannot be made to admit all.

As if to demonstrate the problem concretely, Rawls notes a problem in utilitarianism whereby a large part of society has an irrational abhorrence of certain harmless religious or sexual practices, for which we might substitute the irrational racial prejudices of large percentages of white Americans toward African Americans. Rawls observes that, with a utilitarian perspective, there is nothing to be done about prejudice: "Even when these attitudes are unsupportable on moral grounds, there seems to be no sure way to exclude them as irrational. Seeking the greatest satisfaction of desire may, then, justify harsh repressive measures against actions that cause no social injury." In justice as fairness, however, "this problem never arises. The intense convictions of the majority, if they are indeed mere preferences without any foundation in the principles of justice antecedently established, have no weight to begin with. . . . To have a complaint against the conduct and belief of others we must show that their actions injure us, or that the institutions that authorize what they do treat us unfairly."[68]

Conclusion

What all of the above books emerging around this time show is that affirmative action in its modern sense was an administrative device implied by their analyses, even if they failed to mention it by name. Thus, the utility of an affirmative action-based program for restructing liberalism looms high over its use to its purported benefactors. Affirmative action was possible, available, and, most importantly, became the means by which first the state and then various institutions could demonstrate their allegiance to the national goal of racial equality. Thus, though we have seen that affirmative action developed backwards by destroying the basis of the older, more informal method of allocating jobs, contracts, and college places, it also became the mechanism for the creation of a new basis for doing so. It furnished a sense of continuity with Myrdalian liberalism in the sense that it can be (and often is) justified in the terms of the American Creed.

Inasmuch as it provided demonstrable and, importantly, limited goals and targets, it fit in very well in an era uncomfortable with open-ended goals of the past. Indeed, the terms "goals" and "targets" mirror economic terms, providing a sense of contribution to cultural progress at a time of no economic progress. Though contestable in terms of who it purportedly assisted, it could be endlessly adjusted and tinkered with.

It also fit in well with an era (and with abstract representations of the era) characterized by limits. It chimed with the mindset of risk aversion that developed in an age of limits—something that has not been fully explored in this chapter but is nonetheless relevant. Without the possibility of progress, the concept of "risk" will hold only negative implications.[69] Carving out a social system that is geared toward the needs of the "least advantaged" has little economic rationale, as critics of Rawls pointed out. But, if "moderate scarcity" is assumed, conflict will be in the minds of those attempting to create ruling principles; ensuring that the least advantaged have a stake in the system, as Nixon would have termed it, makes sense. That Nixon's and Rawls' motives are so similar explains the parallel mechanisms put in place, albeit in concrete and abstract forms respectively.

This chapter has dealt with the need for affirmative action in a very abstract sense. The areas that actually implement affirmative action policies—employers, private and public, agencies that award contracts, and educational institutions—involve providing opportunities for the advancement of individuals. They are all (and especially higher education, where most of the public disputes regarding affirmative action occur) related to life chances; hence they may be justified as creating equal opportunities. To adopt these policies in spheres that cannot be seen as related to individual opportunity would be difficult because of the stress laid even now on the importance of individual effort. As Gareth Davies noted: "The language of opportunity has remained central to American discourse . . . a liberal political agenda could not be advanced unless it was seen to respect the nation's dominant social philosophy."[70]

In the differences between the stages of Rawls' thinking, it is possible to see a fairly drastic change in the relationship between the subject and the government that corresponded to what was happening concretely. Rawls' 1967 version contained the blueprint for the new role of victim and indeminifier. Of the two, only the latter is self-defining. Just as Rawls created this new category in order to legitimate his liberal order, so did Nixon. How Nixon contributed to this new relationship in a concrete sense is the subject of the next chapter.

Notes

1. Seymour Martin Lipset, *Political Man: The Social Bases of Politics* (Baltimore: The Johns Hopkins University Press, 1981 [1959]), 31, 45.

2. Louis Hartz, *The Liberal Tradition in America* (London: Harcourt Brace & Company, 1991), 62–63.

3. See Jonathan J. Bean, *Big Government and Affirmative Action: The Scandalous History of the Small Business Administration* (Lexington: University Press of Kentucky, 2001). See Section 9 of the Small Business Act in Addison W. Parris, *The Small Business Administration* (London: Praeger, 1968), 267.

4. See, for instance, Eli Ginzberg et al., *The Negro Potential* (New York: Columbia University Press, 1956).

5. *Report of the National Advisory Commission on Civil Rights* (New York: New York Times Publications, 1968), 411, 414–15.

6. Daniel Bell, *The Cultural Contradictions of Capitalism* (London: Heinemann, 1976), 80.

7. Robert M. Collins, *More: The Politics of Economic Growth in Postwar America* (Oxford: Oxford University Press, 2000), 98.

8. Cited in Collins, *More*, 99.

9. See E. J. Mishan, *The Costs of Economic Growth* (London: Staples Press, 1967).

10. Rachel Carson, *Silent Spring* (London: Penguin, 1965), Ralph Nader, *Unsafe at Any Speed: The Designed-In Dangers of the American Automobile* (New York: Grossman, 1965).

11. Gary Gerstle, "The Protean Character of American Liberalism," *American Historical Review* 99, no. 4 (October 1994): 1045–74.

12. Cited in Collins, *More*, 54.

13. Cited in Christopher Lasch, *The Culture of Narcissism: American Life in an Age of Diminishing Expectations* (London: Abacus, 1980), 19.

14. Dennis L. Meadows, Donella H. Meadows, Jorgen Randers, William W. Behrens III, *The Limits to Growth: A Report for the Club of Rome's Project on the Predicament of Mankind* (London: Potomac Associates, 1972).

15. Meadows et al., *The Limits to Growth*. 23–24.

16. Cited in Arthur M. Schlesinger, *The Crisis of Confidence: Ideas, Power and Violence in America* (London: Andre Deutsch, 1969), 86.

17. Cited in S. Fred Singer, "Do We Dare to Grow?" *Nation* (November 27, 1972): 527–31, esp. 530.

18. Miles, *Awakening from the American Dream*, 2.

19. Singer, "Do We Dare to Grow?" 530.

20. H. S. D. Cole, et al., *Thinking About the Future: A Critique of* The Limits to Growth (London: Chatto and Windus, 1973), 6.

21. Fred Hirsch, *Social Limits to Growth* (London: Routledge and Kegan Paul, 1977), 9.

22. Cited in Stephen Steinberg, *Turning Back*, 105.

23. Cited in Dennis L. Meadows, et al., *The Limits to Growth*, 179.

24. Alvin Toffler, *Future Shock* (London: Pan Books, 1974 [1970]), 2.

25. Toffler, 390.

26. Toffler, 408.

27. E. F. Schumacher, *Small is Beautiful: A Study of Economics as if People Mattered* (London: Blond & Briggs Ltd., 1973), 61.

28. E. F. Schumacher, "Night Thoughts About Progress," *The Nation* (April 6, 1974): 434–36, esp. 434.

29. Collins, *More*, 240.

30. Gian Singh Sahota, "Theories of Personal Income Distribution: A Survey," *Journal of Economic Literature* 16, no. 1 (March 1978): 1–55, esp. 1.

31. Kermit Gordon in the Foreword to Arthur Okun, *Equality and Efficiency: The Big Tradeoff* (Washington, D.C.: The Brookings Institution, 1975), vii.

32. Daniel Bell, *The Cultural Contradictions of Capitalism* (London: Heineman, 1976), 233.

33. See Norman Daniels, "Merit and Meritocracy," *Philosophy and Public Affairs* 7, no. 3 (Spring 1978): 206–23.

34. Of course, this is necessarily a fairly crude summation of entire schools of thought. For a useful and quite lucid introduction into these areas in relation to Rawls, see Wolff, *Understanding Rawls*, 11–15.

35. Chandran Kukathas and Philip Pettit, '*A Theory of Justice*' *and Its Critics* (London: Stanford University Press, 1990), 4.

36. H. Gene Blocker and Elizabeth H. Smith, "Editors' Introduction," Blocker and Smith, eds., *John Rawls' Theory of Social Justice: An Introduction* (Athens: Ohio University Press, 1980), xiii, xvi.

37. Rawls, though studiously avoiding discussions of the concrete in his book, explained in 1980 that throughout his work "the practical social task is primary." Cited in Thomas W. Pogge, *Realizing Rawls*, (London: Cornell University Press, 1989), 3–4. See also Rawls' recent work, *Justice as Fairness: A Restatement* (Boston: Harvard University Press, 2001), edited by Erin Kelly. In another article, Rawls contends that, without consensus, a democratic regime "will not be enduring and secure." "The Domain of the Political and Overlapping Consensus," *New York University Law Review* 64, no. 2 (May 1989): 233–55, esp. 233. See also John Rawls, "Justice as Fairness: Political Not Metaphysical" in J. Angelo Corlett, *Equality and Liberty: Analyzing Rawls and Nozick* (New York: St. Martin's Press, 1991), 145–73. George Klosko also discusses this aspect of Rawls in "Rawls' 'Political' Philosophy and American Democracy," *American Political Science Review* 87, no. 2 (June 1993): 348–59.

38. Robert Paul Wolff, *Understanding Rawls: A Reconstruction and Critique of* A Theory of Justice (Princeton: Princeton University Press, 1977), 16.

39. See Wolff, *Understanding Rawls*, chapter 3, "The Key," 16–21.

40. John Rawls, "Justice as Fairness," *The Philosophical Review* 67, no. 2 (April 1958): 164–94.

41. Rawls, "Justice as Fairness," 165.

42. Rawls, "Justice as Fairness," 167. Here, he uses the baseball analogy.

43. For a useful discussion of the first form of Rawls' model, see Wolff, *Understanding Rawls*, 25–34.

44. John Rawls, "Distributive Justice," in Peter Laslett and Walter G. Runciman, ed., *Philosophy, Politics and Society*, 3rd series, (New York: Barnes and Noble, 1967), 58–82.

45. Rawls, "Distributive Justice," 66.

46. Rawls, "Distributive Justice," 69.

47. Rawls, "Distributive Justice," 66.

48. See Henry David Rempel, who attacks Rawls for his reverential view of efficiency in "Justice as Efficiency," *Ethics* 79, no. 2 (January 1969): 150–55.

49. John H. Schaar, "Equality of Opportunity and the Just Society" in Blocker and Smith, eds., *John Rawls A Theory of Justice: An introduction*, 162–84, 166.

50. Schaar, "Equality of Opportunity and the Just Society," 167.

51. Ian Shapiro, *The Evolution of Rights in Liberal Theory* (Cambridge: Cambridge University Press, 1986), 225.

52. Rawls, "Distributive Justice," 65.

53. John Rawls, *A Theory of Justice* (Cambridge, MA: Harvard University Press, 1971), 75.

54. Rawls, *A Theory of Justice*, 302.

55. Rawls, *A Theory of Justice*, 137; Wolff, *Understanding Rawls*, 72.

56. Rawls does, however, provide a short analysis of libertarianism elsewhere (*A Theory of Justice*, 65–72).

57. Rawls, *A Theory of Justice*, 154; Ian Shapiro, *The Evolution of Rights in Liberal Theory* (Cambridge: Cambridge University Press, 1986), 210–11; Kukathas and Petitt, *A Theory of Justice and its Critics*, 40.

58. Allan Bloom, "Justice: John Rawls vs. The Tradition of Political Philosophy," review of John Rawls' *A Theory of Justice* in *The American Political Science Review* 69, no. 2 (June 1975): 648–62, esp. 659. Other critics have made similar points. See, for instance, John C. Harsanyi, "Can the Maximin Principle Serve as a Basis for Morality? A Critique of John Rawls's *A Theory of Justice* in *The American Political Science Review* 69, no. 2 (June 1975): 594–606; Kukathas and Petitt, *A Theory of Justice and its Critics*, 39.

59. Rawls, *A Theory of Justice*, 141; Shapiro, *The Evolution of Rights in Liberal Theory*, 209.

60. Shapiro, writing from a left-wing perspective, attacks Rawls for his attention to problems of production. Shapiro, *The Evolution of Rights in Liberal Theory*, 250. Anarchist critic Wolff agrees. See Wolff, *Understanding Rawls*, 200. See also libertarian critic Robert Nozick.

61. Wolff, *Understanding Rawls*, 71–75. Michael Sandel, in a communitarian critique of Rawls, shows that those in the original position cannot really be construed as individuals at all, given that they know nothing about themselves but think identically. Michael Sandel, *Liberalism and the Limits to Justice* (Cambridge: Cambridge University Press, 1982), 127. See also David L. Norton, "Rawls's Theory of Justice: A 'Perfectionist' Rejoinder," *Ethics* 85, no. 1 (October 1974): 50–57, esp. 51. See also Kukathas and Petitt, *A Theory of Justice and its Critics*, 96–99.

62. Wolff, *Understanding Rawls*, Shapiro, *The Evolution of Rights in Liberal Theory*, Hans Oberdiek, "Review: A Theory of Justice," *New York University Law Review* 47, no. 5 (November 1972): 1020–22, esp. 1021.

63. Daniel Bell, "On Meritocracy and Equality," *The Public Interest*, no. 29, (Fall 1972): 29–68, esp. 61. See also Bloom, "Justice: John Rawls vs. The Tradition of Political Philosophy." As John Schaar noted in 1980, "work, thrift, enterprise, and profit are defended as moral values only by a few fanatics." Schaar, "Equality of Opportunity and the Just Society," 163.

64. See Hannah Arendt, *The Human Condition* (London: University of Chicago Press, 1958).

65. Daniel Bell, "On Meritocracy and Equality," *The Public Interest*, no. 29 (Fall 1972), 61.

66. Habermas noted this in his 1962 publication, *The Structural Transformation of the Public Sphere: An Inquiry into a Category of Bourgeois Society*, translated by Thomas Burger (Cambridge, MA: The MIT Press, 1989 [1962]). See the discussion on pages 223–24, for example.

67. Jürgen Habermas, "Reconciliation Through the Public Use of Reason: Remarks on John Rawls's Political Liberalism," *The Journal of Philosophy* 92, no. 3 (March 1995): 109–31, esp. 128.

68. Rawls, *A Theory of Justice*, 450.

69. Frank Furedi provides an excellent exposition of this process in *Culture of Fear: Risk-Taking and the Morality of Low Expectations* (London: Cassell, 1997).

70. Gareth Davies, *From Opportunity to Entitlement: The Transformation and Decline of Great Society Liberalism* (Lawrence: University Press of Kansas, 1996), 3.

10

Nixon: The Father of Identity Politics

A LWAYS ON THE LOOKOUT for new constituencies, a memo contained in files
marked "President's Handwriting" gives some indication of just how far
Nixon would go. One of Nixon's aides, Henry C. Cashen, wrote a memorandum regarding a meeting with the winners of the Seventh World International
Bowling Federation Tournament. Cashen noted that there were then fifty-two
million American bowlers, according to the latest poll. Nixon circled the figure and wrote, "H [aide H. R. Haldeman] - note." At least three letters followed
instructing senior staff to note there were fifty-two million bowlers in the
United States. Nixon duly had a publicity shot of himself bowling passed to
the press on September 27 1971. The file shows, however, that the positive impact of Nixon's conversion to the joys of bowling was limited. A flood of letters followed. As Mrs. Ruth M. Mathieu of Wayzata, Minnesota, among many
others, pointed out, the picture clearly showed the president stepping over the
foul line! This was, of course, pure Nixon. The bowling alley in the basement
of the White House, one imagines, fell silent for some time.[1]

On the one hand, this story is about the comically desperate attempts of a
caricature of the postwar politician, always on the make, always looking for
new groups to represent and thus consolidate his base of support. One can almost see the slogans emanating from such a campaign. "Nixon's right up your
alley!" "Don't settle for a spare; a strike every time with Nixon." "Stay out of
the gutter with Nixon" (though, keeping in mind the common Herblock
image of Nixon, this latter suggestion may have backfired).

However, historians and political scientists write off Nixon's occasionally
clownlike political efforts as the obsessive politicing of a chronic campaigner

at their peril. Nixon's chameleonlike appeals to groups old and new, his willingness to jettison most principles and experiment with new formulations not only sum up his true genius but mark his crucial contribution toward creating a new basis for liberalism. His fanatical attention to group politics has had profound effects on the political landscape, creating new political entities and going some way to creating a new relationship between American citizens and the state.

The essential dilemma for Nixon and almost all other political figures (as well as, we have seen, John Rawls) at the turn of the decade was to justify American government in the eyes of its citizens. What was government to do without the goal of national growth and efficiency? Without the encapsulation of progress in economic growth, which Americans could feel more or less a part of, what would government mean to them? Growth had been essential for staving off dissatisfaction in citizens. Disappointment at not achieving a particular policy or policy change could be assuaged by the thought that generating enough resources in the future might result in the implementation of the favored policy. This was a predicament for both government and citizens. However, as this chapter shows, it began with the legitimation crisis in the elite, who projected it on to those below. Of course, that is not to say that those down below did not respond to the clarion call from their betters as they sought an identity within the new arrangements.

There is an abundant literature, especially in the realm of political science, discussing whether or not—and how—the nature of the relationship between state and citizen has changed. Some of the recent literature has concluded that the crises pointed to by Habermas and others have not been sustained or, if they have, they were more superficial than Habermas imagined.[2] Some suggest that a "new" citizen responds to different stimuli. Ronald Inglehart sees "a shift from Materialist to Postmaterialist value priorities . . . from giving top priority to physical sustenance and safety toward heavier emphasis on belonging, self-expression, and the quality of life."[3] Yet, as many have observed, the citizen has moved further away from the public sphere.

This chapter looks at efforts Nixon made to restructure the relationship between the federal government and the citizen and their consequences. In essence he contributed to the process of the "'clientalization' of the citizen's role" as Habermas termed it, whereby the citizen became passive and dependent on the federal government.[4] This client role was implied when, with the active assistance of Nixon, the government role changed from one that rights wrongs—the image of Kennedy and Johnson—to one that indemnifies damages. However, Nixon also actively pushed forward this clientalization by creating a growing list of groups within which Americans might identify themselves.

The point made here is that the basis of the relationship between citizens and the state is more important than the specific groups that formed. Rather than asking who is a minority and who is not, as John D. Skrentny has in his recent publication, *The Minority Rights Revolution*, this chapter focuses upon the basis of the relationship of the state to that minority—or majority—group. Nor were these new groups able to achieve policy change because of the precedent set by the black civil rights movement; it was because of the openness of politicians of all political colors to new constituencies. Some groups were partially self-forming and many formed in bitter opposition to Nixon, but they all called for recognition of their disadvantaged status and state action to compensate it. Few called—as Martin Luther King, Jr. did—for the destruction of their particular identity through the alleviation of the conditions that created it. Here, attention will be paid to the basis upon which they formed, rather than to their exact makeup.[5]

Nixonian affirmative action, with its emphasis on quiet, top-down negotiation, attempted to reduce the political participation of African Americans as a cohesive group. No longer would they be an interest group that mobilized to force change in the system, competing against many other groups for resources. The retreat sounded by Nixon from integration made the second class status suffered by African Americans a permanent feature. However, Nixon knew that a permanent black/white confrontation was potentially destabilizing. Thus, he made furious efforts to dilute black claims of damages by showing that others, too, were victims and deserved the compensation of some sort of affirmative action.

The point made later in this chapter—that, in fact, the Silent Majority were the first group to be defined almost entirely by its victimhood—may be more controversial. Before the civil rights movement entirely gave up their demands for social justice, Nixon (and, before him, Goldwater) created new constituencies of those "who suffered in silence the inequities perpetrated by successive liberal Democratic administrations." If the "culture of complaint" is normally seen in relation to minority groups, Goldwater and Nixon ensured that the political right played a role in creating it.[6]

Expanding Affirmative Action to New Groups

Nixon helped to determine the future of affirmative action by changing the framework within which Americans viewed themselves from white and black terms to a series of groups formulated in various ways but having in common a feeling of grievance. As one article contained in the White House files of Leonard Garment noted: "We need a new way of looking at our bankrupt social and economic policy and our worn-out, black/white human relations programs."[7] Nixon provided it. In previous chapters we saw how Nixon attempted to break the solid wall of resistance in the African-American community into smaller pieces. Here, we see how he divided up what had been the "mainstream" into various different groups, relativizing the experience of African Americans.

In the light of the apparent ingratitude of African Americans for the efforts made by his administration on their behalf, Nixon decided that "benign neglect" should consist of a more solicitous attitude toward other groups. By July of 1970 Nixon instructed his staff to switch priorities in domestic priorities:

> We have, for the last year and one-half, overloaded schedule activity to Blacks, youth and Jews. From here on, until further notice, there are to be no Jewish appointments set up per se. There are to be just enough Blacks to show we care. . . . The concentration is now to be on Italians, Poles, Mexicans, Rotarians, Elks, Middle Americans, Silent Americans, Catholics, etc.[8]

A year later, Nixon had distilled the essential message of his instructions when he instructed White House aide Charles Colson:

Blacks ⎱
Youth ⎰ forget[9]

Nixon explained to the then-up-and-coming staff member Colson at a staff meeting in July 1970 that the administration "won't do Watts thing." An overly concerned approach to blacks, Nixon said, "doesn't win Negroes, could alienate whites. Look at Wallace strength in Gallup [poll?]" He told Colson that the administration must "play more to labor." Colson, who was the administration liaison between the White House and organized labor, readily agreed.[10]

In 1968 the focus of Nixon and everyone else was upon blacks. Despite the fact that the designations "minority" and "disadvantaged" had long been used in relation to civil rights efforts, few looked at the issue in anything other than black and white terms. The civil rights movement, rioting, and the assassination of Dr. Martin Luther King, Jr. had focused the American mind squarely on black civil rights. In the run up to the 1968 election, Nixon had posed the issue in black and white terms. In his famous "Bridges to Human Dignity" speech, Nixon unveiled his "Black Capitalism" idea. This was a black—not a minority—formulation.[11]

In the run up to the 1972 election, however, the Republican Party platform felt able to ignore African Americans in a pamphlet concerning human rights. Here, there were category subheadings for "children," "youth," "women," "older Americans," "working men and women," "Spanish-speaking Americans," "Indians, Alaska Natives & Hawaiians," "consumers," and "veterans." There was one section entitled "ending discrimination" but no reference to black Americans.[12] This was, among other things, a tacit admission by the American political class that they had little or no idea of what their constituents thought or how they viewed themselves. These were, in some ways, banners waved to see who would follow them. But they became counterweights and cross-currents to the divisions between black and white that, with the huge majority of blacks hostile to Nixon and with Wallace still on the scene, it made no sense to heighten.

At least part of the reason for this shift was the actions of the president. Nixon made moves in this direction almost from the day he took office. In 1969, he ditched the "black capitalism" formulation in favor of a more inclusive term: minority business enterprise. In March, the president signaled "the extension of the program to cover all minority groups as opposed to the early emphasis on 'Black Capitalism.'" Nixon's efforts would not be limited "merely to creating business in the ghetto" but would "seek to encourage minority business enterprise everywhere." This change of focus met with approval from civil rights groups who met the new president on March 5, 1969, and were concerned with what they saw as anti-assimilationist implications of Black Capitalism.[13] What they could not have foreseen was that Nixon would use recognition of these additional groups not to assimilate African Americans but to steer them into a competition with other groups, ensuring that black civil rights groups became supplicants within the "system" rather than the vanguard of opposition to it.

When Domingo Nick Reyes quit as a staff member of the Civil Rights Commission in September 1969, saying "the Jewish-dominated Commission is black-oriented to the almost total exclusion of the Chicano and the Indian," Nixon evidently was sympathetic. He scrawled on the news summary carrying the story: "E[hrlichman]—Let's have a report on this. I believe it is probably true—the top staff man, as you recall, is a holdover."[14] Nixon was certainly influenced by his urban advisor, Daniel Patrick Moynihan, on the subject of race relations. Long memos by Moynihan can be found in the President's Handwriting files in the Nixon archives, elaborately annotated by Nixon. In 1969 Moynihan told his boss: "We must dissolve the black urban lower class." He continued the theme in his "Benign Neglect" memo. In order to usher in a quieter, less clamorous period, one where "Negro progress continues and racial rhetoric fades," Moynihan called for "greater attention to Indians, Mexican Americans, and Puerto Ricans." Nixon scribbled "I agree" beside the paragraph.[15]

During the next few years, Nixon acted on his agreement. Embarking on a series of gestures, Nixon ensured that other minorities received his attention.

As Dean Kotlowski has observed, Native Americans were a "safe" minority to help. Nixon preempted concerted demands by Native Americans and helped shape the anti-assimilationist sentiment within the budding Indian rights movement. He restored Blue Lake to the Taos Pueblo in New Mexico and gave the Mount Adams area to the Yakima Nation. The budget of the Bureau of Indian Affairs increased by 214 percent between fiscal year 1969 and fiscal year 1972. Nixon supported the Alaskan Claims Settlement Act that confirmed native title to forty million acres of land, $462.5 million in cash, and a $500 million share of future oil revenues.[16] By such gestures, Nixon attempted to mold Native Americans into a model minority or, at least, into Nixon's model of a minority.

Nixon also nurtured relations with the more numerous group, Hispanic Americans, even before the Moynihan memo. The way the question of bilingual education was posed in a Nixon memo hints at the preemptive nature of Nixon's dealings with them. There was no real demand for it. At a 1966 "preplanning conference" for a White House conference on Mexican-American problems, there was no demand for bilingual education.[17] Though the Bilingual Education Act was signed by Johnson on January 2, 1968, Johnson had recommended no money at all for the new program. But Nixon and his cabinet immediately raised the issue, whether Hispanic Americans wanted it or not. Nixon scrawled at a meeting in February 1969: "Bi Lingual [sic] (do we wait for Mexican Americans?)"[18]

Nixon included Hispanic Americans within EO 11478 and other affirmative action programs. Though they were already listed as a minority and were, therefore, officially an "affected class," Nixon promoted their interest. He announced on November 5, 1970, the adoption by the Civil Service Commission of "a sixteen-point program to assist Spanish-speaking American citizens who are interested in joining federal civilian service."[19]

Certainly, the attention to the Hispanic population of the United States had more electoral relevance than did Native Americans, who numbered less than one million in 1970. Key states such as California and Texas could be swung by the votes of Hispanic Americans, something not lost on Nixon. However, not all Nixon's moves toward Hispanics were gestures designed to accrue votes. When Maurice Stans wrote a letter expressing the wish to appeal the 1973 budget for the OMBE, Nixon wrote in the margin: "Don't announce but double the amt. in Spanish. Keep the black about where it is."[20] This move was almost certainly more of an attempt to set these groups in opposition to each other (and, thus, not united in opposition to the federal government). Here is another example of breaking problems down into more manageable pieces.

The president kept up the attempts to promote Hispanic-American group interests by increasing their representation. His efforts in this direction are undeniable. According to a rather fawning letter from Fidel Gonzalez, Jr., the California State Director of the League of United Latin American Citizens (LULAC), Nixon had made more appointments of Hispanic Americans than all thirty-six of his presidential predecessors. Some Mexican Americans, Gonzalez claimed somewhat generously, have "referred to you as the 'Abraham Lincoln of the Spanish-American.'"[21]

A raft of ethnic entrepreneurs, not blind to the fact that the Nixon administration was open to claims by minorities other than African Americans, wrote in to the administration, hoping for some kind of sponsorship. Not all received a favorable response. Mike Masaoka and David Ushio of the Japanese American Citizens League received very little response to their demand for recognition of the "victim status" of Japanese Americans, despite their warnings of the "explosiveness of the situation."[22] The position of Japanese Americans within affirmative action programs was clearly not promoted or pushed by Nixon—despite the fact that they were ostensibly included in many programs under the term "Orientals." Similarly, women's groups received an ambiguous response from Nixon for their inclusion in programs, again, despite the fact that, in letter, they were included. Nixon clearly promoted the interests of groups that he felt could be an effective counterweight to black claims, who might compete with African Americans. Some groups were "recognized" by Nixon; others were not.

Nixon's attempt to deal with these groups established what would come to be known under Ford as the "Office of Public Liaison." This was a new structure designed to create a direct relationship between groups and the White House, circumventing Congress, which had proved unresponsive to Nixon's programs and initiatives. Especially after the off-year elections of 1970 failed to deliver a Republican majority in Congress, Nixon attempted to galvanize support directly. This was a new initiative. Though since Franklin Delano Roosevelt, presidents sought to forge ties and maintain contact with external constituencies, "not until the Nixon years did systematic efforts emerge to use specialized White House aides to perform this task."[23]

Affirmative action was one way that Nixon attempted to relate to these groups. Even Charles Colson, who had protested vociferously against the Philadelphia Plan and continuously called for the resignation of Arthur Fletcher,[24] suggested a "Philadelphia Plan for Hispanic Americans" to the President in 1971.[25] Several times, the issue of whether to include white ethnics within the affirmative action remit was discussed. As early as January 1970, administration officials Harry Fleming and Peter M. Flanigan debated whether those with ethnic backgrounds should be included within the affirmative action remit. Flanigan, arguing against the proposal, noted: "It's one thing to help the Blacks who are admittedly underprivileged. It's quite another thing to suggest that simply because someone has an ethnic background (like me) he deserves special attention for job placement."[26]

The issue came up again, however. In January 1973 the U.S. Department of Labor, Office of Federal Contract Compliance, issued new guidelines to cover discrimination against persons because of religion or ethnic origin. These guidelines stated:

> Members of various religious and ethnic groups, primarily but not exclusively of Eastern, Middle, and South European ancestry, such as Jews, Catholics, Italians, Greeks, and Slavic groups continue to be excluded from executive middle management, and other job levels because of discrimination based on their religion and/or national origin. These guidelines are intended to remedy such unfair treatment. (60–50.1 of Chapter 60, Title 41, Code of Federal Regulations)

In the end, it was decided that affirmative action would deal only with "unchanging physical characteristics."[27] Also in 1973, however, affirmative action was extended to the physically and mentally handicapped. In 1974, nonnative speakers of English were included. Within SBA's 8(a) program, the original definition for the purposes of classification had been "Negroes, Spanish-speaking, Indians, Eskimos, and Aleuts" but, at least potentially, members of all races could benefit provided they were "deprived."[28] In 1979, the program was expanded to include "Asian Pacific Americans." In the 1980s the SBA accepted petitions from representatives of the following groups for inclusion within the 8(a) program: (East) Indians, Sri Lankans, Tonganese, Indonesians, Nepalese, and natives of Bhutan. It rejected petitions from Hassidic Jews, women, disabled veterans, Iranians, and Afghans.[29]

Thought of as a political category, it is difficult to determine whether the inclusion of women as a beneficiary of affirmative action programs has been successful. Of course, as some have demonstrated, women have benefited more than any other category in terms of jobs provided, though it would be difficult to determine whether the great increase in women working since the 1970s is the result of affirmative action or lower wages forcing more wives out to work to supplement the family income.[30] Yet affirmative action cannot be said to be the basis of the relationship between the federal government and women, especially after the highlighting of sexual violence in the late 1970s and 1980s.

Another less than successful political constituency appeal by both parties was to "white ethnics." Democrats attempted to co-opt them into a new progressive coalition on the basis of shared victimhood. In 1967, Irving M. Levine began the National Project on Ethnic America. Levine, urban affairs director of the American Jewish Committee, sought to "push whites off a strictly negative anti-black agenda" and to make them "conscious of their own realities."[31]

In other words, Levine hoped that if whites could be made aware of their own oppression, they might stop oppressing blacks. Similarly, the National Center for Urban Ethnic Affairs (NCUEA), developed in 1969, presented the complaints of blue-collar Americans in language more redolent of African Americans: "These 'middle Americans' earning their 'moderate income' are often the *victims* of a stereotype—the hardhats, the silent majority, racists."[32]

This group, referred to generally as "white ethnics," though little more than a historical curiosity today, was a key target group for politicians of all stripes in the early 1970s. Journalist Peter Hamill penned an article entitled "The Revolt of the White Lower Middle Class" which was published in *New York Magazine* on April 14, 1969. In it, Hamill brought out the identification as victims of at least a segment of the Silent Majority: "The working-class white man sees injustice and politicking every-where in this town, with himself in the role of victim. . . . The working-class white man spends much of his time complaining almost desperately about the way he has become a victim." Nixon certainly noticed this trend. He had a memo sent to Moynihan asking him to analyze the article, saying: "I find this to be a very disturbing article. What is our answer?"[33] As indicated above, the fact that Colson was put on to the case indicates the seriousness with which Nixon took these new groups.

White ethnics—the "almost-minority"—failed ultimately to be recognized as disadvantaged, perhaps because they were difficult to cohere as a group. Were they "ethnics," or Catholics, or Italian/Polish/Irish? How did they view themselves? This was an experiment that did not ultimately work because these ethnics were being subsumed within a new group whose claim of victimhood emanated from the claims made by minorities. Later, they would feel that they were disadvantaged by the affirmative action machinery meant, ostensibly, to alleviate the disadvantage of others.[34] The competition for disadvantaged status, or contest of victimhood, thus came from opposition to affirmative action as well as from those within its remit.

Nixon and the White Victim

Besides acknowledging the existence of other minority groups, Nixon formed a "minority group" of the majority. He took those that had loosely counted themselves within the great coalition and directed the resentment they felt, as the institutions through which they had related to government lost their importance, against liberalism itself. Rather than, like Wallace, encouraging these Americans to blame civil rights gains and African Americans directly, Nixon acknowledged that African Americans had suffered, admitting their complaints without agreeing to take any real action to alleviate their condition.

But he also led a section of white Americans to list their own complaints, creating a counterweight to African-American complaints and reducing the case
of the civil rights movement from a transforming crusade to make America
true to her own creed to a list of grievances. In this way, Nixon made American society appear unjust not only to African Americans, Mexican Americans,
and Native Americans but to those at the heart of America, the Silent Majority. His adeptness at manipulating the "New Politics" for his own purposes ensured his election in 1968. The Silent Majority became a victim of the noisy
few but also, by implication, of the existing arrangements that had allowed the
noisy few the platform in the first place.

Nixon's political opportunism, in fact, created the prototype of the "victim" image so berated by some generally right-wing pundits today. However,
it was not his embrace of affirmative action but his molding of the resentments of blue-collar Americans that began the process. Before indicating
how Nixon did this, it is necessary to show that resentment to affirmative
action—like the source of its resentment—shifted dramatically from when
the first debates arose in 1963 to the mid-1970s. Indeed, resentment against
affirmative action was probably not generalized until the *Bakke* decision was
handed down in 1978.

The remarkable thing about affirmative action policies, given how many
Americans have been affected by them, is that little comment greeted their arrival. Exceptions to quotas in the past tended to be argued in very general
terms, usually invoking democratic principles. As discussed previously, objections to quota-based affirmative action policies rested primarily on their perceived divisiveness and "unAmericanness," or that they abrogated traditional
union and management prerogatives. After the travails of 1968, these objections were largely overcome. No new objections, at that time, replaced them.

Though the issue of "discrimination against whites" arose early on, the primary objections to employment quotas came, as discussed in previous chapters, from employers and unions, who were fearful of loss of control over the
processes of hiring, firing, and promotions. Though in 1963 the issue had
made headlines, by 1970, few people remained interested.[35] There is simply no
evidence that anyone in the media thought the new involuntary affirmative action warranted comment rather than simply reportage for nearly three years
after the Philadelphia Plan and Order No. 4 were implemented. None of the
leading liberal publications mention the issue once until the latter half of 1972.
Though the *New Republic* does mention the controversy in 1972, the *Nation*
contains no comment at all on the matter throughout Nixon's first term of office. Nor do conservative publications such as the *Christian Science Monitor,
U.S. News and World Report, Business Week,* and *Forbes* magazine contain anything more than routine reports about affirmative action or quotas in the two

years following the implementation of the Philadelphia Plan. A survey of the *Readers' Guide to Periodical Literature*, indexing of contemporaneous media coverage, contained no reference categories for "quotas," "affirmative action," or "Philadelphia Plan" in 1969, 1970, or 1971.[36] The only other programs that had any prominence—the OMBE and the SBA's 8(a) programs encouraging black business—received praise from conservatives like California Governor Ronald Reagan, who praised SBA "boot straps" programs to assist minority entrepreneurs, and criticism from liberals as distractions from real civil rights.[37] For most Americans, affirmative action was simply not yet an issue.

There were few objections to preferential treatment for minorities in colleges and universities, despite the fact that many openly ran preferential policies. When objections were made, it was on an entirely different basis than recent objections to affirmative action. As Richard P. McCormick noted, quotas of both staff and student admissions were initiated with few difficulties at Rutgers in 1968 after black students demanded them.[38] Macklin Fleming, Justice of the Court of Appeal, State of California, and Louis Pollak, Dean of the Yale Law School, published their argument over preferential treatment in *The Public Interest* in the spring of 1970.[39] Yale Law School initiated a system of quotas for the first year class of the fall of 1969 whereby forty-three black students were admitted, of whom five qualified under the regular standards and thirty-eight did not. Fleming objected that this would lead to separate law schools and legal institutions—one black and one white—that the under-qualified black students would suffer in such a highly competitive atmosphere (leading to "aggressive conduct" by black students), that Jews and "Orientals" would suffer from the inevitable extension of quotas to other groups. Fleming stated that "the American Creed, one that Yale has proudly espoused, holds that an American should be judged as an individual and not as a member of a group." Justice Fleming, however, admitted "racial quotas may serve a purpose in some contexts."[40]

Jews had reasons to fear quotas, given the interwar restrictions at Ivy League colleges on how many Jews could attend. Restrictions of many social clubs against Jews ended only in the 1960s. Antagonism had occurred between black Americans and Jews sporadically since the 1930s in New York City, often due to the proximity of the two communities and Jewish ownership of businesses in black areas. In the late 1960s some black leaders made blatantly anti-Semitic comments in a dispute over the control over public schools that peaked between September and November 1968. S. Ardhil Frieberg, in an article entitled "Negroes and Jews—Confrontation or Cooperation?" written in *The Crisis* in February 1969, hinted at the direct competition between Jews and blacks resulting from black demands in colleges. However, this passage also indicates that, to most people, affirmative action remained part of a still-vital civil rights effort: "People of good will consider it fair and equitable to provide this 'compensation.'"[41]

In fact, it was in higher education that the first real controversies about affirmative action broke out. In 1970 *The Wall Street Journal* reported that demonstrations at the University of Michigan led by black students resulted in the Board of Regents voting to set a 10 percent Negro admissions quota. "The action presumably was well-intentioned, but it was nonetheless unfortunate," the paper complained, worried about white backlash. Needless to say, there was no discussion of victimized white students.[42]

A debate arose on quotas from late 1971 on the pages of the American Jewish Committee's publication, *Commentary*. However, much of the early criticism of quotas on the pages of *Commentary* simply implied that a worthy program was in danger of being taken too far. It clearly had an eye on the pernicious effects of earlier quotas. Stephen Steinberg, in an article on quotas appearing before the storm had broken, told readers: "One can only speculate on whether this will significantly diminish educational opportunities for Jews." Steinberg imagined that wealthy students admitted on the basis of family contacts might be the ones to suffer.[43]

Though it may fairly be objected that the implications of affirmative action programs—and the direction in which they would move—was not entirely clear by 1971–1972 when these articles were written, the "white victim" thesis, whereby affirmative action attacks the civil rights of whites, had yet to be made persuasively.[44]

Conservative publications were either silent on the issue or critical of Nixon, as was *The Wall Street Journal*. After Nixon's letter to Philip Hoffman became news, an editorial worried only that "the likely result [of Nixon's *volte face* on quotas] will be that the public and the bureaucracy will conclude that there is now no real policy to combat job discrimination."[45] Even the DeFunis case, whereby Marco DeFunis sued Washington State University when he was denied a place in its law school was originally launched not as an anti-preferences case but on the basis that DeFunis's family had paid taxes in the state of Washington for fifty years. It was only after his lawyers noticed that minorities with lesser test scores had been admitted that DeFunis changed the basis of his case to an abridgement of his Fourteenth Amendment rights.[46]

In fact, the sense of "white victimhood" has only recently identified itself against affirmative action. It has become generalized since Nixon, rather than during his tenure of office. As Stanley Rothman and Amy E. Black noted in 1998, "while in 1980, very few whites (less than one in twenty) expressed the view that minority gains came at the expense of whites, almost half our white respondents support that view now."[47] However, though it had yet to be generalized, it was Nixon's politically entrepreneurial forays that created the basis for today's victimhood before African Americans, other minorities, or women presented themselves or were presented in similar terms.

The Origins of the Silent Majority

The raw material of anger and resentment that would make up the Silent Majority and later provide the basis for the "white victim" of affirmative action did exist in the 1960s. Specifically, the American working class had been a recognizable entity during World War II and before, holding an honored and important position, as Nathan Glazer and Daniel Patrick Moynihan noted in 1970: "Radicals fought over his allegiance, the Democratic party was happy in his support, one could even see workers portrayed in the movies by men such as Humphrey Bogart, John Garfield, [and] Clark Gable."[48] In the postwar period, though, the concept of the worker was downgraded. As the 1960s progressed, those who had been at the center of the Rooseveltian Democratic coalition found that many elements of American society seemed to be reorienting itself around the needs of African Americans. No more the heroes and increasingly fingered as the villains, they experienced a destruction of their sense of place in the world.

But the anger and resentment of those who had formerly been the working class did not immediately translate automatically into white victimhood. In no sense could a conservative or racial response be presupposed. They might, theoretically, have been reorganized politically on the side of the civil rights movement. They might have reacquired an ethnic identity. The temporary nature of labels used to describe this group—"forgotten Americans," "silent Americans," "Silent Majority," "New Majority"—indicates their inexact nature and that an evolution was taking place as Nixon and others grasped for some way to pin them down. Since Franklin Roosevelt's time, the working class had been aligned to the Democratic Party. As the identity lost its meaning, political parties competed to use formulations that might reach the unaligned, blue-collar Americans. It was largely the success of Nixon in reaching this group—after much trial and error—that created the white victim.

Policy makers—even Republicans—did not experience the dissolution of this group simply as an opportunity. They perceived the existence of an unaligned group with no fixed identity as a threat, as a potentially destabilizing force in American society. Throughout the 1960s, the destruction of postwar institutions disoriented blue-collar Americans. Trade unions in particular had played a key role, organizing them, regulating relationships within the workplace and even, in the Myrdalian sense, educating their members, promoting patriotism and progressive perspectives among them.

Thus, the paniced reaction identified by Habermas ensued, as the White House sought to replace the institutional influence by establishing its own direct relationship with this group. At least one part of the origins of affirmative action lies in the failure of trade unions to successfully "educate" their members to accept African Americans. Thus, instead of regulating their behavior through these institutions, the federal government would regulate it directly (as Hugh Davis Graham points out, the amount of new federal regulations increased fivefold during Nixon's tenure).[49]

The first to experiment with new ways of relating to the working class was actually the spectacularly unsuccessful Republican presidential candidate of 1964, Barry Goldwater. Few of Goldwater's appeals worked until he tried a set of tactics that were new to conservative campaigning. He used lines such as "We want to make it safe to live *by* the law; enough has been done to make it safe to live life *outside* the law." The issue of crime created a constituency that felt victimized by a liberal approach by liberal policy makers and especially by the Supreme Court's *Miranda* decision. One pamphlet asked "Are you safe on the streets? What about your wife? Your kids? Your property? What about after dark? Why should we have to be afraid? This is America."[50] These sentiments struck a chime with those who increasingly felt helpless, powerless, and lost as the world they knew unraveled.

Nixon was, as Tom Wicker observed, one of them, ideally suited to relate to angry blue-collar Americans. His manner was like that of the smart kid at a rough school, despised by his peers and loathed by his superiors. His facial expression was often that of a whipped dog who clearly anticipated more whipping. His background was blue collar; his life was a series of snubs and resentments; he, too, carried a chip on his shoulder. He had played by the rules—his magnanimous gesture toward his country in the 1960 election springs to mind—but had lost and received no credit. He had been "kicked around" by the press. He could, more convincingly than most politicians, personify the victim.

As *de facto* Republican candidate by 1966, Nixon inherited Goldwater's most successful tactics. He pointed to the civil rights movement's alleged role in the breakdown of law and order. In an article published in 1966, provocatively called "If Mob Rule Takes Hold in the U.S.," he argued that "the deterioration [of respect for the rule of law] can be traced directly to the spread of the corrosive doctrine that every citizen possesses an inherent right to decide for himself which laws to obey and when to disobey them." However, he carefully drew a line separating him from Wallace.[51]

In the run up to the 1968 election, Nixon played on the issue for all it was worth: "I say that doubling the conviction rate in this country would do far more to cure crime in America than quadrupling Humphrey's war on poverty."[52] The Republican Party formed a "Crusade Against Crime" in the run-up to the 1968 elections.[53]

The increased sense of vulnerability was not restricted to blue-collar workers but found a resonance within the elite, though they, unlike blue-collar Americans, continued to look to liberal reforms to offset the danger. It was the same sentiment that led John Rawls to insist on rules that would ensure the well-being of the least advantaged. However, there was also a partial recognition that a community's victimization gave various institutions a new role to play. The way the Nixon administration picked up on the problem of heroin addiction indicates its use for the authorities. Clayton Riley, the arts editor of *Liberation*—needless to say, no great fan of Nixon—noted: "While we take time to program the destruction of the 'pig' ('Off him') and cheer the small inconveniences we construct against whitey's existence, and even as we walk tall in a new and valid sense of our own beauty, the Mighty Horse gallops through our neighborhoods; heroin arrives as the genuine ruler of our lives." "The drug problem" was given a separate section in a report about minorities and was the sole source of congratulations to the Nixon administration from the Congressional Black Caucus. Nixon staff member Brad Patterson felt that "the Black Caucus grudgingly had kind comments on the drug responses" and thought "the Administration was making some progress in this area." Accordingly, the budget proposed to increase money for drug rehab centers in urban areas from $28.5 million in 1969 to $88 million in 1972.[54] Here was a small justification for the presence of some sort of authority in the ghetto.

The issue of crime was important in the evolution of the white victim. The Republicans, anxious to avoid the nakedly racial politics of the Wallace campaign, deliberately concentrated on the "victim" rather than the alleged "criminal." The blame for the perceived social breakdown was kept as diffuse as possible. As James Sundquist observed, "In the public's perception, all these things merged. Ghetto riots, campus riots, street crime, anti-Vietnam marches, poor people's marches, drugs, pornography, welfarism, rising taxes, all had a common thread: the breakdown of family and social discipline, of order, of concepts of duty, of respect for law, of public and private morality."[55]

Politicians blindly searched for new ways of relating to voters, for new political formulations, for ways of characterizing them so that they could connect with them. Nixon's success came from what Garry Wills pointed to as his best asset—his "iron butt."[56] This was Nixon's strength, his virtue as a politician rather than his vice. He mounted a relentless search for new constituencies and new ways to relate to old ones. By doing so, Nixon was able to outmanoeuver his opponents.

Perhaps Nixon's most crucial move in the construction of the victim was the identification of silence as a virtue in the face of so many problems. At first, it was a sign of frustration that they could mobilize so few on their own side. Nixon would often ask when faced with a demonstration, "Where are our people?" They concluded that they had been cowed into silence by the vociferous minority, the "big mouths." In order to summon up some psephological authority, Nixon began claiming the support of all those who did not protest; he would champion them. A sign of disengagement, resentment rather than real anger, Nixon made this alienation a virtue. He experimented with a number of terms but thematically all were contrasted with activist protestors. In one of his radio speeches in 1968, Nixon called for a new "alignment of ideas" that included Republicans, "New Liberals," the "New South," "Black Militants," and a fifth element, "a non-voice, if you will." "That is the silent center, the millions of people in the middle of [the] American political spectrum who do not demonstrate, who do not picket or protest loudly."[57]

At this stage, Nixon had no idea how significant the formulation would be. In 1970 he reflected that "the most significant line of the speech was the one that dealt with 'silent Americans.'" Certainly, he repeated it often, pledging in his 1968 acceptance speech to represent "the non-shouters, the non-demonstrators."[58]

He clearly still hoped that he could form a meaningful, *activist* counterweight to the demonstrators that dogged him. Some of Nixon's pleas were for more Americans to take responsibility. At a meeting discussing campus disorders on March 18, 1969, Nixon ruefully concluded: "Students and faculty must recognize what the real issue is; only if they take the responsibility on each campus will the problem be solved. The great mass of students must stand up and be counted since a denial of their point of view is really an issue."[59] Unfortunately, they sat and counted themselves out. Taking the pragmatic view that if the mountain would not come to Mohammed, Mohammed would go to the mountain, Nixon increasingly identified them by their silence. This formulation of "silent Americans" undoubtedly made a virtue out of inaction, passivity, and disengagement, qualities that had been condemned as vices in prior decades.

The Silent Majority

On November 3, 1969, Nixon made a speech on Vietnam where he appealed to the Silent Majority. It contained no new policy but an appeal to Americans to support Nixon's continuing efforts to find an honorable end to the Vietnam War. It was essentially a rebuff to those who both predicted and called repeatedly for immediate withdrawal, to the peace demonstrators. "And so tonight—to you the great silent majority of my fellow Americans—I ask for your support."[60]

Somewhat unexpectedly, the speech generated a huge response from the American public. Nixon modestly recalled: "Very few speeches actually influence the course of history. The November 3 speech was one of them." The White House mail room reported the biggest response ever to any presidential speech.[61] More than 50,000 telegrams and 30,000 letters had poured in, and the percentage of critical messages among them was low. A Gallup phone poll taken immediately after the speech showed 77 percent approval.[62] True, eager aide Charles Colson had manufactured some of the response but no one could deny that the speech had a large effect. The most important effect—the way that the speech did change history—was that it identified the center of American politics, the representative man or woman, as silent.

The concept of "Silent Majority" was evidently something to which many Americans now related. The files show that there were many versions of the Silent Majority. The Black Silent Majority Committee appeared alongside the awkwardly titled Spanish-surnamed Silent Majority (its name indicates that its origin was not quite at the grassroots level), and a Chinese group called itself the Silent Minority.[63]

The difficulties in mobilizing such a constituency would soon become apparent. However, Nixon and his team did not understand that it was silence that held the Silent Majority together and tried many ways of coaxing them to speak. Shortly after the speech, Nixon told his aides, "I hope we can use every possible device to keep this very real asset from wasting away."[64]

The truth, as both Nixon and more liberal groups courting the Silent Majority would find out, is that they tended to concentrate on issues rather than giving political allegiance one way or the other. Great hope was placed in the 1970 off-year elections. In its run up, Nixon called "for the silent majority to speak out with power far greater than four letter or any other kind of words—the power of their votes."[65] Especially after hardhats marched in New York in May of 1970, protesting at the lowering of the American flag after the shooting dead of four students in Ohio, the Nixon team assumed the Silent Majority expressed old-fashioned cold-war patriotism.

They were mistaken, as the stinging results of the 1970 election indicated. As Richard M. Scammon and Ben J. Wattenberg show, response to the "social issue" was no return to the past but an entirely new phenomenon. "At the same time that white fear and resentment were growing, white attitudes towards civil rights for blacks were probably *liberalizing*," they noted about the 1960s. These contradictory impulses were best reached by issue politics. Despite not entirely understanding the process (though perceptive Nixon staff highlighted the book and Scammon became a *de facto* advisor to Nixon on busing), Nixon's relentless work rate and more flexible principles ensured that he was in a strong position in 1972. Especially with the issue of busing, Nixon was able to offset the political damage that economic problems had inflicted on his popularity among blue-collar Americans.[66]

Busing represented an excellent opportunity for creating a sense of victimization from resentment. Here was an apparent conspiracy from above and below that attacked the innocent—the bewildered white school child turned away from that important American symbol, the neighborhood school, to be bused across the city. And all because of some liberal do-gooder in city hall! Not only was this child's education put at risk but the control of the neighborhood was taken away from those that lived there.

After hedging his bets on busing, supporting the Senate's removal of anti-busing provisions in an education bill eventually passed in the spring of 1971, Nixon took a much more firm stand against it in the summer of 1971.[67] He had, in some ways, drawn the analogy between *de facto* segregation in the North and *de jure* segregation in the South during the 1968 election campaign. Nixon asked in January 1970: "Why should we continue to kick the South + hypocritically ignore the same problem in the North?" His support in the South would always be difficult but he portrayed those in the North as victims of busing much more effectively.[68]

In January of 1972 the *Richmond* decision ordered busing across city boundaries into the suburbs. Before leaving to go to Peking in mid-February, Nixon decided to go down the legislative route. In a memo to Haldeman and Ehrlichman ("no distribution beyond these two"), Nixon confirmed: "I am convinced that while legal segregation is totally wrong that forced integration of housing or education is just as wrong." He continued: "I realize that this position will lead us to a situation in which blacks will continue to live for the most part in black neighborhoods and where there will be predominantly black schools and predominantly white schools in the metropolitan areas."[69] Before Nixon could act, a Denver court decision ordered busing from the city to the suburbs.

Nixon finally delivered his busing speech on March 16, 1972. In it he called for an immediate congressional moratorium on the federal courts to prevent them from ordering any further busing. He also called for passage of the Equal Educational Opportunities Act of 1972, which would direct $2.5 billion in federal aid to improve the education of inner-city children without busing them to the suburbs. Of course, as many observers pointed out, there was little to the speech. The television network CBS called the reaction of the GOP "lukewarm." Others thought the president gained politically by "dumping" the program on a divided Congress, "leaving his rivals scrambling."[70]

The effort was entirely political. It had been from the start. In February Nixon had noted: "Busing has become #1 Domestic issue. . . . Dems are squirming."[71] Accordingly, shortly after the speech, Nixon launched the "Busing Roadshow," with an all-star cast, including Pat Buchanan. Their job was to convey Nixon's hostility to busing. By May, Nixon was fairly confident that the strategy was working. He told Colson: "Blue collar vote will decide election. Fed Courts will reelect RN. . . . Busing may be the 'crossing bridge' for Blue Collars. Cannot muddle this issue; have to be clear."[72] And the strategy did work—aided by Wallace's decision to run for Democratic Party candidate, potential candidate Edmund S. Muskie's apparent tears on the campaign trail, eventual candidate George McGovern's self-destructive campaign, and, of course, the sterling efforts of the Campaign to Re-elect the President (CREEP).

Busing was not finally the "crossing bridge" around which a new constituency was shaped. First, at the same time as the courts were ordering busing, black leadership was moving away from busing as any real solution. Busing—along with housing integration—was by that time doomed by its association with integration. As John Kaplan observed, "while preferential treatment in employment serves a whole series of values, the benign quota [in education and housing] advances just one—integration."[73] Such integrative sentiments that had been regarded as articles of faith in the 1960s were now increasingly rejected by African-American leaders and theorists concerned with the issue of race. The National Black Political Caucus condemned busing in 1972 as "racist" and "suicidal."[74] In 1978 influential sociologist James Coleman—the thinker behind the 1967 Coleman Report—recanted his earlier view that black children's performance would improve in majority white schools.[75]

This rejection of integration began to be reflected in law. The 1974 Supreme Court decision in *Milliken v. Bradley* held that suburban public schools outside of Detroit did not have to participate in a metropolitan busing plan, greatly limiting the ability of lower courts to insist on busing plans. Most central cities in the United States had, by the 1970s, very few whites left within them after "white flight" to the suburbs.

Second, without powerful sponsors like Nixon, the activism inevitably attracted negative publicity in the media. The protestors were (often rightly) castigated for their crude racial antipathies toward those who would be bused to their areas, putting off many moderates who might have been sympathetic to their cause, especially among the most articulate groups of Americans. Nixon's almost entirely political reasons for his opposition to busing became very apparent when he appeared to forget about the issue after the election.

The busing issue, however, helped transform the Silent Majority. Ronald Formisano, in an interesting book about the busing crisis in Boston in the

mid-1970s, noted the appropriation of the symbols of the civil rights move-
ment by the anti-busers. Anti-busing rallies "frequently broke into chants of
'No! No! We Won't Go!' echoing the draft resisters who protested the Vietnam
War." Pat Russell, leader of Powder Keg, the local ROAR (Restore Our Alienated
Rights, a local antibusing movement) chapter, shouted as she led a mothers'
march: "If Martin Luther King could do it, so can the women of Charleston."
The women then sat down in the street and sang, "We Shall Overcome."[76] The
form of these struggles—bereft of any progressive content—survived.

The cry of "police brutality" was generally heard on civil rights marches,
anti-war demonstrations, and hippie "happenings." The Silent Majority
doubtless cheered the police when they attacked protesters outside of the
Democratic Party Convention in Chicago in 1968. However, when Boston's
Special Tactical Force went in against the anti-busing protesters, that was exactly the cry they heard. The backbone of the nation, as administration officials had called blue-collar Americans, became victims of police repression.[77]

Conclusion

By the end of the 1970s, as Hugh Davis Graham observed, two of the nation's
great postwar crusades in civil rights policy, the racial integration of America's
schools and housing, had largely failed. Affirmative action remains the one
focal point for the heirs of the Silent Majority. Ironically, this creation of a
constituency hostile to affirmative action because it feels victimized by it may
be one reason for the longevity of affirmative action. Though many principled
reasons for opposing affirmative action exist, most of the public cases involved the claim of victimization by the policy, adding to the basis for its existence. Put another way, though particular policies may be contested, the
principle of compensation (and thus the need for some sort of redistribu-
tional policies beyond merit and efficiency) remains.

The recent Supreme Court case involving Jennifer Gratz, a policeman's
daughter from Southgate, a working-class Detroit suburb who sued the University of Michigan when she was not admitted to its prestigious medical
school, illustrates Nixon's legacy fairly perfectly. Here was a true contest to see
who was the least advantaged. Gratz represented the "white victim." Ms. Gratz
publicly announced that she thought that her life would probably be better
had she been admitted to Ann Arbor. After her rejection, she lost so much confidence in herself that she gave up her intention to become a doctor, even before she had enrolled as a college freshman. "To me, this was a failure," said Ms.
Gratz. She graduated with a math degree from the University of Michigan in
Dearborn and took a job as a manager at a technology company in San

Diego.[78] What she resented is not so much the special consideration of African Americans, minorities, and women but the fact that her victimization has not been recognized. As Edward Blum, legal director of the American Civil Rights Institute, who sponsored Gratz, said: "We're not out to kill these programs. What we're out to do is expand them to everyone."[79] Similarly, Dinesh D'Souza, Seymour Martin Lipset, and Richard D. Kahlenberg all argue that affirmative action should be "refocused."[80] This does not challenge the whole idea of preferential treatment but creates an argument about who should get it.

This chapter also has suggested, in what is also sure to be a contentious point, that the culture of complaint had its origins with Republicans and that the joys of victimhood were first experienced by the Silent Majority. When Goldwater and Nixon first related to blue-collar Americans as "victims" of crime, the liberal establishment, and the noisy few, the civil rights movement still spoke of redeeming the soul of America, of correcting the one wrong in American society. They did not see themselves as helpless but as a strong, activist movement that would transform the country. They organized themselves from the ground up. In contrast, the silent Americans, Silent Majority, and their ilk had to be given voice—recognized—by Nixon. Their powerlessness was defined by the issues, like crime and domination by the "noisy few," around which they formed. As Garry Wills noted, those who wished to turn back the clocks in the 1960s never had a hope, "just a chance to scream into the darkness."[81]

Notes

1. See memorandum for the president from Henry C. Cashen, no date (September 1971), President's Handwriting, September 16–31, 1971, box 13, and letter and attached article from Ruth M. Mathieu of Wayzata, Minnesota, to Nixon, September 30, 1971, President's Handwriting, September 16–30, 1971, box 14, WHSF: POF: President's Handwriting, NPMP.

2. See, for instance, Russell J. Dalton, *Citizen Politics: Public Opinion and Political Parties in Advanced Industrial Democracies* (London: Chatham House Publishers, 2002 [1988]). See also David O. Friedrichs, "The Legitimacy Crisis in the United States: A Conceptual Analysis," *Social Problems* 27, no. 5 (June 1980): 540–55.

3. For example, see Ronald Inglehart, *Culture Shift in Advanced Industrial Society* (Princeton: Princeton University Press, 1990), and Dieter Fuchs and Hans-Dieter Klingemann, "Citizens and the State: A Changing Relationship?" in Hans-Dieter Klingemann and Dieter Fuchs, ed., *Citizens and the State* (Oxford: Oxford University Press, 1995), 1–23.

4. Cited in Will Kymlicka and Wayne Norman, "Return of the Citizen: A Survey of Recent Work on Citizenship," *Ethics* 104, no. 2 (January 1992), 352–81, esp. 369.

5. John D. Skrentny, *The Minority Rights Revolution* (Cambridge, MA: The Belknap Press of Harvard University Press, 2002).

6. This point is made by sociologist Frank Furedi in *Culture of Fear: Risk-Taking and the Morality of Low Expectations* (London: Cassell, 1997), 101. In a paragraph on this page, Furedi first made the point explicated in this chapter: "Long before the advocates of the abused pointed to the invisible and unacknowledged victim, the silent majority was in existence."

7. Monsignor Geno Baroni, "The Unmeltable American: He Will Be Heard," *Journal of Current Social Issues* (Summer 1972): 6–9, esp. 6, in Ethnic Studies [1 of 2] [CFOA 928], box 83, WHSF: SMOF: Leonard Garment, NPMP.

8. Memo for Mr. Chapin from H. R. Haldeman, July 13, 1970, mtg. with president, Sec. Volpe, P. Flanigan, Dick Moore 7/13/70, folder 2 of 6, documents from boxes 10–30: WHSF: SMOF: Colson, Contested Files, NPMP.

9. Handwritten notes of telephone conversation with president, June 23, (presumably 1971), Meetings/Phone Conversations with President: CWC's notes—Mtg. With the President [2 of 2], box 14, WHSF: SMOF: Colson, NPMP.

10. Handwritten notes of a meeting held on 7/23, H Notes July–September 1970 [July–August 6, 1970], part I, box 42, folder 1 of 25, documents from boxes 1 to 45: WHSF: SMOF: H. R. Haldeman, Contested Files, NPMP.

11. "Bridges to Human Dignity," an address by Richard M. Nixon on the NBC Radio Network, April 25, 1968, 1968 presidential campaign: RNC news releases 8/23/68–9/25/68, comment 8/26/68–11/4/68, Nixon speeches 10/67–9/25/68, box 5, 1968 Nixon Campaign: Press Releases and Nixon Speeches, Records of the RNC.

12. Republican Platform: *A BETTER FUTURE FOR ALL*, ['Taking the Lead' and 'Republican Platform'], box 3, Records of the RNC.

13. Memo for the president from Robert J. Brown, March 6, 1969, files of John Ehrlichman re: EEOC # 379 [CFOA 7730], box 86, WHSF: SMOF: Garment.

14. News Summaries—September 1969, box 30, WHSF: POF: ANS, NPMP.

15. Memorandum for the president from Moynihan, January 16, 1970, President's Handwriting: January 16–31, 1970, box 5, WHSF: POF: President's Handwriting.

16. Kotlowski, *Nixon's Civil Rights*, 202 (see Chapter 7, 188–221). "Four Year Report: Section on American Indians," November 21, 1972, box 4: [Ex] HU 2 1972 Onwards, WHCF: Subject Files: HU (Human Rights), NPMP.

17. See Skrentny, *Minority Rights Revolution*, 198.

18. President's handwritten notes 2-17-[69], President's Handwriting, February 1969, box 1: White House Notes—April 1969, WHSF:POF: President's Handwriting. For a detailed account of bilingual education and language rights, see chapter 7 (129–229) of Skrentny, *Minority Rights Revolution*.

19. Attached copy of M. Barta, "The representation of Poles, Italians, Latins, and Blacks in the Executive Suites of Chicago's Largest Corporations," *Minority Report* (1970), box 17, WHCF: Subject Files: HU (Human Rights); [Ex] HU2-2 Employment, NPMP.

20. Memorandum for the president from George Shultz, September 17, 1971, President's Handwriting, September 16–30, 1971, box 13, WHSF: POF: President's Handwriting, NPMP.

21. Letter to Nixon from Fidel Gonzalez, Jr., California State Director of the League of United Latin American Citizens (LULAC), March 29, 1973, box 17, WHCF: Subject Files: HU (Human Rights); [Ex] HU2-2 Employment, NPMP.

22. Letter to Nixon from Mike Masaoka and David Ushio of the Japanese American Citizen's League, November 16, 1971, Civil Rights—Domestic Council Committee on [1 of 2] [CFOA 908], box 58, WHCF: SMOF: Leonard Garment, NPMP.

23. Karen M. Hult and Charles E. Walcott, *Empowering the White House: Governance under Nixon, Ford, and Carter* (Lawrence: University Press of Kansas, 2004), 78.

24. See, for instance, memo to the president from Colson, June 26, 1971, meetings/phone conversations with president: CWC's notes—Mtg. With the President [2 of 2], box 15, WHSF: SMOF: Charles W. Colson, NPMP.

25. Memo for Bob Finch from Colson, December 21, 1971, Ethnics [3 of 3], box 62, WHSF: SMOF: Charles W. Colson.

26. Memorandum to Harry Fleming from Peter M. Flanigan, January 27, 1970, box 18, WHCF: Subject Files: HU (Human Rights); [Ex] HU2-2 Employment [Gen], NPMP.

27. M. Barta, *Minority Report*, Box 18, WHCF: Subject Files: HU (Human Rights), [Ex] HU2-2 Employment, [Gen], NPMP. See also Skrentny, "Affirmative Action: Some Advice for the Pundits," 882.

28. Anonymous memo to Mr. Terrence M. Scanlon, Office of Minority Business dated December 15, 1969, Equal Employment Opportunities Commission (EEOC)—1970 [2 of 2] [CFOA 7730], Garment: Alpha Subject Files, box 35, WHSF: SMOF: Garment, NPMP.

29. See Hugh Davis Graham, "Unintended Consequences: The Convergence of Affirmative Action and Immigration Policy," *The American Behavioral Scientist* 41, no. 7 (April 1998): 898–912, esp. 905.

30. John Fiske contends that affirmative action policies have benefited white women at the expense of African-American males. See the chapter entitled "Race and Gender in U.S. Politics" in *Media Matters: Everyday Culture and Political Change*, (Minneapolis: University of Minnesota Press, 1994), 99–128.

31. Graham, "Unintended Consequences," 278.

32. "The Metropolitan Washington Project," newsletter of The National Center for Urban Ethnic Affairs, Ethnic Studies, [2 of 2] [CFOA 928], box 83, WHCF: SMOF: Garment, NPMP.

33. Photocopied article attached to Memo to Moynihan from the staff secretary, Stephen Bull, May 16, 1969, president's handwriting, April 1969, box 2, WHSF: POF: President's Handwriting, NPMP.

34. Skrentny, *Minority Rights Revolution*, 275.

35. Thomas J. Sugrue, "Affirmative Action from Below: Civil Rights, the Building Trades, and the Politics of Racial Equality in the Urban North, 1945–1969," *The Journal of American History* 91, no. 1 (June 2004): 145–73.

36. See *Reader's Guide to Contemporary Literature* (New York: H. W. Wilson Co., 1969–1972).

37. Ward Thomas and Mark Garrett, "U.S. and California Affirmative Action Policies, Laws, and Programs," pp. 25–58, in Paul Ong, ed., *Impacts of Affirmative Action: Policies and Consequences in California* (London: AltaMira Press, 2000), 40.

38. Richard P. McCormick, *The Black Student Protest Movement at Rutgers* (London: Rutgers University Press, 1990).

39. Macklin Fleming and Louis Pollak, "The Black Quota at Yale Law School," *The Public Interest*, no. 19 (Spring 1970): 44–52.

40. Fleming and Pollak, "The Black Quota at Yale Law School," 46–47, 49.

41. S. Ardhil Frieberg, "Negroes and Jews—Confrontation or Cooperation?" *The Crisis* (February 1969): 64–66, esp. 65.

42. Editorial, "Reactions to Racial Quotas," *Wall Street Journal*, July 22, 1970, 10.

43. Stephen Steinberg, "How Quotas Began," *Commentary*, September 1971, 68–76.

44. Although see the reactionary diatribe against quotas in Lionel Lokos, *The New Racism: Reverse Discrimination in America* (New Rochelle, NY: Arlington House, 1971), chapter 14, "Black Help Wanted," 360–88.

45. Editorial "Those Nixon 'Goals,'" *Wall Street Journal*, September 10, 1972, 8.

46. *DeFunis v. Odegaard*, 94 S. Ct. 1704, 1974. See also chapter 9, "Reverse Discrimination" in Ronald Dworkin, *Taking Rights Seriously* (London: Duckworth, 1977), 185–206.

47. Cited in Liv Goodwin, "The Causation Fallacy: Bakke and the Basic Arithmetic pf Selection Admissions," *University of Michigan Law Review* 100 (2001–2002): 1045–1107, 1047n.

48. Nathan Glazer and Daniel Patrick Moynihan, *Beyond the Melting Pot: The Negroes, Puerto Ricans, Jews, Italians, and Irish of New York City* (London: The MIT Press, 1970 [1963]), xxxiv, xxxv.

49. Hugh Davis Graham, *The Civil Rights Era: Origins and Development of National Policy 1960–1972* (New York: Oxford University Press, 1990), 463.

50. Rick Perlstein, *Before the Storm: Barry Goldwater and the Unmaking of American Consensus* (New York: Hill and Wang, 2001), 483, 486–87.

51. Cited in Katherine Beckett, *Making Crime Pay: Law and Order in Contemporary American Politics* (Oxford: Oxford University Press, 1997), 31.

52. "Nixon on the Campaign Trail," *The Republican* 3, no. 9 (September 20, 1968), "The Republican," RNC Publications, box 99, RNC records.

53. "The Crusade Against Crime," RNC news releases 8/23/68–9/25/68, Comment 8/26/68–11/4/68, Nixon speeches 10/67–9/25/68, box 5, RNC records.

54. Copy of Clayton Riley, "Nickel Bags of the Mighty Horse," *New York Times*, January 26, 1971, folder 3, part III, box 47, NUL Manuscripts, LOC. Cited in memo for Ed Harper from Jeff Donfeld, May 26, 1971, Black Caucus I [2 of 2] [CFOA 463], box 46, WHCF: SMOF: Leonard Garment: NPMP.

55. Cited in Jonathan Reider, "The Rise of the 'Silent Majority'" in Steve Fraser and Gary Gerstle, eds, *The Rise and Fall of the New Deal Order* (Princeton: Princeton University Press, 1989), 243–68, esp. 257.

56. See Garry Wills' brilliant, if at times snobbish, *Nixon Agonistes: The Crisis of the Self Made Man* (Boston: Houghton Mifflin Company, 1970).

57. "A New Alignment for American Unity, Address by Nixon on CBS Radio Network," May 16, 1968, box 5, 1968 Nixon Campaign: Press Releases and Nixon Speeches, RNC Records.

58. Memo for HRH [from Nixon], November 30, 1970, Memos—November 1970, box 2, PPF: NPMP Memoranda from the President, 1969–1974: RN memo re 1968 to Memos—December 1969, PPF: NPMP.

59. Memorandum for the President's Personal File, March 29, 1969, files of John Ehrlichman re: EEOC [CFOA 7730], box 86, White House Central Files: Staff Member and Office Files: Leonard Garment, NPMP.

60. Cited in Stephen E. Ambrose, *Nixon: Volume Two: The Triumph of a Politician, 1962–1972* (London: Simon and Schuster, 1989), 286.

61. The mail room (and Nixon, who repeated the claim in his autobiography *RN*) perhaps forgot the fact that Franklin Roosevelt's inaugural speech generated nearly half a million letters.

62. Richard Nixon, *RN: The Memoirs of Richard Nixon* (London: Book Club Associates, 1978), 409–10.

63. Memo for Tom Huston from Ehrlichman, February 10, 1971, box 3, White House Central Files; Subject Files HU [Ex] HU, NPMP.

64. Memo for Haldeman, December 30, 1969, memos—December 1969, President's Personal File: Memoranda from the President, 1969–74: RN memo re: 1968 to memos—December 1969, NPMP.

65. September 21, 1970, memos—September 1970, box 2, President's Personal File: Memoranda from the President, 1969–1974, NPMP.

66. Richard M. Scammon and Ben J. Wattenberg, *The Real Majority* (New York: Coward-McCann, Inc., 1970), 42.

67. See Editorial, "More on the President's 'Anti-Busing' Program," *Washington Post*, March 22, 1972, A19.

68. Memorandum for the president from Buchanan, January 30, 1970, president's handwriting, January 16–31, 1970, box 5, WHSF: POF: President's Handwriting.

69. Memorandum for John Ehrlichman, January 28, 1972, [Integration—Housing and Education], folder 2 [box 20], Contested Files: WHSF: SMOF: Ehrlichman. See also Ambrose, *Nixon: Volume Two*, 521–522.

70. Reactions to President's Speech (Busing) (Press et al) [CFOA 10177], Box 54, WHCF: SMOF: Leonard Garment.

71. Notes of a meeting held on February 17, 1972, notes of a meeting held on February 28, 1972, Presidential Meetings and Conversations [1 of 6], box 17, WHSF: SMOF: Charles W. Colson.

72. Presidential Meetings and Conversations, May 18, box 18, WHSF: SMOF: Charles W. Colson.

73. John Kaplan, "Equal Justice in an Unequal World: Equality for the Negro—the Problem of Special Treatment," *Northwestern University Law Review* 61, no. 3 (July–August 1965): 363–410, esp. 389.

74. Copy of *Washington Post*, March 13, 1972, contained in file marked "Busing–Amendments–Public Reaction to [CFOA 10177]," box 51, WHCF: SMOF: Leonard Garment.

75. Diane Ravitch, Frank J. Battisti Memorial Lecture, "School Reform: Past, Present, and Future," *Case Western Reserve Law Review* 51 (2000–2001): 187–200, esp. 191.

76. Ronald P. Formisano, *Boston Against Busing: Race, Class, and Ethnicity in the 1960s and 1970s* (London: University of North Carolina Press, 1991), 140–41.

77. *Ibid.*, 145.

78. Jacques Steinberg, "3 See College Suit as a Way to Show They Belonged," *New York Times*, February 23, 2003, A3.

79. Greg Winter, "Attack on Colleges' Aid to Minorities Widens," *New York Times*, March 30, 2003, A3.

80. Cited in the introduction to Francis J. Beckwith and Todd E. Jones, *Affirmative Action: Social Justice or Reverse Discrimination?* (Amherst, NY: Prometheus Books, 1997), 21–33, esp. 29. See also Seymour Martin Lipset, *American Exceptionalism: A Double Edged Sword* (London: W. W. Norton and Co., 1996); Richard D. Kahlenberg, *The Remedy: Class, Race, and Affirmative Action* (New York: Basic Books, 1996).

81. Wills, Garry, *Nixon Agonistes: The Crisis of the Self Made Man* (Boston: Houghton Mifflin Company, 1970), 35.

Conclusion

TO CONCLUDE, IT IS FITTING to return to the question asked at the beginning: Why was Nixon the one to implement affirmative action and, even more, oversee its massive expansion? This small and seemingly insignificant question, the preceding pages have hopefully demonstrated, demands a reconstruction of different historical time periods and extensive rummaging through the cupboards of philosophy, sociology, political science, economics, and perhaps even psychology, as well as history. The answer may be considered nearer to historical sociology than any other discipline by those who like to draw lines of distinction between disciplines.

The point made above is that affirmative action should be divided into at least four different phases and the question should be, why did the final phases—the repaid expansion of affirmative action-based programs and its elevation into a contentious national issue—happen on Nixon's watch? As the first part of this book indicated, there were barriers to affirmative action in its modern sense that had to be removed. When civil rights groups called for affirmative action or when the phrase was used during the Kennedy and Johnson administrations, it was part of a larger, political project to integrate African Americans into the mainstream of American society. Forcibly implementing affirmative action would have jeopardized the Myrdalian project of converting all Americans to the cause of racial equality. When Nixon took office, this dream was dying and the first phase of affirmative action was over.

When this political project ended, serious consideration could be given to implementing an enforceable affirmative action plan for the first time in the postwar period. The institutions Myrdal identified as crucial in leading

Americans away from their outdated, outmoded racial beliefs, which created racial divisions, had patently failed. Their educative leadership, seriously compromised by affirmative action, no longer functioned. Business, which had jealously guarded its management prerogatives to hire and fire who it wished, declared itself willing to give up this prerogative in order to restore racial peace. Trade unions, demoralized and growing weaker, could no longer resist affirmative action effectively. After the tumult of the 1960s, the possibility of a violent reaction against affirmative action measures by reactionary whites—the great fear of liberals during the 1950s—looked less threatening than more rioting by African Americans. Finally, the civil rights movement, which had insisted on equality at every level and, hence, resisted policies that would divide blacks from whites, was already fragmenting when its most important leader Martin Luther King, Jr. was assassinated. No longer did it drive the response of the government to racial problems.

Once these barriers fell, Nixonian reasons for experimenting with affirmative action came into view. It represented the most conservative civil rights option at a time when campaigns to integrate schools and neighborhoods continued to attract the support of many. Affirmative action covered a retreat; it allowed Nixon to back away from the grand promises of the 1960s, to break up the big problems into little pieces, to manage rather than reform race relations. Affirmative action could be implemented quietly, rewarding those with more of a stake in the system—the black middle class—rather than those shouting from the ghettos. Nixon's 1968 call to "lower our voices" was thus answered by affirmative action and it was controlled not from the streets or by civil rights activists but from the boardrooms and by upper echelon personnel managers.

The Habermasian theory of legitimation crisis also gives insight into the negative reasons why Nixon was the one. Habermas showed how policy makers tend to back in to progressive intervention into hitherto informally administered areas. The theory, not elaborated in previous treatments of the history of affirmative action, makes Nixon's actions more understandable. As Habermas understood, the act of attempting to restore legitimacy to hiring systems in one area undermined all existing systems and created a need for more formal regulation to replace them.

Not only did it stretch the resources of the government (Habermas's theory gives a pretty good indication why the foreign and domestic projects of the early and mid-1960s suddenly looked frighteningly impossible only a few years later), it resulted in a rolling process whereby merit, a fairly automatic impetus for personnel decisions, became suspect. In the short term, it simply threw other systems into confusion. In September 1973, Jersey Central Power and Light decided to lay off 200 workers but had contracts with both a union and the Equal Employment Opportunities Commission. In order to clear up the confusion, it asked a federal court to review its list. Decisions that would have been made fairly automatically in the past had now to be micromanaged by the government.[1]

Beside the above reasons why affirmative action backed into existence, what might be called positive reasons exist, especially in relation to at least temporarily resolving the crisis in legitimacy. Here, this book departs from the existing literature (and points out the limitations to Habermas's *Legitimation Crisis*, which did not foresee the possibility of an entirely new basis for legitimacy being created) in adumbrating affirmative action's role in a new liberal polity. At one level, this policy suited an age of limits, whereby "moderate scarcity" was assumed. In some ways, as sociologists Sutton, Dobbin, Meyer, and Scott have noted, affirmative action directly replaced union-controlled personnel systems.[2] Its focus on distribution replaced the automatic discipline of the market, especially in areas one step removed from the dictates of profit, loss, and productivity. Affirmative action was an ideal alternative system when constantly increasing production no longer ruled.

But the less tangible benefits of an affirmative action system, those that concern legitimation of the elite at a broader level, have been most important in determining the path of affirmative action. The deciding tendency that underwrote the massive expansion of affirmative action beginning in the Nixon years has been the shift in the relationship between Americans and their government, the "clientization," as Habermas put it, of the citizen's role. Affirmative action's expansion outside of the government appears to be a function of this new relationship between the elite and the masses of Americans. Public consciousness of affirmative action on the part of Americans replicates this relationship. Americans either imagine themselves as administrators of the system or as beneficiaries and potential beneficiaries. Even those who oppose affirmative action nearly always argue for expansion of the program to white men, be it through affirmative action based on economic class or on some other nonracial criteria. All enter into this relationship between victim and indemnifier of damages. The elite thus legitimates itself within this latter role.

Nixon helped to generalize this clientization as he backed away from efforts to extend a hand to the most alienated elements. In reaching out to others, he made a virtue of the sense of powerlessness among many in American society, setting up new "client" groups dependent on the government. Though Nixon hardly oversaw the day-to-day implementation of affirmative action programs, he undoubtedly contributed more to this phase of affirmative action than any bureaucrat. Ironically, through opposition to the gains of other groups, he brought disgruntled whites into the clientization process without bringing them under the administrative umbrella of affirmative action.

Though this study has stressed the discontinuity between the various "affirmative actions," the common ideological hinge is in the attempt of all policies and potential affirmative action policies to restore equality of opportunity at a time when it does not appear to be automatically guaranteed by American capitalism. It kept alive the American Creed as Gunnar Myrdal defined it, the "inalienable right to fair opportunity," the idea that America was a fair and moral nation and that the opportunity to better oneself and one's children was open to all.[3] The close connection with opportunity should be noted; all affirmative action was justified primarily by its ability to give individuals of various different groups a chance to succeed.

Having suggested answers to the question of why Nixon, what other implications emerge from this study?

Methodologically, this study has shown the limited analytical value of left and right. The bipolar framework hides the way debates about affirmative action (especially) continuously evolve. Scholars should also reassess the role of Richard M. Nixon in less emotive terms. Nixon led a slow retreat from both the Vietnam War and the promises of the Great Society and, as Walter Lippman noted, "he's done pretty good at it." Nixon's obsessive politicking and his "iron butt" should be recognized not simply as part of a psychological flaw but as the essential characteristics of a president who was able to give history a nudge, even if he failed to control which way it fell. Though personally not involved in civil rights issues, Nixon's actions in giving up on the ghettos, encouraging the stability of the black middle class and preventing the issue of race from being used as a weapon against the "system" should receive some attention.

The 1970s, often ridiculed as a nadir in fashion, music, and politics, and sometimes presented as an intermission between the radical 1960s and the conservative 1980s, is beginning to be reassessed and this study, I hope, has contributed to this reassessment. Beside being the height of a crisis of legitimacy, it should also be understood as a richly experimental period for policy where new bases for legitimacy were tried out.

Finally, there are important implications in this analysis for how affirmative action should be understood. The important points made throughout this book are first, that the *underlying* relationship between the elite and citizen "clients"—not the individual minorities involved, nor the merit of their claims—has determined how the affirmative action story has unfolded. Moreover, the beneficiaries of this client relationships are not the clients but those who legitimate themselves by adopting the "enabler" role.[4] This is not restricted to the state. Hence, affirmative action appears on the "mission statements" of just about all large corporations and public institutions. This explains the resistance of large corporations to Ronald Reagan's attack on affirmative action and why so many of the normally-reticent American elite lined up behind the University of Michigan in the recent *Gratz* case. It is also possible to see that the opposition to affirmative action usually objects to purported victimization of white males, fitting into the same clientization model from the other side.

A caveat is perhaps necessary at this point. Though this study has had one eye upon affirmative action in the present, it has only done the historical groundwork for the period of the Nixon presidency. The 1970s may have only been a rehearsal for trends that would develop later on; the story of the way they actually developed remains to be told.

Having said that, it is possible from this analysis to predict that, at least in the short term, affirmative action is here to stay. The most important reason is that all agree that some sort of affirmative action—whether it be on the basis of race, class, sex differences, or whatnot—is appropriate. President Bush's recent opposition to the University of Michigan's affirmative action program in *Gratz*, for instance, included the Texas program based on an alternative but even less merit-related system. As soon as someone proposes that a merit or efficiency-based system is reinstated, vociferous questioning of whether or not true merit existed before affirmative action—or whether it can exist at all—can be heard. With very little faith in the curative aspects of economic growth, it seems unlikely that any persuasive arguments for efficiency and merit will come to light.

As important if not even more so, the clientization of Americans remains, ensuring that most Americans view themselves as either clients or potential clients. This means that opposition to affirmative action, with a few honourable exceptions, will be on the basis that it does not adequately serve the needs of this or that group. The "therapeutic" nature of many relationships between the state and the individual has been noted by some sociologists.[5] The affirmative action "client" is dependent on recognition and appropriate restitution by the state or some quasi-state organization.

The analysis here of affirmative action is negative, not because of affirmative action as a strategy *per se*. It certainly does not victimize anyone any more than other hiring, contract award, or college place decisions that consider the needs of the institution above the needs of the individuals concerned. Even using efficiency and generation of maximum profits as the prime consideration, individual merit has always come second to institutional needs. There is no right to a college place, as Ronald Dworkin has persuasively argued.[6] As part of a larger political strategy that has as its goal the integration of African Americans or another group into the mainstream of American society, it might have been and still might become a useful tool.

The problem is that affirmative action, in its most recent phases, has covered a retreat from a commitment to real racial equality, writing off political efforts at tackling the problem of racial inequality. In other words, the adoption of affirmative action implied that democratic political efforts to convince whites that they must eradicate racism are hopeless and substituted bureaucratic methods. Liberation of any people is unlikely to be accomplished in boardrooms and offices.

Perhaps worse, though, is affirmative action's role in institutionalizing the clientization of citizens. As long as Americans remain cramped, risk-fearing individuals who fear the future, rue the past, and have no aspiration other than to survive the present, they lack the ability to change anything, let alone a huge but eminently resolvable problem like racial inequality.

Notes

1. Marylin Bender, "Job Discrimination: Ten Years Later," *New York Times*, November 10, 1974, III, 1.

2. See John R. Sutton, Frank Dobbin, John W. Mayer, and W. Richard Scott, "The Legalization of the Workplace," *American Journal of Sociology* 99, no. 4 (January 1994): 944–71.

3. Gunnar Myrdal, *An American Dilemma: The Negro Problem and American Democracy* (Harper & Brothers Publishers: New York, 1944), 25.

4. See Jonathan Leonard, "The Impact of Affirmative Action on Employment," *Journal of Labor Economics* 2, no. 4 (October 1984): 439–63.

5. See James L. Nolan, Jr., *The Therapeutic State: Justifying Government at Century's End* (New York: New York University Press, 1998) and, more recently, Frank Furedi, *Therapy Culture: Cultivating Vulnerability in an Uncertain Age* (London: Routledge, 2004).

6. Ronald Dworkin, *Taking Rights Seriously* (London: Duckworth, 1977), esp. chapter 9, "Reverse Discrimination," 223–39.

Bibliography

Books, Essays, and Articles

Aberbach, Joel D. and Bert A. Rockman, "Clashing Beliefs Within the Executive Branch: The Nixon Administration Bureaucracy," *The American Political Science Review* 70, no. 2 (June 1976): 456–68.

Abrahamsen, David, *Nixon vs. Nixon: An Emotional Tragedy* (New York: Farrar, Strauss and Giroux, 1977).

Abrams, Elliot, "The Quota Commission," *Commentary* 54, no. 4 (October 1972): 54–57.

Adorno, T. W. et al. *The Authoritarian Personality* (New York: Harper and Brothers, 1950).

Aitken, Jonathon, *Nixon: A Life* (Washington, D.C.: Regnery, 1993).

Allport, Gordon W., *The Nature of Prejudice* (Reading, MA: Addison-Wesley, 1954)

Ambrose, Stephen E., *Nixon, Volume II: The Triumph of a Politician 1962–1972* (London: Simon and Schuster, 1989).

———, *Nixon: The Education of a Politician 1913–1962* (New York: Simon and Schuster, 1987).

———, ed., *Institutions in Modern America: Innovation in Structure and Process* (Baltimore: John Hopkins Press, 1967).

Anderson, Terry, *The Pursuit of Fairness: A History of Affirmative Action* (New York: Oxford University Press, 2004).

Aptheker, Herbert, *The Negro People in America: A Critique of Gunnar Myrdal's An American Dilemma* (New York: Kraus Reprint, 1977 [1946]).

Arendt, Hannah, *The Human Condition* (Chicago: University of Chicago Press, 1958).

Armor, David J., "The Evidence on Busing," *The Public Interest*, no. 28 (Summer 1972): 90–126.

Baldwin, James, Nathan Glazer, Sidney Hook, and Gunnar Myrdal, "Liberalism and the Negro: A Roundtable Discussion," *Commentary* 37, no. 3, (March 1964): 25–42.

Barkan, Elazar, *The Retreat of Scientific Racism* (Cambridge: Cambridge University Press, 1992).

Bell, Daniel, "On Meritocracy and Equality," *The Public Interest*, no. 29 (Fall 1972): 29–68.

———, *The Coming of Post-Industrial Society* (New York: Basic Books, 1973).

———, *The Cultural Contradictions of Capitalism* (London: Heinemann, 1976).

———, *The End of Ideology* (Glencoe, IL: The Free Press, 1960).

Belz, Herman, *Equality Transformed: A Quarter-Century of Affirmative Action* (London: Transaction Publishers, 1992).

Benedict, Ruth, *Race and Racism* (London: Routledge, 1942).

Benokraitis, Nijole V. and Joe R. Feagin, *Affirmative Action and Equal Opportunity: Action, Inaction, Reaction* (Boulder, CO: Westview Press, 1978).

Bergmann, Barbara R., *In Defense of Affirmative Action* (New York: Basic Books, 1996).

Berlin, Isaiah, "Two Concepts of Liberty," in *Four Essays on Liberty* (Oxford University Press: Oxford, 1979), 118–73.

Berman, Ronald, *America in the Sixties: An Intellectual History* (New York: The Free Press, 1968).

Berman, William C., *America's Right Turn: From Nixon to Bush* (Baltimore: Johns Hopkins University Press, 1994).

Bickell, Alexander, *The Least Dangerous Branch: The Supreme Court at the Bar of Politics* (New York: Bobbs-Merrill Co., Inc., 1962).

Blocker, H. Gene and Elizabeth H. Smith, "Editors' Introduction," in H. Gene Blocker and Elizabeth H. Smith, eds., *John Rawls, A Theory of Justice: An Introduction* (Athens: Ohio University Press, 1980).

Bloom, Alan, "Justice: John Rawls vs. The Tradition of Political Philosophy," *The American Political Science Review* 69, no. 2 (June 1975): 648–62.

Blumrosen, Alfred, *Black Employment and the Law* (New Brunswick, NJ: Rutgers University Press, 1971).

Bobo, Lawrence, "Race, Interests, and Beliefs about Affirmative Action: Unanswered Questions and New Directions," *American Behavioral Scientist* 41, no. 7 (April 1998): 985–1003.

Bochin, Hal, *Richard Nixon—A Rhetorical Strategist* (New York: Greenwood Press 1990).

Brauer, Carl M., *John F. Kennedy and the Second Reconstruction* (New York: Columbia University Press, 1977).

Brazziel, William F., "Manpower Training and the Negro Worker," *Journal of Negro Education* 35, issue 1 (Winter 1966): 83–87.

Brennan, Mary C., *Turning Right in the Sixties: The Conservative Capture of the GOP* (Chapel Hill: University of North Carolina Press, 1995).

Brinkley, Alan, *End of Reform: New Deal Liberalism in Recession and War* (London: Harvard University Press, 1998).

———, *Liberalism and Its Discontents* (London: Harvard University Press, 1998).

Brodie, Fawn M., *Richard Nixon: The Shaping of His Character* (London: W. W. Norton & Company, 1981).

Buchanan, Allen, "A Critical Introduction to Rawls," in H. Gene Blocker and Elizabeth H. Smith, eds., *John Rawls, A Theory of Justice: An Introduction,* 5–41.

Buchanan, Pat, *The New Majority* (Philadelphia: Girard Bank, 1973).

Burk, Robert F., *The Eisenhower Administration and Civil Rights* (Knoxville: University of Tennessee Press, 1984).

Burke, Vincent, *Nixon's Good Deed: Welfare Reform* (New York: Columbia University Press, 1974).

Burner, David, *Making Peace With the '60s* (Princeton: Princeton University Press, 1996).

Burstein, Paul, *Discrimination, Jobs and Politics: The Struggle for Equal Employment Opportunity in the United States Since the New Deal* (London: University of Chicago Press, 1985).

Cahn, Edmund, *The Sense of Injustice: An Anthropocentric View of Law* (London: Oxford University Press, 1949).

Califano, Joseph, *The Triumph and Tragedy of Lyndon Johnson: The White House Years* (New York: Simon and Schuster, 1991).

Carleton, William G., "The Second Reconstruction: An Analysis from the Deep South," *Antioch Review* XVIII (Summer 1958): 171–80.

Carmichael, Stokely and Charles V. Hamilton, *Black Power: The Politics of Liberation in America* (New York: Random House, 1967).

Carmines, E. G., and Stimson, Johnson. A., *Issue Evolution: Race and the Transformation of American Politics* (Princeton: Princeton University Press, 1989).

Carter, Dan T., *The Politics of Rage: George Wallace, the Origins of the New Conservatism, and the Transformation of American Politics* (London: Simon and Schuster, 1995).

———, *From George Wallace to Newt Gingrich: Race in the Conservative Counterrevolution, 1963–1994* (London: LSU Press, 1996).

Case, Frederick E., *Black Capitalism: Problems in Development* (New York: Praeger, 1972).

Chafe, William H., *The Unfinished Journey: America Since World War II* (New York: Oxford University Press, 1986).

Chalmers, David, *And the Crooked Places Made Straight: The Struggle for Social Change in the 1960s* (London: Johns Hopkins University Press, 1996).

Chappell, David, *Inside Agitators: White Southerners in the Civil Rights Movement* (Baltimore: Johns Hopkins University Press, 1994).

Chávez, Lydia, *The Color Bind: California's Battle to End Affirmative Action* (Berkeley: The University of California Press, 1998).

Chereminsky, Erwin, "Making Sense of the Affirmative Action Debate," John Higham, ed., *Civil Rights and Social Wrongs: Black–White Relations Since World War II* (University Park: The Pennsylvania State University Press, 1997).

Chesen, Eli S., *President Nixon's Psychiatric Profile: A Psychodynamic–Genetic Interpretation* (New York: P. H. Wyden, 1973).

Chester, Lewis, Godfrey Hodgson, and Bruce Page, *An American Melodrama: The Presidential Campaign of 1968* (New York: Dell, 1969).

Chin, Gabriel, "Series Introduction," *Affirmative Action Before Constitutional Law, 1964–1977* (London: Garland Publishing, Inc., 1998).

Cole, H. S. D. et al., *Thinking About the Future: A Critique of the Limits to Growth* (London: Chatto and Windus, 1973).

Cole, Richard L., and David A. Caputo, "Presidential Control of the Senior Civil Service: Assessing the Strategies of the Nixon Years," *The American Political Science Review* 73, no. 2 (June 1979): 399–413.

Colson, Charles W., *Born Again* (Old Tappan, NJ: Chosen Books, 1976).

Combs, Michael W. and John Gruhl, eds., *Affirmative Action: Theory, Analysis, and Prospects* (Jefferson, NC: McFarland & Company, Inc., 1986).

Conlan, Timothy J., "The Politics of Federal Block Grants: From Nixon to Reagan," *Political Science Quarterly* 99, no. 2 (Summer 1984): 247–70.

Cook, Robert, *Sweet Land of Liberty? The African-American Struggle for Civil Rights in the Twentieth Century* (London: Longman, 1998).

Costello, William, *The Facts About Nixon: A Candid Biography* (London: Hutchinson & Co., 1960).

Cothran, Tilman C., "The Negro Protest Against Segregation in the South," *The Annals of the American Academy of Political and Social Science* 357 (January 1965).

Cox, Oliver, *Caste, Class and Race: A Study in Social Dynamics* (New York: Doubleday, 1948).

Cross, Theodore L., *Black Capitalism* (New York: Atheneum, 1969).

Cruse, Harold, *Plural But Equal: A Critical Study of Blacks and Minorities and America's Plural Society* (New York: William Morrow and Co., Inc., 1987).

Dahlberg, Gunnar, *Race, Reason and Rubbish: An Examination of the Biological Credentials of the Nazi Creed* (London: Allen and Unwin, 1942).

Dallek, Robert, *Flawed Giant: Lyndon Johnson and His Times* (Oxford: Oxford University Press, 1998).

Danzig, David, "The Meaning of Negro Strategy," *Commentary* 37, no. 2 (February 1964): 41–46.

Davies, Gareth, *From Equal Opportunity to Entitlement: The Transformation and Decline of Great Society Liberalism* (Lawrence: University Press of Kansas, 1996).

Dent, Harry S., *The Prodigal South Returns to Power* (New York: John Wiley and Sons, 1978).

Depoe, Stephen P., *Arthur M. Schlesinger and the Ideological History of American Liberalism* (London: University of Alabama Press, 1994).

Douglass, John Aubrey, "Anatomy of a Conflict: The Making and Unmaking of Affirmative Action at the University of California," *American Behavioral Scientist* 41, no. 7 (April 1998): 938–59.

Dudziak, Mary L., *Cold War Civil Rights: Race and the Image of American Democracy* (Princeton: Princeton University Press, 2000).

Dworkin, Ronald, *Taking Rights Seriously* (London: Duckworth, 1978).

Dye, Thomas R. and L. Harmon Zeigler, *The Irony of Democracy: An Uncommon Introduction to American Politics* (Belmont, CA: Wadsworth Publishing Company, Inc., 1970).

Eagles, Charles, *The Civil Rights Movement in America* (London: University Press of Mississippi, 1975).

Edsall, Thomas Byrne and Mary D. Edsall, *Chain Reaction: The Impact of Race, Rights and Taxes on American Politics* (New York: Norton, 1992).

Ehrlich, Paul R., *The Population Bomb* (London: Pan Books, 1971, originally published in New York by Ballantine, 1968).

Ehrlichman, John E., *Witness to Power: The Nixon Years* (New York: Simon and Schuster, 1982).

Eleanor Holmes Norton, "Civil Rights: Working Backwards" in Alan Gartner, et al., *What Nixon is Doing to Us* (New York: Harper and Row, 1973), 201–15.

Ellison, Ralph, *Shadow and Act* (New York: Signet Books, 1966).

Evans, Roland, Jr. and Robert D. Novak, *Nixon in the White House: The Frustration of Power* (New York: Random House, 1971).

Fairclough, Adam, *To Redeem The Soul of America: The Southern Christian Leadership Conference and Martin Luther King, Jr.* (Athens: University of Georgia Press, 1987).

Farmer, James, *Lay Bare the Heart: An Autobiography of the Civil Rights Movement* (New York: Plume, 1985).

Finch, Minnie, *The NAACP: Its Fight For Justice* (London: Scarecrow, 1981).

Fleming, Harold C., "The Federal Executive and Civil Rights: 1961–1965," in Talcott Parsons and Kenneth B. Clarke, eds., *The Negro American* (Boston: Beacon Press, 1966), 88–105.

Fleming, Macklin and Louis Pollak, "The Black Quota at Yale Law School," *The Public Interest*, no. 19 (Spring 1970): 44–52.

Fletcher, Arthur, *The Silent Sell-Out: Government Betrayal of Blacks to the Craft Unions* (New York: The Third Press, 1974).

Foner, Philip S., ed., *The Black Panthers Speak* (New York: J. B. Lippincott Company, 1970).

Formisano, Ronald P., *Boston Against Busing: Race, Class and Ethnicity in the 1960s and 1970s* (Chapel Hill: University of North Carolina Press, 1991).

Fraser, Steve and Gary Gerstle, *The Rise and Fall of the New Deal Order* (Princeton: Princeton University Press, 1989).

Fredrickson, H. George, "Toward a New Public Administration," in Frank Marini, ed., *Toward a New Public Administration* (Scranton, PA: Chandler, 1971), 309–31.

Friedman, Leon and William F. Levantrosser, ed., *Richard M. Nixon: Politician, President, Administrator* (New York: Greenwood Press, 1991).

Friedman, Milton, "Capitalism and Freedom," in Felix Morley, ed., *Essays on Individualism*, (Philadelphia: University of Pennsylvania Press, 1958).

Fullinwider, Robert K., *The Reverse Discrimination Controversy: A Moral and Legal Analysis* (Totowa, NJ: Rowman and Littlefield, 1980).

Furedi, Frank, *Culture of Fear: Risk-Taking and the Morality of Low Expectation* (London: Cassell, 1997).

———, *The Silent War: Imperialism and the Changing Perception of Race* (London: Pluto Press, 1998).

———, *Therapy Culture: Cultivating Vulnerability in an Uncertain Age* (London: Routledge, 2004).

Galbraith, John Kenneth, *The Affluent Society* (Harmondsworth, England: Penguin Books, 1962).

Garment, Leonard, *Crazy Rhythm: My Journey From Brooklyn, Jazz, and Wall Street to Nixon's White House, Watergate, and Beyond* (New York: Times Books, 1997).

Garrow, David J., *Bearing the Cross: Martin Luther King, Jr., and the Southern Christian Leadership Conference, 1955–1968* (New York: William Morrow and Co., 1986).

Genovese, Michael A., *The Nixon Presidency: Power and Politics in Turbulent Times* (New York: Greenwood Press, 1990).

Gerstle, Gary, "The Protean Character of American Liberalism," *American Historical Review* 99, no. 4 (October 1994): 1045–74.

Ginzberg, Eli, "The Changing Manpower Scene," *Journal of Negro Education* 38, no. 3, (Summer, 1969): 315–23.

Glazer, Nathan and Daniel Patrick Moynihan, *Beyond the Melting Pot: The Negroes, Puerto Ricans, Jews, Italians and Irish of New York City* (London: The MIT Press, 1970).

Glazer, Nathan, "A Breakdown in Civil Rights Enforcement?" in *The Public Interest* (Spring 1971): 106–15.

——, *Affirmative Discrimination: Ethnic Inequality and Public Policy* (London: Harvard University Press, 1987).

Glover, Robert W. and Ray Marshall in Leonard Hausman, et al., "The Response of Unions in the Construction Industry to Antidiscrimination Efforts," *Equal Rights and Industrial Relations* (Madison, WI: Industrial Relations Research Association, 1977): 120–40.

Goldman, Alan H., *Justice and Reverse Discrimination* (Princeton: Princeton University Press, 1979).

Goldman, Eric F., *The Tragedy of Lyndon Johnson* (London: McDonald, 1968).

Goldwater, Barry, *Conscience of a Conservative* (New York: Hillman Books, 1960).

Gomberg, William, "The Job as Property," *The Nation* (November 26, 1960): 410–12.

Goodwin, Richard, *Remembering America: A Voice from the Sixties* (New York: Harper and Row, 1988).

Gossett, Thomas F., *Race: The History of an Idea in America* (New York: Harper and Brothers, 1964).

Gould, Louis L., *1968: The Election that Changed America* (Chicago: Ivan Dee, 1993).

Graham, Hugh Davis, "Civil Rights Policy in the Carter Presidency" in Gary M. Fink and Hugh Davis Graham, *The Carter Presidency: Policy Choices in the Post-New Deal Era* (Lawrence: University Press of Kansas, 1998), 202–23.

——, "Legacies of the 1960s: The American 'Rights Revolution' in an Era of Divided Governance," *Journal of Policy History* 10, no. 3, (1998): 159–72.

——, "Race, History, and Policy: African Americans and Civil Rights Since 1964" in Hugh Davis Graham, ed., *Civil Rights in the United States* (University Park: The Pennsylvania State University Press, 1994): 12–39.

——, "Richard Nixon and Civil Rights: Explaining and Enigma," *Presidential Studies Quarterly* XXVI, no. 1 (Winter 1996): 163–80.

——, "The Incoherence of the Civil Rights Policy in the Nixon Administration" in Leon Friedman and William F. Levantrosser, ed., *Richard M. Nixon: Politician, President, Administrator* (New York: Greenwood Press, 1991), 159–72.

——, "Unintended Consequences: The Convergence of Affirmative Action and Immigration Policy," *The American Behavioral Scientist* 41, no. 7 (April 1998): 898–912.

———, *The Civil Rights Era: Origins and Development of National Policy, 1960–1972* (New York: Oxford University Press, 1990).

Graubard, Stephen R., Preface to the Issue "An American Dilemma Revisited," *Daedalus* 124 (Winter 1995): V–XXXIV.

Greenberg, Jack, *Race Relations and American Law* (New York: Columbia University Press, 1959).

Greene, John Robert, *The Limits to Power: The Nixon and Ford Administrations* (Bloomington: Indiana University Press, 1992).

Habermas, Jürgen, "Citizenship and National Identity: Some Reflections on the Future of Europe," *Praxis International* 12, no. 1 (April 1992): 1–19.

———, *Legitimation Crisis*, translated by Thomas McCarthy (London: Heinemann Educational, 1976).

———, "Reconciliation Through the Public Use of Reason: Remarks on John Rawls' Political Liberalism," *Journal of Philosophy* 92, no. 3 (March 1995): 109–31.

———, *The Structural Transformation of the Public Sphere: An Inquiry into a Category of Bourgeois Society*, translated by Thomas Burger (Cambridge, MA: The MIT Press, 1989 [1962]).

Hacker, Andrew, *Two Nations: Black and White, Separate, Hostile, Unequal* (New York: Scribner's, 1992).

Haldeman, H. R. and Joseph DiMona, *The Ends of Power* (New York: Times Books, 1978).

Haldeman, H. R., *The Haldeman Diaries* (Sony CD-ROM, 1994).

Hamby, Alonzo L., *Liberalism and Its Challengers: FDR to Bush* (New York: Oxford University Press, 1992).

———, *Beyond the New Deal: Harry S. Truman and American Liberalism* (London: Columbia University Press, 1973).

Handlin, Oscar, "The Goals of Integration," in Talcott Parsons and Kenneth B. Clarke, ed., *The Negro American* (Boston: Beacon Press, 1966).

———, *Race and Nationality in American Life* (Boston: Little, Brown and Company, 1957 [1948]).

Harmon, Michael M., "Social Equity and Organizational Man: Motivation and Organizational Democracy," *Public Administration Review* 34, no. 1 (January–February 1974), A Symposium: Social Equity and Administration, 11–18.

Harsanyi, John C., "Can the Maximin Principle Serve as a Basis for Morality? A Critique of John Rawls's *A Theory of Justice*, *The American Political Science Review* 69, no. 2. (June 1975): 594–606.

Herman, Ellen, *The Romance of American Psychology: Political Culture in the Age of Experts* (London: University of California Press, 1995).

Hess, Stephen, *Organizing the Presidency* (Washington, D.C.: Brookings Institution, 1988).

Hill, Herbert and James E. Jones, Jr., eds., *Race in America* (Madison: University of Wisconsin Press, 1993).

Hill, Herbert, "The Construction Industry: Evading the Law," *Civil Rights Digest* (Quarterly Publication of the United States Civil Rights Commission, April 1975): 22–36.

Hirsch, Arnold R., "Massive Resistance in the Urban North: Trumbull Park, Chicago, 1953–1966," *Journal of American History* 82, no. 2 (September 1995): 522–50.

Hirsch, Fred, *The Social Limits to Growth* (London: Routledge and Kegan Paul, 1977).

Hoeveler, J. David, *The Postmodernist Turn: American Thought and Culture in the 1970s* (New York: Twayne Publishers, 1996).

Hodgson, Godfrey, *In Our Time: America from World War II to Nixon* (London: Macmillan, 1976).

Hoff, Joan, 'Researchers Nightmare: Studying the Nixon Presidency', *Presidential Studies Quarterly* XXXVI, no. 1 (Winter 1996): 259–75.

———, *Nixon Reconsidered* (New York: Basic Books, 1994).

Holmes, Michael S., "The New Deal and Georgia's Black Youth," *The Journal of Southern History* 38, no. 3 (August, 1972): 443–60.

Holub, Robert C., *Jurgen Habermas: Critic of the Public Sphere* (London: Routledge, 1991).

Hood, J. Larry, "The Nixon Administration and the Revised Philadelphia Plan for Affirmative Action: A Study in Expanding Presidential Power and Divided Government" *Presidential Studies Quarterly* 23 (1993): 145–67.

Hook, Sidney, James Baldwin, Sidney Nathan Glazer, and Gunnar Myrdal, "Liberalism and the Negro: A Round-Table Discussion," *Commentary* 37, no. 3 (March 1964): 25–42.

Hooks, Benjamin L., "'Self-Help' Just Won't do it All," in Nicolaus Mills, ed., *Debating Affirmative Action, Race, Gender, Ethnicity and the Politics of Inclusion* (New York: Delta, 1994), 304–8.

Jackson, Walter A., "White Intellectuals and Civil Rights," in Brian Ward and Tony Badger, eds., *Martin Luther King and the Making of the Civil Rights Movement* (Basingstoke: Macmillan, 1995): 96–114.

Jacoby, Tamar, *Someone Else's House: America's Unfinished Struggle for Integration* (New York: Basic Books, 2000 [1998]).

Jencks, Christopher, *Rethinking Social Policy: Race, Poverty and the Underclass* (New York: Harper Perennial, 1992).

Jones, Hardy, "A Rawlsian Discussion of Discrimination" in H. Gene Blocker and Elizabeth H. Smith, eds., *John Rawls, A Theory of Justice: An Introduction* (Athens: Ohio University Press, 1980): 270–88.

Jones, James E., Jr., "The Bugaboo of Employment Quotas," *Wisconsin Law Review* (1970): 341–403.

Kahlenberg, Richard D., *The Remedy: Class, Race, and Affirmative Action* (New York: Basic Books: 1996).

Kelley, Erin and Frank Dobbin, "How Affirmative Action Became Diversity Management," *American Behavioral Scientist* 41, no. 7 (April 1998): 960–83.

Kersten, Andrew Edmund, *Race, Jobs, and the War: The FEPC in the Midwest, 1941–1946* (Chicago: University of Illinois Press, 2000).

Key, V. O., *Southern Politics in State and Nation* (New York: Vintage Books, 1949).

Kimball, Penn, *The Disconnected* (New York, Columbia University Press, 1972).

King, Desmond, *Separate and Unequal: Black Americans and the U.S. Federal Government* (Oxford: Clarendon Press, 1995).

King, Martin Luther Jr., *Why We Can't Wait* (New York: Harper & Row, 1963).

King, Richard H., *Civil Rights and the Idea of Freedom* (Oxford: Oxford University Press, 1992).

——, *Race, Culture, and the Intellectuals, 1940–1970* (Baltimore: Johns Hopkins University Press, 2004).

Klehr, Harvey, *The Heyday of American Communism: The Depression Decade* (New York: Basic Books, 1984).

Klosko, George, "Rawls' 'Political' Philosophy and American Democracy," *American Political Science Review* 87, no. 2 (June 1993): 348–59.

Knowles, Louis L. and Kenneth Pruitt, eds., *Institutional Racism in America* (London: Prentice-Hall, 1969).

Kotlowski, Dean, *Nixon's Civil Rights: Politics, Principle, and Policy* (London: Harvard University Press, 2001).

Krasner, Stephen D., "Approaches to the State: Alternative Conceptions and Historical Dynamics" *Comparative Politics* 16 (1984): 217–40.

Krikorian, Mark, "Affirmative Action and Immigration," in Nicolaus Mills, ed., *Debating Affirmative Action: Race, Gender, Ethnicity and the Politics of Inclusion* (New York: Delta, 1994), 300–3.

Kukathas, Chandran and Phillip Pettit, *Rawls: A Theory of Justice and its Critics* (Cambridge: Polity Press, 1990).

Kull, Andrew, *The Color-Blind Constitution* (London: Harvard University Press, 1992).

Kutler, Stanley, *The Wars of Watergate: The Last Crisis of Richard Nixon* (New York: Norton, 1992).

Kymlicka, Will and W. J. Norman, "Return of the Citizen: A Survey of Recent Work on Citizenship Theory," *Ethics* 104, no. 2 (1994): 352–81.

Landman, J. H., "Sterilization and Social Betterment" in *Survey Graphic Magazine* (March 1936): 7–10.

LaNoue, George R. and John C. Sullivan, "Deconstructing the Affirmative Action Categories, *American Behavioral Scientist* 41, no. 7 (1998): 913–26.

Lasch, Christopher, *The Culture of Narcissism: American Life in an Age of Diminishing Expectations* (London: Abacus, 1980).

Lemann, Nicholas, "Taking Affirmative Action Apart," in Francis J. Beckwith and Todd E. Jones, *Affirmative Action: Social Justice or Reverse Discrimination?* (Amherst, NY: Prometheus Books, 1997), 34–55.

——, *The Promised Land: The Great Black Migration and How it Changed America* (London: Macmillan, 1991).

Leonard, Jonathan, "The Impact of Affirmative Action on Employment," *Social Forces* 2, no. 4 (Oct. 1984): 388–401.

Lipset, Seymour Martin and Earl Raab, *The Politics of Unreason: Right-Wing Extremism in America, 1790–1977* (Chicago: University of Chicago Press, 1978).

Lipset, Seymour Martin, *American Exceptionalism: A Double-Edged Sword* (London: W. W. Norton and Co., 1996).

Loevy, Robert D., *To End All Segregation: The Politics of the Passage of the Civil Rights Act of 1964* (London: University Press of America, 1990).

Lokos, Lionel, *The New Racism: Reverse Discrimination in America* (New Rochelle, NY: Arlington House, 1971).

Lovell, Catherine, "Three Key Issues in Affirmative Action" in "A Mini-Symposium: Affirmative Action in Public Employment," *Public Administration Review* no. 3 (May–June 1974): 235–36.

Lowi, Theodore, *The End of Liberalism: Ideology, Policy, and the Crisis of Public Authority* (New York: W.W. Norton & Company, Inc., 1969).

Lukas, Anthony, *Nightmare: The Underside of the Nixon Years* (New York, Bantam Books, 1977).

Lyman, Stanford, "Race Relations as Social Progress," in Herbert Hill and James E. Jones, Jr., eds., *Race in America* (Madison: University of Wisconsin Press, 1993): 78–99.

——, *The Black American in Sociological Thought* (New York: Capricorn Books, 1972).

Malik, Kenan, *The Meaning of Race: Race, History and Culture in Western Society* (London: MacMillan, 1996).

Marcuse, Herbert, *One Dimensional Man* (London: Routledge, 1991 [1964]).

Massey, Douglas S. and Nancy A. Denton, *American Apartheid: Segregation and the Making of the Underclass* (London: Harvard University Press, 1992).

Matusow, Alan, J., *The Unravelling of America: A History of Liberalism in the 1960s* (New York: Harper & Row, 1984).

——, *Nixon's Economy: Booms, Busts, Dollars, and Votes* (Lawrence: University of Kansas Press, 1998).

Mayhew, David, *Divided We Govern: Party Control, Lawmaking and Inverstigations, 1946–1990* (New Haven: Yale University Press, 1991).

Mazlish, Bruce, *In Search of Nixon: A Psychohistorical Inquiry* (London: Basic Books, Inc., 1972).

McGinnis, Joe, *The Selling of the President: 1968* (New York: Trident Press, 1969).

McKee, James B., *Sociology and the Race Problem: The Failure of a Perspective* (Chicago: University of Illinois Press, 1993).

McPherson, Harry, *A Political Education* (Boston: Houghton Miflin Co., 1988).

Meadows, Dennis L., Donella H. Meadows, Jorgen Randers, and William W. Behrens III, *The Limits to Growth: A Report for the Club of Rome's Project on the Predicament of Mankind* (London: Potomac Associates, 1972).

Meier, August and Elliott Rudwick, *CORE: A Study in the Civil Rights Movement, 1942–1968* (New York: Oxford University Press, 1973).

Miles, Rufus E., Jr., *Awakening from the American Dream: The Social and Political Limits to Growth* (New York: Universe Books, 1976).

Milkis, Sidney M., "Remaking Government Institutions in the 1970s: Participatory Democracy and the Triumph of Administrative Politics," *Journal of Policy History* 10, no. 1 (1998): 53–70.

Miller, Loren, "Farewell to the Liberals: A Negro View," *The Nation* (October 20, 1962): 235–38.

Mills, C. Wright, *The Power Elite* (London: Oxford University Press, 1956).

Mills, Niclaus, ed., *Debating Affirmative Action, Race, Gender, Ethnicity and the Politics of Inclusion* (New York: Delta, 1994).

Moreno, Paul D., *From Direct Action to Affirmative Action: Fair Employment Law and Policy in America, 1933–1972* (London: Louisiana State University Press, 1997).

Morgan, Iwan W., *Beyond the Liberal Consensus: A Political History of the United States Since 1965* (London: Hurst and Company, 1994).

Morgan, Iwan W., *Nixon* (London: Arnold, 2002).

Moynihan, Daniel P., *Maximum Feasible Misunderstanding: Community Action in the War on Poverty* (New York: The Free Press, 1969).

——, *The Politics of a Guaranteed Income: The Nixon Administration and the Family Assistance Plan* (Random House: New York, 1973).

——, *Towards a National Urban Policy* (New York: Basic Books, 1970).

Moynihan, Daniel Patrick, "Policy vs. Program in the '70s," *The Public Interest* no. 20 (Summer 1970): 90–100.

Murphy, Reg and Hal Gulliver, *The Southern Strategy* (New York: Scribner, 1971).

Murray, Charles, *Losing Ground: American Social Policy, 1950–1980* (New York: Basic Books, 1984).

Myrdal, Gunnar, *An American Dilemma: The Negro Problem and American Democracy,* (New York: Harper & Brothers Publishers, 1944).

Nash, Peter G., "Affirmative Action Under Executive Order 11,246," *New York University Law Review* 46, no. 2 (April 1971): 225–61.

Nathan, Richard P., *Jobs and Civil Rights: The Role of the Federal Government in Promoting Equal Opportunities in Employment and Training* (United States Civil Rights Commission Clearinghouse Publication by the Brookings Institution, April, 1969).

——, *The Plot That Failed: Nixon and the Administrative Presidency* (London: John Wiley and Sons, Inc., 1975).

Nixon, Richard, *In the Arena: A Memory of Victory, Defeat, and Renewal* (New York: Pocket Books, 1990).

——, *RN: The Memoirs of Richard Nixon* (New York: Grosset and Dunlap, 1978).

——, *Seize the Moment: The Challenge for America in a One-Superpower World* (New York: Simon and Schuster, 1992).

——, *Six Crises* (Garden City, NY: Doubleday, 1962).

Nolan, James L., Jr., *The Therapeutic State: Justifying Government at Century's End* (New York: New York University, 1998).

Norton, David L., "Rawls's Theory of Justice: A 'Perfectionist' Rejoinder," *Ethics* 85, no. 1 (October 1974): 50–57.

O'Neill, William L., *Coming Apart: An Informal History of America in the 1960s* (New York: Times Books, 1971).

O'Reilly, Kenneth, *Nixon's Piano: Presidents and Racial Politics from Washington to Clinton* (New York: Free Press, 1995).

Oberdiek, Hans, "Review: A Theory of Justice," *New York University Law Review* 47, no. 5 (November 1972): 1020–22.

Olson, Mancur, "Introduction," in Mancur Olson and Hans H. Landsberg, *The No-Growth Society* (London: The Woburn Press, 1975, originally published by the American Academy of Arts and Sciences, 1973): 7–10.

Orfield, Gary, "Race and the Liberal Agenda: The Loss of the Integrationist Dream, 1965–1974" in *The Politics of Social Policy in the United States,* Margaret Weir, Ann Shola Orloff, and Theda Skopcol, eds. (Princeton: Princeton University Press, 1988): 72–90.

Ostrom, Vincent, *The Intellectual Crisis in American Public Administration* (Tuscaloosa: University of Alabama Press, 1974).

Oudes, Bruce, ed., *From: The President* (New York: Harper and Row, 1989).

Outhwaite, William, ed., *The Habermas Reader* (Cambridge: Polity Press, 1996).

———, *Habermas: A Critical Introduction* (Oxford: Polity Press, 1994).

Panetta, Leon E. and Peter Gall, *Bring Us Together: The Nixon Team and Civil Rights* (New York: J. B. Lippincott Company, 1971).

Parikh, Sunita, *The Politics of Preference: Democratic Institutions and Affirmative Action in the United States and India* (Ann Arbor: The University of Michigan Press, 1997).

Parmet, Herbert S., *Richard Nixon and His America* (London: Little, Brown and Company, 1990).

Parsons, Talcott, *Essays in Sociological Theory* (Free Press: New York, 1964).

Patterson, James T., *America's Struggle Against Poverty, 1900–1980* (London: Harvard University Press, 1981).

———, *Grand Expectations: The United States 1945–1974* (New York: Oxford University Press, 1991).

Pearl, Arthur, *Landslide: The How and Why of Nixon's Victory* (Secaucus, NJ: Citadel Press 1973).

Pelezynski, Z. A., *The State and Civil Society: Studies in Hegel's Political Philosophy* (London: Cambridge University Press, 1984).

Petrocik, John R., *Party Coalitions: Realignments and the Decline of the New Deal Party system* (Chicago: University of Chicago Press, 1981).

Phillips, Kevin, *The Emerging Republican Majority* (New York: Arlington House, 1969).

Pogge, Thomas W., *Realizing Rawls* (London: Cornell University Press, 1989).

Pole, J. R., *The Pursuit of Equality in American History* (Berkeley: University of California Press, 1978).

Price, Ray, *With Nixon* (New York: Viking, 1977).

Quadagno, Jill, *The Color of Welfare: How Racism Undermined the War on Poverty* (New York: Oxford University Press, 1994).

Raab, Earl, "Quotas by Any Other Name," *Commentary* (January 1972): 41–45.

Rainwater, Lee and William L. Yancey, *The Moynihan Report and the Politics of Controversy* (Boston: MIT Press, 1967).

Rawls, John, "Distributive Justice," in Peter Laslett and Walter G. Runciman, ed., *Philosophy, Politics and Society*, 3rd series (New York: Barnes and Noble, 1967): 58–82.

———, "Justice as Fairness," *The Philosophical Review* 67, no. 2. (April 1958): 164–94.

———, "The Domain of the Political and Overlapping Consensus," *New York University Law Review* 64, no. 2 (May 1989): 233–55.

———, *A Theory of Justice* (London: Oxford University Press, 1973).

Reed, Linda, *Simple Decency and Common Sense: The Southern Conference Movement, 1938–1963* (Indianapolis: Indiana University Press, 1991).

Reichley, A. James, *Conservatives in an Age of Change: The Nixon and Ford Administrations* (Washington, D.C.: The Brookings Institution, 1981).

Rosenbloom, David H., "Equal Employment Opportunity: Another Strategy," *Personnel Administration/Public Personnel Review* 1, no. 1 (July–August 1972): 38–41.

Rustin, Bayard, "From Protest to Politics: The Future of the Civil Rights Movement," *Commentary* 39, no. 2 (February 1965): 25–31.

Safire, William, *Before the Fall: An Inside View of the Pre-Watergate White House* (New York: Doubleday and Co., 1975).

Sandel, Michael, *Liberalism and the Limits to Justice* (Cambridge: Cambridge University Press, 1982).

Scammon, Richard M. and Ben J. Wattenberg, *The Real Majority* (New York: Coward, McCann & Geoghegan, Inc., 1970).

Schaar, John H., "Equality of Opportunity and the Just Society" in H. Gene Blocker and Elizabeth H. Smith, eds., *John Rawls, A Theory of Justice: An Introduction*, 162–84.

Schaefer, David Lewis, *Justice or Tyranny? A Critique of John Rawls' "A Theory of Justice"* (Port Washington, NY: Kennikat Press, 1979).

Schell, Jonathon, *Observing the Nixon Years* (New York: Pantheon Books, 1989).

———, *The Time of Illusion* (New York: Knopf, 1976).

Schlesinger, Arthur M., Jr., *The Vital Center: The Politics of Freedom* (Boston: The Riverside Press, 1949).

Schulz, George P., *Turmoil and Triumph* (New York: Charles Scribner's Sons, 1993).

Schuman, Howard, Charlotte Steeh, Lawrence Bobo, and Maria Krysan, *Racial Attitudes in America: Trends and Interpretations* (London: Harvard University Press, 1997).

Schutt, Russell K., "Craft Unions and Minorities: Determinants of Change in Admission Practices," *Social Problems* (1987): 388–401.

Schuwerk, Robert P., "The Philadelphia Plan: A Study in the Dynamics of Executive Power," *University of Chicago Law Review* 39 (1971–1972): 723–60.

Shafer, Byron E., *Quiet Revolution: The Struggle for the Democratic Party and the Shaping of Post-Reform Politics* (New York: Russell Sage Foundation, 1983).

Shapiro, Ian, *The Evolution of Rights in Liberal Theory* (Cambridge: Cambridge University Press, 1986).

Sheatsley, Paul, "White Attitudes Towards the Negro," *Daedalus*, no. 1 (Winter 1966): 217–38, 234.

Sher, George, "Justifying Reverse Discrimination in Employment," *Philosophy and Public Affairs* 4, no. 2. (Winter 1975): 159–70.

Silberman, Charles E., "The Businessman and the Negro," *Fortune* (September 1963): 97–99, 184–94.

Sitkoff, Harvard, *The Struggle for Black Equality 1954–1980* (New York: Hill and Wang, 1981).

Skowronek, Stephen, *The Politics Presidents Make: Leadership from John Adams to George Bush* (Cambridge, MA: Harvard University Press, 1993).

Skrentny, John D., *The Minority Rights Revolution* (Cambridge, MA: The Belknap Press of Harvard University Press, 2002).

———, "Affirmative Action: Some Advice for the Pundits," *American Behavioral Scientist* 41, no. 7 (April 1998): 876–85.

———, *The Ironies of Affirmative Action: Politics, Culture, and Justice in America* (London: University of Chicago Press, 1996).

Small, Melvin, *The Presidency of Richard Nixon* (Lawrence: Kansas University Press, 1999).

Smith, Robert C., *We Have No Leaders: African Americans in the Post-Civil Rights Era* (New York: SUNY Press, 1996).

Sniderman, Paul M. and Michael Gray Hagen, *Race and Inequality: A Study in American Values* (New York: Chatham House, 1985).

Southern, David W., *Gunnar Myrdal and Black–White Relations: The Use and Abuse of An American Dilemma, 1944–1969* (London: Louisiana University Press, 1987).

Stampp, Kenneth, *The Peculiar Institution* (London: Eyre and Spottiswoode, 1964 [1956]).

Stanley, David T., "Whose Merit? How Much?" in "A Symposium: The Merit Principle Today," *Public Administration Review* 34, no. 5 (September–October 1974): 2–3.

Stans, Maurice, *One of the President's Men: Twenty Years with Eisenhower and Nixon* (Washington, D.C.: Brassey's, 1995).

Steinberg, Stephen, "How Quotas Began," *Commentary* 52, no. 3 (September 1971): 68–76.

———, *Turning Back: The Retreat from Racial Justice in American Thought and Social Policy* (Boston: Beacon Press, 1995).

Strober, Gerald S. and Deborah Hart Strober, *Nixon: An Oral History of His Presidency* (New York: HarperCollins, 1994).

Sugrue, Thomas J., "Affirmative Action from Below: Civil Rights, the Building Trades, and the Politics of Racial Equality in the Urban North, 1945–1969," *The Journal of American History* 91, no. 1 (June 2004): 145–73.

———, "Crabgrass-Roots Politics: Race, Rights and the Reaction against Liberalism in the Urban North, 1940–1964," *Journal of American History* 82, no. 2 (September 1995): 551–78.

———, "The Tangled Roots of Affirmative Action," *The American Behavioral Scientist* 41, no. 7 (April 1998).

Teles, Steven M., "Why is There No Affirmative Action in Britain?" *American Behavioral Scientist* 41, no. 7 (April 1998): 1004–1026.

Thomas, R. Roosevelt, "From Affirmative Action to Affirming Diversity," *Harvard Business Review* 90, no. 2 (March–April, 1990): 107–17.

Thompson, Daniel C., "The Rise of the Negro Protest," in *The Annals of the American Academy of Political and Social Science*, 357 (January 1965).

Tobin, James "On Improving the Economic Status of the Negro" in Talcott Parsons and Kenneth B. Clarke, eds., *The Negro American* (Boston: Beacon Press, 1966): 451–71.

Trotsky, Leon, *Leon Trotsky on Black Nationalism and Self-Determination* (New York: Pathfinder Press, 1978).

Tushnet, Mark V., *The NAACP's Legal Strategy Against Segregated Education, 1925–1950* (Chapel Hill: University of North Carolina Press, 1987).

Unger, Irwin and Debi Unger, *Turning Point: 1968* (New York: Scribner, 1988).

Vatter, Harold and John F. Walker, *The Inevitability of Government Growth* (New York: Columbia University Press, 1990.

Vieira, Norman, "Racial Imbalance, Black Separatism and Permissible Classification by Race," *Michigan Law Review* 67 (June 1969): 1603–18.

Waddan, Alex, "A Liberal in Wolf's Clothing: Nixon's Family Assistance Plan in the Light of 1990s Welfare Reform," *Journal of American Studies* 32 (August 1998): 203–18.

Walker, John F. and Harold G. Vatter, *The Rise of Big Government in the United States* (London: M. E. Sharpe, 1997).

Walton, Hanes, *When the Marching Stopped: The Politics of Civil Rights Regulatory Agencies* (New York: SUNY Press, 1988).

Whalen, Charles W. and Barbara Whalen, *The Longest Debate: A Legislative History of the 1964 Civil Rights Act* (Washington, D.C.: Seven Locks Press, 1985).

Whitcover, Jules, *The Resurrection of Richard Nixon* (New York: Putnam, 1970).

White, Theodore H., *The Making of the President: 1968* (New York: Atheneum, 1969).

———, *The Making of the President: 1972* (New York: Atheneum, 1973).

Wicker, Tom, "Introduction" to the *Report of the National Advisory Commission on Civil Disorders* (the Kerner Commission Report) (New York: Bantam Books, 1968).

———, *One of Us: Richard Nixon and the American Dream* (New York: Random House, 1991).

Wills, Garry, *Nixon Agonistes: The Crisis of the Self-Made Man* (Boston: Houghton Mifflin Company, 1970).

———, *The Second Civil War: Arming for Armageddon* (New York: New American Library, 1968).

Wilson, William Julius, *The Declining Significance of Race: Blacks and Changing American Institutions* (Chicago: University of Chicago Press, 1978).

———, *The Truly Disadvantaged: The Inner-City, the Underclass, and Public Policy* (London: University of Chicago Press, 1987).

Winant, Howard, *Racial Conditions: Politics, Theory, Comparisons* (London: University of Minnesota Press, 1994).

Wofford, Harris, *Of Kennedys and Kings: Making Sense of the Sixties* (New York: Farrar, Strauss, Giroux, 1980).

Wolfe, Alan, *Limits of Legitimacy: Political Contradictions of Contemporary Capitalism* (New York: Free Press, 1977).

Wolff, Robert Paul, *Understanding Rawls: A Reconstruction and Critique of A Theory of Justice* (Princeton: Princeton University Press, 1977).

Wolk, Allen, *The Presidency and Black Civil Rights* (Cranbury, NJ: Associated University Presses, Inc., 1971).

Yinger, J. Milton and George E. Simpson, "Can Segregation Survive in Industrial Society?" *Antioch Review* XVIII (Spring 1958): 10–20.

Yuill, Kevin, "The 1966 White House Conference on Civil Rights," *Historical Journal* 41, no. 1 (May 1998): 259–82.

Serials

AFL-CIO News
Antioch Review
Chicago Tribune
Christian Science Monitor
Commentary
Congressional Record

Daedalus
Fortune
Harper's Magazine
Harvard Business Review
Liberation
Los Angeles Times (available at www.latimes.com/archives/).
Michigan Law Review
New Republic
New York Times
Ramparts
Survey Graphic
The Annals of the American Academy of Political and Social Science
The Crisis
The Republican
Washington Post

Microfilm

Steven F. Lawson, ed., "Records of the White House Conference on Civil Rights, 1965–1966," *Civil Rights During the Johnson Administration 1963–1969* [microfilm], part IV.

Official and Semi-Official Publications

A Report on the 1966 Plans for Progress Fourth National Conference, held at the Washington Hilton Hotel on January 24–25, 1966 (Washington, D.C.: US GPO, 1966).
Five Years of Progress, 1953–1958: A Report to President Eisenhower by the President's Committee on Government Contracts (Washington, D.C.: US GPO, 1958).
Pattern for Progress: Final Report to President Eisenhower from the President's Committee on Government Contracts (Washington, D.C.: US GPO, 1960).
Public Papers of the Presidents of the United States: Richard Nixon, 1969 (Washington, D.C.: US GPO, 1970).
The Nixon Presidential Press Conferences (New York: Coleman Enterprises, 1978).
The President's Committee on Government Employment Policy, *Some Questions and Answers on the Non-Discrimination Policy of the Federal Government* (Washington, D.C.: US GPO, 1955).
United States Civil Rights Commission, *Affirmative Action in Higher Education: A Consultation Held in Washington, D.C., September 9–10, 1975* (Washington, D.C.: US GPO, 1976).
United States Civil Rights Commission, *Federal Civil Rights Enforcement* (Washington, D.C.: US GPO, 1969).
United States Civil Rights Commission, *Federal Civil Rights Enforcement* (Washington, D.C.: US GPO, September 1970).

United States Civil Rights Commission, *Making Civil Rights Sense Out of Revenue Sharing Dollars* (Washington, D.C.: USCRC Clearinghouse Publication 50, February 1975).

United States Civil Rights Commission, *The Challenge Ahead: Equal Opportunity in Unions* (Washington, D.C.: US GPO, May 1976).

United States Civil Rights Commission, *The Federal Civil Rights Effort: Seven Months Later* (Washington, D.C.: US GPO, May 1971).

United States Civil Rights Commission, *The Federal Civil Rights Enforcement Effort: A Reassessment* (Washington, D.C.: US GPO, January 1973).

United States Civil Service Commission, *Preliminary Report of Minority Group Employment in the Federal Government* (Washington, D.C.: US GPO, 1969) SM-70-69A.

United States Civil Service Commission, *Preliminary Report of Minority Group Employment in the Federal Government, 1969* (Washington, D.C.: US GPO, 1969).

United States Department of Health, Education and Welfare, Office of Education, *Equality of Educational Opportunity* (Coleman Report): (Washington, D.C.: US GPO, 1966).

United States Department of Labor, *Service to Minority Groups*, U.S. Department of Labor Employment Office Training Program: Instructor's Guide (Washington, D.C.: US GPO, December 1951).

United States Equal Employment Opportunities Commission (EEOC): *Minorities and Women in Referral Units in Building Trade* (Washington, D.C.: US GPO, 1972).

National Archives and Records Administration, College Park, MD

Records of the Committee on Government Contract Compliance: RG325, National Archives and Records Administration, College Park, MD

Nixon Presidential Materials Project (National Archives and Records Administration, College Park, MD)

White House Central Files: Subject Files: HU (Human Rights)

White House Central Files; Subject Files: HU [Ex] HU

White House Special Files: SMOF: Charles W. Colson

White House Special Files: Staff Member and Office Files: John D. Ehrlichman

White House Central Files: Staff Member and Office Files: Leonard Garment:

White House Special Files: Staff Member and Office Files: H. R. Haldeman: Haldeman Notes

White House Special Files: Staff Member and Office Files: H. R. Haldeman: Talking Papers

White House Special Files: Staff Member and Office Files: H. R. Haldeman: Alpha Subject Files

White House Special Files: Subject Files, 1969–1974: Oversize Attachments

White House Special Files: President's Office Files: President's Handwriting
White House Special Files: President's Office Files: Annotated News Summaries
White House Special Files: President's Personal File: Memoranda from the President
White House Special Files: White House Central Files: Subject Files: Confidential Files
White House Special Files: Staff Member and Office Files: Harry S. Dent
White House Special Files: Staff Member and Office Files: John W. Dean III
White House Central Files: Staff Member and Office Files: Charles L. Clapp
White House Central Files: Subject Files [Ex] HU (Human Rights)
White House Central Files: Subject Files: HU (Human Rights)

Nixon Presidential Materials Project:
Contested Material (Presidential Materials Review Board:
Review on Contested Documents: released October 1996)

White House Special Files: Staff Member and Office Files: Harry S. Dent
White House Special Files: Staff Member and Office Files: John D. Ehrlichman
White House Special Files: Staff Member and Office Files: President's Personal Files
White House Special Files: Staff Member and Office Files: President's Office Files
White House Special Files: Staff Member and Office Files: White House Special Files:
   White House Central Files: SubF: [Confidential Files]
White House Special Files: Staff Member and Office Files: Charles W. Colson
White House Special Files: Staff Member and Office Files: H. R. Haldeman

National Archives and Records Administration, Washington, D.C.

Records of the Republican National Committee transferred to the Office of Presidential Libraries on June 30, 1978

Library of Congress, Washington, D.C.

Papers of Edward W. Brooke
National Urban League Manuscripts

Index

About the Author

Kevin Yuill is Senior Lecturer in American Studies at the University of Sunderland in the United Kingdom.